46

GAYLORD MG

ANNUALS
for
CONNOISSEURS

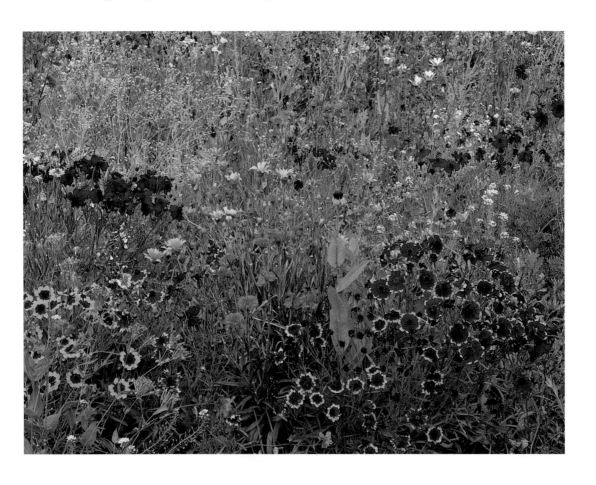

ANNUALS
for
CONNOISSEURS

Wayne Winterrowd

Foreword by Christopher Lloyd
Photographs by Cynthia Woodyard

A **Horticulture** Book

PRENTICE HALL

New York   London   Toronto   Sydney   Tokyo   Singapore

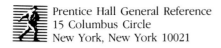 Prentice Hall General Reference
15 Columbus Circle
New York, New York 10021

PRENTICE HALL and colophon are registered trademarks of
Simon & Schuster, Inc.

A **Horticulture** Book
An Affiliate of *Horticulture*, The Magazine of American
Gardening

Library of Congress Cataloging-in-Publication Data

Winterrowd, Wayne.
    Annuals for connoisseurs / Wayne Winterrowd.
       p.   cm.
    Includes bibliographical references (p.   ) and Index
    ISBN 0-13-038175-6
    1. Annuals (Plants)   I. Title.
SB422.W55   1992
635.9'312--dc20   91-48215
                                      CIP

Manufactured in the United States of America

10 9 8 7 6 5 4 3 2 1

First Edition

PHOTOGRAPHY CREDITS
Thomas C. Cooper: pages 5, 7, 11, 12, 21, 31, 90, 99, 131,
177, 181, 194.
Michele and Jean-Claude Lamontagne: pages 15, 50, 60, 86,
129, 133.
Joe Eck: pages 25, 76, 80.
Pamela Harper: pages 54, 112.

Cover photo: The well-stocked annual garden draws on every corner of the globe and every habitat from
steamy tropical jungles to arid sunbaked deserts to wide temperate grasslands. But few annuals originate
from such chilly places as Papaver nudicaule, *the iceland poppy, which is native wherever the high summer*
sun shines at midnight. In addition to this haunting pink, flowers may occur in white, greenish white, ivory,
coral, salmon, yellow or orange. No flower of iceland poppy is ever one single color, for all show a complex
overlay of shade on shade, which is a great part of their beauty.

Page i: Many gardeners who crave a flower meadow will want a rich tapestry of many species in many
colors, all rioting together. Such meadows may be established by adding handfuls of seeds saved from
elsewhere in the garden to a standard annual meadow mix.

For Tom Cooper

ACKNOWLEDGMENTS

Only another book writer can realize, perhaps, how hopeless a task it is to write a proper set of acknowledgments, for any book owes its existence to the help of so many people. Some provide massive encouragement and untiring daily assistance, some provide knowledge, and some, by a word or chance observation, provide just the beginning to an essay that redeems a whole day from loss. "Words pay no debts," Shakespeare says; but still they must be spoken.

My first thanks goes to all the gardeners who allowed us to photograph in their gardens, and particularly to Hardy Amies, Bill Baker, Suzanne Bales, John Bates, Geoff Beasley, Ruth Borun, Bob Fletcher, Allen C. Haskell, Penelope Hobhouse, David Huston, Mary Keen, Faith Mackiness, Nancy McCabe, Mrs. Ralph Merton, the late Jane Platt, Kathy Pufhal, Chris Rosmini, Marco Polo Stufano at Wave Hill, Graham Stuart Thomas, and Rosemary Verey.

From their gardens the images that illustrate and ornament this book were taken by my seeing-eye friend Cynthia Woodyard, who in addition to being principal photographer for this book was also a cheerful, knowledgeable, and tireless collaborator in its making. Occasionally, because she could not be in the right place at the right time, images were supplied by other photographers. Thanks for them goes to Joe Eck, to Michele and Jean-Claude Lamontagne, to Tom Cooper, and especially to Pam Harper, who generously drew from her vast slide library at the last moment to supply the stubbornest customers.

Several seed companies provided both information and valuable packets of seed. I extend my thanks to Suzanne Bales and Chela Kleiber at Burpee, Steve Frowine at White Flower Farm, to John Elsley at Park Seed and to Mark Jenner-Parsons at Thompson & Morgan. But the seeds might have stayed in their packets had it not been for Jack Manix at Walker Farm in Dummerston, Vermont, who was willing to sow anything and to keep records on its germination.

Like any other child, a book has its family friends, its godparents, its doctors and teachers. Among those I must thank my agent and friend, Helen Pratt, who with her assistant Beatrice Tosti always provided encouragement and always laughed at my jokes. At Prentice Hall, I am grateful to Anne Zeman, who enthusiastically bought my idea, and to Rebecca Atwater, who patiently saw it into reality. The tireless efforts of her staff, particularly Rachel Simon, have earned my enormous gratitude.

But more than any other force, it is *Horticulture* magazine that deserves my thanks for giving me a curious and wonderful career as a garden writer in my middle age. In the making of this book, more support than I could ever have dared to ask for has come from its staff, and particularly from Tom Cooper and Tom Fischer, who provided hours of patient editing, often in the anxious light of early dawn. On every page, I can see what a poor thing this book might have been without their skill, taste, and erudition.

This book, because it depended on close observation, had to be written in high summer, when the beauties, and more, the chores of the garden were always beckoning. So I must thank Stuart Aylin and Darren Bernard, who pulled the weeds that should have been mine, and who responded with patience and humor to my rantings when I wandered from the typewriter into the garden.

My thanks to Joe Eck, Faith Sprague, and Martha Ronk are really beyond words.

CONTENTS

This beautiful field of English flax, which draws the sky to earth, can teach us the value of simplifying our garden designs. Plantings of annuals, often vivid of color as they are, benefit from the generous use of a single species.

FOREWORD

It is a great privilege to have been asked to write this foreword; I have seldom enjoyed a gardening book more.

First there is the subject. Annuals are thought of far too often as stopgaps, or as material (weasel word for living plants) wherewith to fill a new garden before more important plants have taken up the space. In their freshness and gaiety, their cheerful greeting on a summer's day: "here we are; make the most of us; we can't stay long"—they bring a gladness into our lives for which there is no substitute.

Then the author, Wayne Winterrowd, has the essentials of enthusiasm and the ability to communicate. He loves every plant he writes on and he writes delightfully. He is a great proselytizer. If you didn't know the plant before you read about it, you'll certainly want to give it a try. Likewise, if you half knew and thought you disliked it, you'll want to give it another, better chance. Many of the plants will already be your favorites, but how warming it is to read nice things about them; things, moreover, that you'd not thought of putting into words just like that. "How right!" you'll exclaim, as though you'd been saying the same for years.

The choice of annuals is entirely personal to the author. And, of course, they're not all annuals. I once asked a pillar of this Alpine Garden Society for his definition of an alpine. "Any plant I enjoy growing," he said promptly. Winterrowd has included biennials and plenty of tender perennials, my favorite cannas among them. After telling us how to germinate their iron-hard seed, he drops all that, which few of us want to be bothered with anyhow (I've never grown one from seed in my life and now he's gone and sent me a packet—a bit unfair, surely) and then describes them as the perennials they are. Salvias, too. How right he is to go overboard on them.

He often recommends lifting plants at summer's end, cutting them back, potting them up, and bringing them in, either to continue flowering through winter, or so as to have strong stock for planting out next year. Windowsills won't get you far; you need a conservatory and he has one. Why don't more Americans? The greenhouse is a rarity with you. I suppose it's a question of priorities. In Britain, where nearly everyone has a greenhouse, we shiver in our dwellings through winter but reserve enough heat to keep precious plants alive. In America the dwellings are overheated and the plants can die. It wants examining.

This book gains immensely from having been written, at least in part, in summer. This must have been hell for Winterrowd (it's something I have never achieved) but it means that he has been able to convey the details of what a plant looks like and just how it is attractive with a directness that can never quite be achieved by writing from memory. Plant and scene here reach us as actuality.

There are some lovely turns of phrase. Of love-lies-bleeding (*Amaranthus caudatus*), "In the right place it can be a stunning accent, both dignified and slightly giddy, looking like nothing else in the summer garden." Of *Argemone*, the prickly poppy, "It is the birthright of all poppies to bear flowers of ephemeral beauty, as fragile as the finest silk." Of *Eustoma*, "They are five-petaled cups, possessing the *art nouveau* grace that some tulips and many poppies have, with the same silken sheen, as if they were cut from satin and molded of wax." I liked the expression of a way "to mask the shanks of shrub or tea roses" with the annual mallow, *Lavatera trimestris*, "in rich drifts of deep rose, pale pink, and white," adding "beauty to a spot in the garden that could otherwise most charitably be described as resting." When it self-sows, "sweet alyssum seems to have an instinct for coming up where it looks best." Exactly so.

Writing from experience, Winterrowd is exact on practical detail in the cultivation of annuals; it would be rash to argue with him. There is a large nuts-and-bolts section in the last part of this book with much sound advice and instruction which would apply equally to many kinds of plants. On setting annuals out, "young plants should be watered in, even if the surrounding soil is already moist." That is just as relevant to trees and shrubs, in order to settle the soil around their roots and fill in large air spaces. And he has many suggestions on ways to use the plants to look effective with their partners. There is none of that fashionable distancing of the author from his subject. "Here are the facts; you are all sufficiently adult to draw your own conclusions," is the attitude taken. Which is a cop-out. Winterrowd is totally biased, which is surely right. It's a viewpoint that we like, not dry-as-dust presentation.

Nuggets of wisdom are continually thrown out. On weeding among the quaking grass, *Briza maxima*: "Once one has learned to distinguish their compact little tufts . . . they may be left in place, if they are in the right place." We depend on its self-sown seedlings, after the first year. They just look like grass. It is essential to weed among and thin them yourself, otherwise you'll proudly be told, "I've cleared that patch" and it'll be all too true. And isn't this wise? "Part of the excitement of gardening is an endless altering of one's plans and a shifting around of plants for ever more refined effects." Follow that advice and you'll never look back. The imagination is set free.

Christopher Lloyd

Gardeners turn to annuals first for the wealth of color they offer, often in shades more brilliant than those possessed by most plants grown in temperate gardens. But many annuals are also beautifully crafted in leaf or flower shape. None is more engaging than love-in-a-mist (Nigella damascena), seen here in lonely splendor among California poppies (Eschscholzia californica).

INTRODUCTION

Most gardeners begin their love of plants with annuals, usually in childhood. The seed is readily available, and it puts no great strain on a childish pocket, crammed with the wealth of patiently accumulated small change. All children love the dirt, for they are nearer to it than are adults, and though the child's imagination can always find serious reasons for digging holes in the earth and getting them wet, a real purpose, rather than a merely imagined one, adds value to the endeavor. What's in the packet of seed is often comfortably large in a small hand, and germination is rapid enough to be gratifying to those who have experienced little of time and so are impatient of it. So the passion for gardening often starts in a plot, splendid with marigolds and zinnias, with great-faced sunflowers, and the daily breathless event of opening four o'clocks.

As they mature in sophistication, however, many gardeners put away annuals with other pursuits of childhood gardening. The thrill of seeing a seed germinate and grow to thriving maturity never departs; but instead of petunias, zinnias, and marigolds, the seed comes to be of *Meconopsis betonicifolia*, or *Saxifraga longifolia*, or *Heptacodium miconoides*. The gardener's sense of time expands as well, comprising not just a season but many seasons. Perennials, shrubs, and even trees come to seem the essential components of the garden, according to a paradox well known among gardeners, that as one's allotment of time decreases, one's garden schemes tend to reflect the assumption of an unbroken store of years. Interest turns away from the growing merely of flowers to the growing of plants, for groundcover, for subtle combi-

nations of mass and form, for the endless fascination of leaves, shades of green on green or fantastically variegated. The garden comes to be a permanent but ever-changing creation rather than the diversion of a single summer, or even a single lifetime.

Still, either from sentiment or from desperation, a few annuals hold their place. The winsome, thoughtful stare of pansies is always irresistible in spring, and the soft, never-tiring beauty of impatiens cannot really be bettered for brightening the shady retreats of summer. Even the most sophisticated gardeners will fall for a well-grown hanging basket of begonias or browallias, or—for one never completely forgets one's first love—for a six-pack of shining marigolds, each with a single flower in two neat rows, and with leaves that, brushed casually as one is debating whether or not to give in, settle the question with their smell, quintessentially of summers past. But mostly, in those gardens one calls "established," annuals, when they are grown at all, are grown because one couldn't resist. They are quickly planted in a bare spot, and quickly thrown away when a choice perennial is acquired or when something good needs dividing. At best, annuals come to seem to gardeners rather as cake mixes to serious cooks, either an embarrassing indulgence or a quick solution.

That is a pity. Of all the major groups of plants (trees, shrubs, perennials, grasses, and ferns) annuals have as much to offer as any, and it could be argued, more. They come in all sizes, from the two-inch ground-hugging mats of *Lobularia maritima* to brawny giant castor beans 14 feet tall. Though some can tax the skills of the most experienced gardener, most are amiable and undemanding, ready to accept without complaint conditions far below the best. They are *carpe diem* plants, prepared to seize and make the most of their short day, bridging the span from seed to flower and back to seed again in 12 months or less. Like the grasshopper in the fable, they have no care to store up their resources underground in root or tuber or woody crown as do perennials, the smug ants of the garden. Rather, they put their energies into the production of as much flower as they can, hoping thereby to insure their continuity not through their own lives but through their seed-born progeny. The result is an abundance of flower rivaled in the plant kingdom only by forest trees, and a length of blooming time more extensive than almost any perennial can boast. There is no color, shade, or tint, and no shape—whether daisy, spike, umbel, panicle, raceme, or cymem that cannot be found in some annual or another. The possibilities for combination are infinite.

Even with all these virtues, it is surprising that the range of annuals grown in most gardens is so small. There arc always the ten or 15 stalwarts that appear in garden centers every spring and in an ever-increasing range of colors—the pansies, petunias, impatiens, marigolds, zinnias, cosmos, and so forth. About none of these sturdy veterans of the garden-center display bench should ever a bad word be said; for they are all excellent plants, and if we do not choose to grow them ourselves, our

*Sublime effects can often be achieved by limiting plantings of annuals to one or two species. Such restraint is apparent here in the massive planting of purple violas divided by a narrow ribbon of white China asters (*Callistephus chinensis*). So beautiful is it that it might bear repeating, but a great joy of annual plants is that new combinations can always be contrived from year to year.*

Zinnia angustifolia *flowers from late June until frost, and remains clean and bright throughout the hottest days of summer. Here its clear color is given added value by a companion planting of* Petunia *'Azure Pearls'.*

summers would be the poorer if no one else did. For all that, annuals are for most gardeners a vast unexplored dominion, as rich in "finds" as was China when the first plant explorers visited it in the last century. There are great treasures, some grown long ago in gardens and now forgotten, and others hardly ever known. Among the rich diversity of annuals are plants that can fill a niche in the most sophisticated planting schemes, giving the gardener one of the greatest of garden pleasures, that of having a visitor walk round and suddenly exclaim,

"What in the world is *that* beautiful plant?" Even in the most familiar species there are refined varieties, worthy of a place in any garden, such as the lime-green zinnia called 'Envy' or the delicate, single-flowered, fine-foliaged marigold called 'Irish Lace'. Annuals are adapted to endless uses, and they contribute, by the beauty and gaiety of their flowers and often even by their very transitoriness, an element missing from too many gardens—a sense of lightness, of spontaneity, of heart.

Though often confined to rigid bedding schemes, Zinnia elegans *has many other garden uses. Here, with the signet marigold (*Tagetes tenuifolia*) and the stately American native perennial* Lobelia cardinalis, *it adds arresting color to a streamside setting.*

What Is an Annual?

What is or is not an annual, though a fairly easy question for the botanist, is a surprisingly vexing one for the gardener, unless he or she is content with the blunt definition that an annual is anything bought in the garden center in spring (or later) to bloom quickly, and discarded in the fall (or earlier) when it finishes. Technically, an annual is any plant that completes its natural life cycle, from germinated seed through growth, flower, seed production, and into death, in a single growing season. But many plants treated as annuals throughout much of North America are in fact tender perennials, native to climates so mild that they can regenerate from woody crowns or even from stray bits of root for many seasons. Others produce corms, rhizomes, or tubers that can, if lifted and stored in a cool dark place over the winter, become family heirlooms. Then there are shrubs and subshrubs that can be potted to flower on a sunny windowsill throughout the long dark months and returned to the garden for a fresh summer of bloom. Finally, there are biennials, universally frustrating to gardeners and to garden writers alike, and to the inexperienced, who may believe that they are plants that bloom every other year. In fact, they are mostly only "annuals," too, though they need one full calendar year to mature.

To many gardeners, these technical distinctions will be irrelevant. They will be content to purchase plants each spring, enjoy them for one

Annuals and perennials may often be combined, as here in a corner of the author's garden in Vermont, for a full summer of exuberant bloom.

full summer of glorious bloom, and bid them farewell when the first frosts have blackened their flowers and leaves, and the deeper freezes of late autumn have blasted their stems and roots. To gardeners who have the will to try and the necessary facilities, however, it is useful to know a plant's technical classification, for it can lead to the knowledge that will allow them to carry over an "annual" plant from year to year. From a tender perennial lifted and potted up in autumn, or a shrub or subshrub cut back and regrown on a sunny windowsill, or even from a cutting or stray bit of rooted stem found beneath a true annual and cosseted in a pot, the gardener may even get some flowers through the long months of winter, a shy but precious memory of summer past. And from such plants there are always divisions to take, or new cuttings in early spring, for a fresh supply of bloom in the summer to come. With some plants, such as the beautiful double blue form of *Lobelia erinus* that does not set seed, or the finer forms of *Verbena × hybrida* that are not common in commerce, overwintering may be the only way to preserve one's stock. And with all annuals saved from the black frost and patiently carried through the winter, the gardener achieves a sense of continuity that, to cold-climate gardeners, is precious in itself. (Instructions on carrying annuals through the winter are offered in the section "Techniques," page 153.)

HARDY, HALF-HARDY, AND TENDER

Traditionally, plants grown as annuals are also subdivided into three classes that cut across the botanist's distinctions of true annual, biennial, perennial, shrub, and subshrub. For the convenience of gardeners, plants grown as annuals are divided into "hardy," "half-hardy," or "tender," depending on their tolerance for cold. This division is one of many bits of garden lore American gardeners have inherited from

England, where the climate, though certainly subject to its vagaries, tends to be more uniform and settled than ours. Even so, one doubts that this rough-and-ready classification is any more useful to English gardeners than to us, for plants are individuals, and in their treatment there is no real substitute for considering their particular needs (and the hard-won knowledge of one's own patch and gardening practices).

Nevertheless, knowing a plant's general tolerance to cold is always helpful. Hardy annuals are those that will accept frost, sometimes only a little and sometimes a surprising amount. They can usually be planted out early or seeded directly in the garden, just about the time the forsythias fade. In this class belong many plants that are intolerant of transplanting, such as larkspurs and annual poppies, and most of the familiar biennials gardeners crave, notably foxgloves, forget-me-nots, and hollyhocks. It includes as well less-known but wonderful plants, such as Mexican horned poppies (*Argemone* species), some of the annual garden mallows such as *Lavatera trimestris*, and the startling eight-foot-tall Himalayan jewel weed (*Impatiens glandulifera*). Many hardy annuals will self-seed even in a cold garden such as ours in Vermont (USDA Zone 4), choosing their own wise time to sprout from seed born of the previous year's planting.

Any self-seeder can usually be assumed to be hardy. Still, the best effects are often achieved not from volunteers but from plants that are started early and put in place once they are well on their way. Bloom will be earlier, thus offering the long season of flower that is the chief reason for planting most annuals in the first place. So even when plants are classed technically as hardy, gardeners in cold climates would be wise to start them early indoors, in peat pots if they are difficult to transplant. Their quick lush growth, however, will not be inured to even a degree or two of frost, and they should thus be treated as half-hardy.

Half-hardy annuals are those that tolerate no frost and may even sulk for a time in a cold

Almost more valuable for its leaves than for its great white trumpets of flower is the single specimen of Datura metel *in this planting of perennials. Just beginning its development in late June when this photograph was taken, it eventually filled its allotted space and tumbled gracefully onto the grass. With the help of a single pot of* Gomphrena *'Lavender Lady', this section of the garden remained interesting long after the daylilies and campion had ceased to bloom.*

damp garden in early June. They must be seeded or transplanted into the garden when all danger of frost is past, which is about the time the petals of the apple blossoms fall, or when good farmers know it is reasonable to plant tomatoes. In a good year, one never looks back. The corn thrives, and promises to be ready by the Fourth of July. But the last frosts and the first ones are always capricious things, and one must be ready with old sheets, blankets, paper bags, whatever one has, to shield the young plants from a sudden dip in temperature. In the half-hardy class belong most of the familiar annuals, such as petunias, marigolds, and cosmos, and many less well-known plants grown as annuals, such as *Ammi majus*, daturas, and *Eustoma grandiflorum*.

Tender annuals all originate in climates that never know a touch of frost, which would surely do them in. But they are also intolerant of the "sweater days" of early summer, when temperatures are well above freezing but still chill enough to justify an extra layer of clothing. In this group belong many tender shrubs and several wonderful vines, notably *Solanum jasminoides* and *Dolichos lablab*. They will sit still and stare reproachfully at the gardener in the cold drizzles that sometimes come in June.

However, when the beach days arrive in early July, they will take off, making up for lost time, and they may stand the hot muggy days of August better than many hardy or half-hardy annuals. For this reason, it is never wise to hurry their planting; they will fare far better if kept in roomy pots in warm quarters and fertilized well to encourage lush growth, to be planted out when settled warmth arrives.

In this book, plants have been designated as hardy, half-hardy, or tender according to the traditional classifications. But care has been taken to respect the individuality of the plants, and to pass on cultural knowledge gathered from experience of their tolerance to the vicissitudes of the weather. There are always surprises, as any good gardener knows, born of the infinite flexibility of growing things.

Kochia scroparia *and* Salvia splendens *are often passed over by the discriminating gardener. Used imaginatively, even in a somewhat self-conscious way, they add both wit and beauty to this otherwise restrained garden planting.*

Using Annuals in the Garden

Annuals are plants perfectly suited to spontaneity, to the magic hours all gardeners know in early morning or just at dusk, when even the weeds are glorified by fresh dew or pleasantly blurred in the falling light. Then the garden looks its most beautiful, and its most promising, and the gardener's invention runs high. Annuals suit these moments, for planting them is no great effort, and if, in the harsh clear light of noon, one feels one has made a mistake, they can be transplanted, either to another part of the garden or to the compost pile. One can always do better by them next year. Though there are good and very learned gardeners who take the planting of annuals very seriously, and work out their color harmonies, heights, and bloom times on charts and graph paper, for most gardeners, annuals are a sort of garden play, reminding them of the time they first came to love plants, and gardening itself.

But despite—or perhaps even because of—their essential spontaneity, annuals cannot of themselves make a garden. In certain circumstances, when a garden is very young or when the lease at the shore is only for a single summer, they must serve in place of more permanent elements. But a garden should convey a sense of timelessness and settled repose at all seasons of the year. Trees, shrubs, hedges, walls, fences, and pavement are its main players. For all their indispensable charm, annuals exist only in supporting roles or, to vary the metaphor, they are the spices and condiments that enliven the feast. And so, in an established garden, they always seem to look best when grouped among other elements, and in single species. Planted in sunny bays of shrubbery, in natural-looking clumps among perennials, or scattered in seemingly random patterns along paths as if they had spontaneously seeded in, they may come to rest peacefully against and among their companions.

The magic of planted terraces is not often seen in American gardens, perhaps because a love of tidiness is our greatest horticultural virtue. Many annuals are quite happy growing among pavement, where they can often be directly seeded between the cracks, and where they will self-seed for many years to come.

This is, of course, not how American gardeners most often see annuals used. Abundant examples of their mishandling are one of the persistent facts of the American summer landscape, where, before almost any filling station or restaurant specializing in "Surf 'n' Turf," red pelargoniums or *Salvia splendens* alternate with orange marigold and white petunias, with an occassional silver artemisia or cineraria stuck among them in some recognition of the need to keep the peace. At filling stations, the result is to make one want to get out quick, which is perhaps desirable to the owners; but before restaurants, the consequence is a case of visual indigestion that bodes ominously for those who choose to enter. When one adds to this

*Annuals are often best for creating a feeling of romantic abandon in a garden. In this famous planting of common nasturtium (*Tropaeolum majus*) in Monet's garden at Giverny, the path is almost, but not quite, obscured by luxuriant growth.*

insatiable lust for color the most persistent of all aesthetic desires, that for pattern, the result is often a madly rhythmic planting, in which each single element is alternated on a principle of one of this, one of that, and one of the other, or perhaps fashioned into swirls of low, medium, and tall, with a single exclamation point in the middle—a cordyline, or a fountain of purple amaranthus. It is no wonder that most sensitive gardeners turn away with a shudder from such plantings, and from the plants that compose them.

But there is no annual, even among the brashest of color and the most frequently abused, that cannot be beautiful if respected for itself alone. It is no more true of annuals than of any other plants that they will automatically look good together, simply because they fit the same rough and largely arbitrary category. The misuse of any plant is a challenge to the gardener, to see if he or she could (if only in imagination) do better by it. And so the ubiquitous scarlet bedding geranium, if detached from its orange marigolds and *Cineraria* 'White Diamond', might glow splendidly planted all alone against a bank of black-green English ivy. Marine-blue *Salvia farinacea*, once freed from "patriotic" plantings of white petunias and red *Salvia splendens*, can be wonderful in the perennial border among yellow-flowered perennials—for example, *Anthemis tinctoria* in the softest shades of butter yellow. Those white petunias could themselves take one's breath away—quite literally, for their scent is magical—when planted in a mass around a terrace at twilight with no other shades to muddy their purity. And even *Salvia splendens*, planted in a colony of irregular dimensions with plenty of green or silver around, could add tropical splendor to a hot summer morning. (As for those cordylines, sold in thousands each spring as "spike plants," they can be superbly elegant all alone in capacious pots, liberated from the niggling fringe of blooming things that is usually clustered about their delicate ankles.).

The trick with annuals, whether rare or common, is to see them as plants rather than as flowers, or worse, as merely "color." Of course the flowers matter, and color is a positive appetite, particularly in summer. But many an excellent plant has been squandered for these values alone, when it could contribute as well its own dignity as a growing thing. Many annuals are beautiful in leaf and stem as well as in flower, and when planted so as to give full significance to all their claims, they can come to be plants as treasured as the choicest perennials or the rarest shrubs or evergreens.

Though from sentiment or sheer beauty many familiar annuals return to the garden year after year, there are always new discoveries to make. All gardeners know marigolds, in the heavy tall "African" form or in the bushy, lower-growing "French" sorts. New to many gardeners, however, are varieties of the delicate species Tagetes tenuifolia, *with fine ferny leaves and tiny single buttons of yellow, bronze, or mahogany.*

Above: The unimproved species form of Nicotiana alata *gains distinction when planted in a colony in a bay of shrubbery with no competition from other flower shapes or colors. At night this planting is luminescent.*

Right Top: Hybridizers are constantly at work on familiar annuals, and sometimes their work leaves the gardener wondering why the old unimproved or species forms were not good enough. New hybrids of Zinnia elegans *reflect true progress, however, for the colors are purer, the flower shapes finer, and, best of all, resistance to mildew has been bred in. Among the best of the new zinnias is this form called 'Red Sun'.*

Right Bottom: More than other classes of plants, it seems that annuals are subject to the vicissitudes of fashion. Cannas, much loved by Victorian gardeners, fell sharply from popularity 30 years ago. Now many gardeners are reevaluating them, for their bold foliage, a counterweight to the sometimes fiddly quality in plantings, and for their brilliant flowers. This canna is the very old variety 'Le Roi Humbert', which grows to 10 feet and produces a wealth of scarlet flowers.

Annuals in Pots

A garden that hasn't a few handsome pots placed about seems to lack something of its soul, and annuals have always been treasured for pot culture. Their limited root mass, their tolerance for dry soil between waterings (which many species actually demand), and their gratitude for supplementary feeding allow the gardener to cram all sorts of containers gloriously full of them. It is true, of course, that pots are always a trial for the busy gardener, since the plants in them are entirely dependent on him for food and moisture. This often means hauling about a watering can once a day in the hot summer months (and even twice in good "laundry weather") and remembering at least every two weeks to throw in some water-soluble fertilizer according to the manufacturer's directions. To look their best, also, plants in pots require frequent grooming, since a pot calls attention to anything in it, including a yellowed leaf or spent flower. Still, nothing more quickly suggests a deep love of gardening, or is so evocative of other places and other times, as containers of well-grown plants.

Some annuals, such as the stiff but gorgeous prairie gentian (*Eustoma grandiflorum*), never seem to settle well in the garden, looking often like plastic flowers stuck in "for the occasion." But in an old weathered sap bucket or a good clay pot, planted in single colors and thickly, to suggest a clump, they can be very beautiful. Other annuals are too brash for many bedding uses, such as the simple marigold or calendula; but they are glorious in pots, where they can add a dash of sunlight and some of the magic scents of summers past without posing problems of composition. And many annuals simply look their best in pots. Nothing, no matter how sophisticated, can ever replace the charm of a cascade of white petunias; but a petunia draggled in the mud after a summer shower is a petunia in abasement, whereas, in a container,

A few annual plants, left over perhaps from bedding elsewhere in the garden, can be established in a pot for an interesting (and portable) note of color. Often pots are loveliest when limited to a single species, and even a single color. It would be difficult to find another plant that would reflect the tint of this old weathered sap bucket as closely as does Gomphrena *'Lavender Lady'.*

it can spread its white sails unmarred. There are annuals, also, that relish root restriction and a moderately dry soil, even what gardeners call a "baking" soil. Neither the lovely lemon-and-orange-drop species zinnia, *Zinnia laterifolius*, nor the gorgeous, jewel-colored portulaca, (*Portulaca oleracea*), will do much but pout and rot off in the heavy wet soil in a cold garden. But in a pot they will show for the great beauties they are.

Pots also offer the great advantage that they can be shifted about at will and when they are at their best, to add a note of welcome at an entrance, or a bit of color on a terrace. If the pot is very large and handsome, one can isolate it at the turning of a path or in a leafy bay of

*When planted in containers, annuals are often most beautiful if they are limited to one or two species. Here the Swan River daisy (*Brachycome iberidifolia*) is paired with a single scented-leaved pelargonium, and asks for no further companions.*

An undue concern for good taste often prevents gardeners from exercising imagination in the combination of annual plants. No such restraint is initially evident in this garden, though one note of yellow would destroy its effect.

shrubbery like a piece of sculpture. And finally, making a collection of pots, of really good and beautiful ones, is one more way gardeners can exercise their passion, particularly in the depths of winter when it is not safe or pleasant to poke things in outdoors and when gardening pockets tend to be the deepest.

Pots should be large, since small ones look fiddly and distracting, and the plants in them, no matter how well grown, seem as if they would be more comfortable in the ground. Pots should also be made of natural materials, clay or wood or stone, materials that are unassertive in themselves and can take on a soothing patina with age. Highly glazed pots, painted with bright colors, are always charming in sun-drenched Mexican and Mediterranean gardens. But in our cool northern one, where light is soft and drizzles are regular, they look like souvenirs brought home from vacation; the attention they call to themselves distracts from the attention one gives to the plants. Plastic, for all its convenience of portability and its retention of evenly moist soil, simply won't do, for as a material it is the antithesis of all I feel about gardens. And half whiskey barrels, though I fell in love with and bought the first one I ever saw, have become so ubiquitous as to amount to a garden cliché. A simple box of good proportions, with feet perhaps and finials at each corner to make it fancy, is a much more pleasing alternative where a large wooden planter is wanted.

*Though most plants trained as standards are grown in pots, these standard heliotropes (*Heliotropium arborescens*) are planted directly in the ground, adding both height and dignity to the exuberant growth of annuals at their feet. Hardy only to USDA Zone 10, they should be lifted and potted before frost.*

Half the beauty of growing plants in pots is inherent in the pots themselves. Even weeds would look beautiful in this magnificent collection of antique English containers, originally made to exhibit florists' carnations.

All these are of course matters of taste, and there are thousands of found objects—old paint cans, rusted pot-bellied stoves, fractured Victorian urns with rapt, ambiguous faces—that can in the right hands form wonderful containers for annuals. For annuals lend themselves to such whimsy, and wit, when it is tactful and a little tongue-in-cheek, contributes a rare effect in the garden. I myself could fall for just the right battered enamel dishpan, such as I remember from childhood on the front porch of an old country woman who grew legendary achimenes in just such a container. But generally speaking, the best containers are those that convey a sense of dignity and settled antiquity, against which the spontaneity of annuals achieves a perfect counterpoise.

On the way in which annuals are planted in containers I also have strong opinions. The vast realm of annuals offers infinite possibilities for combining colors and textures. In containers, as in the garden, restraint is essential to the most beautiful effects. Too often, every bright thing the gardener can find or grow gets crammed in all together, and the effect is rather like the *hors d'oeuvres variés* of a pretentious cocktail party, leaving us at once sated and hungry. Plants from different hemispheres, and sometimes with very different cultural requirements, all end up in the same container, with

An effulgent combination of plants can sometimes carry its own sense of lightheartedness. The secret of success with this planting lies in its superb culture, maintained by frequent applications of liquid fertilizer and by the daily removal of spent flowers.

The somber dignity of this planting perfectly suits this house, acting as both a complement and a contrast to its ancient facade. Like so many successful garden effects, one suspects that it is somewhat accidental, resulting from the thriving growth of the purple heart (Setcreasea purpurea) *and the geraniums at the expense of the marigolds, barely visible to the rear.*

only the survival of the fittest controlling the end result. It is better usually to limit plants in pots to a single species, or at the most to two species that one knows to be suavely complementary. In that way, "blenders," which bore everybody, can be dispensed with. And "trailers," which always look in a crowded container as if they had plunged over the rim for more room, are unnecessary. For if the pot is really worth standing about as an ornament, it should not need to be hidden or softened. Planting pots with single species allows one to focus on the beauty of an individual plant, on its own peculiar claims of flower and stem and leaf. And as containers arc portable, combinations can be made and unmade simply by shifting the pots about.

Finally, a word should be said about the title of this book and about its essential contents, the plants described within it. The book is entitled *Annuals for Connoisseurs*, but such a title should not suggest only plants that are impossible to find, hard to grow, and appealing only to the most discerning gardeners (to the exclusion of all others). There are some things, like good bread, that cannot be bettered, however sophisticated one's taste; so anyone who loves annuals will find within the following pages names that are quite familiar, such as nicotiana, zinnia, or digitalis. Often, however, familiar genera are represented by unfamiliar species, as in the case of the genus *Nicotiana*, for example, where the subtle green-belled *N. langsdorfii* and the stately, sweet-scented *N. sylvestris* have been unaccountably passed over for the more familiar (and ever more bunchy and brightly tinted) alata hybrids. There are old-fashioned plants, also—bells of Ireland, datura, and lettuce poppy—that have been suddenly rediscovered and brought into fashion. There are also excellent American native plants such as *Eustoma grandiflorum*, the prairie gentian, and *Gaura lindheimeri*, a perennial of the Southwest treated as an annual in cold gardens. Both have until recently been

Our love of plants and color often causes us to cram containers full of bright plants in many species. Restraint, though hard to practice, often results in effects of quiet beauty that are more pleasing, as with this splendid display of impatiens in a fine old pot.

neglected in preference to exotic species. Finally, it is hoped there will be a few new plants, unknown to readers and justifying their attention. In every case, however, the plants selected for portraiture possess some extra distinction, some fineness of color or form or fragrance, that makes them particularly worthy of garden room.

It is of course an arbitrary selection. One of the most exciting aspects of the gardening enthusiasm that is now sweeping North America, and that shows no signs of abating, is that it has

Sometimes an oversized pot can perform the function of a piece of garden sculpture, focusing attention on a corner of the garden and adding interest to it. Lucky indeed is the gardener who owns a pot as distinguished as this, designed by Gertrude Jekyll and now in the possession of the great English plantsman, Graham Stuart Thomas.

returned to our consideration a serious attitude toward annual plants. They no longer require apology. The result has been that seed companies have begun to find that they can list unfamiliar plants with some hope of not going bankrupt, and even garden centers are offering six-packs of melampodiums or *Salvia vir-* *idis* with an eye toward something other than the end-of-the-season compost heap. Given these developments, the number of plants offered in this book seems quite small. But it is a start, and, I hope, an introduction. I am very fond of all the plants described. I hope you will be, too.

In the minds of many gardeners, annuals are still associated with the rigid, unromantic bedding schemes of public parks. In this California garden, however, they have been planted to create a feeling of spontaneity and lushness.

I.
THE PLANT
PORTRAITS

Towering to six feet and blooming from late July to frost, Nicotiana sylvestris *is invaluable for prolonging the garden's beauty through the dull days of August. The bright red of Flanders poppy (*Papaver rhoeas*) is not so enduring, but fresh crops of flowers may be produced all summer from repeat sowings.*

ABELMOSCHUS MANIHOT; A. MOSCHATUS

The fragile, five-inch-wide flowers of Abelmoschus manihot *do not appear until August in northern gardens, but are worth the wait. Even before they appear, the rick dark palmate leaves give good garden value. Two other fine annual plants, the airy purple* Verbena bonariensis *and the graceful quaking oat grass (*Briza maxima*), add their elegance to this planting.*

If it were really true, as wise people have said to reassure us, that there is nothing new under the sun, it would be a black thought for gardeners. For a large part of the wonder of gardening consists of the fact that there is always some marvelous new plant to grow. Annuals, particularly, are rich with the delightful shock of surprise, and as they are transitory plants, one can continue to experiment without ever running out of room. There are always new ones to try.

Sometimes they are fine old-fashioned plants that one remembers seeing as a child, but that have been unaccountably neglected by seed companies and kept alive by being passed among the gardeners that loved them. Sometimes they are familiar species that one long ago ceased growing, but that have suddenly been bred into new flower shapes, arresting colors or stripes or splotches, or that have reverted through self-seeding to a greater poise and grace than one ever dreamed they could possess. Or they might be neglected species in a genus, looking a little like but subtly different from other excellent plants. Among all these discoveries, however, none is more thrilling than a plant that has simply, for whatever reason, never been grown before. In this latter category belong two species of *Abelmoschus*,

Abelmoschus moschatus and *A. manihot*, both of which were almost unknown in American gardens until the mid-1980s.

Abelmoschus manihot borrows its odd specific name from a Brazilian native word for several plants in the genus *Euphorbia*, from which casava meal and tapioca are manufactured. It is a showy cousin of okra, a vegetable treasured in the warmer parts of the world. It resembles okra in tropical stateliness, and it might actually be thought of as an "improved" form of its vegetable cousin for ornamental purposes. It grows to five or six feet tall by summer's end, producing a stout, almost woody plant with many secondary bud-bearing branches. Its leaves are dark green, as much as a foot long and as broad, deeply lobed into seven sections, the two smallest at the stem end and the longest in the center of the palm. They are born singly on petioles as much as two feet in length, and they turn up gracefully to expose their entire surface to the full force of the sun. For its stature and for its beautiful leaves alone one might grow the plant, as a component of a "tropical" bedding scheme that could include tall canna lilies and species of *Ricinus,* the castor bean.

But it is the flowers of *A. manihot* that are its greatest glory. They do not appear until mid- to late August, for like many mallows, *A. manihot* does not really burgeon until the weather is warm and settled; its early energies are expended in the production of its thick stems and magnificent leaves. When the flowers do come, however, they are worth the wait. Each is borne singly, first in the leaf axils of the top third of the plant and later in great abundance (assuming frosts allow) in the tight cobs of buds that form at the top of its central stem and its secondary branches. Each is five or six inches across, made up of five broad overlapping petals, colored a fine pale yellow shading to rich butter-yellow. In the center of the blossom, yellow gives way to a deep burgundy, marked with garnet-red where the petal edges fuse to the calyx. And in the heart is a prominent inch-long

column of fertile parts, made up of a dusting of bright-yellow stamens along its length and crowned at the top by a five-branched pistil of Victorian plush red. Each flower lasts only a day, and though in northern gardens flowers will never be very numerous, one or two is enough to give special luster to a hot late-summer morning.

The other species of *Abelmoschus* that has recently burst into gardens is *A. moschatus*. It is a much smaller plant, hardly two feet tall, though its resemblance to *A. manihot*, and indeed to all mallows, is apparent in its two-inch dark leaves, typically five fingered, and in its five-petaled hibiscus flowers. Against *A. manihot*, or the eight-inch blossoms of the tender shrubby *Hibiscus rosa-sinensis*, or the vast Frisbees of the hardy perennial *Hibiscus moscheutos*, those flowers might appear quite small. But they are in fact large for so diminutive a plant, and very showy. They are about three inches across, flat-faced, and fashioned like a star or a wheel, each petal distinct from its neighbor. The flowers are an endless play upon a single shade of orange-pink; those of some plants may deepen almost to scarlet and others will lighten to salmon. In every blossom, however, there is a suggestion of other possibilities in the range it might have assumed, for the deepest are veined with a paler tincture, particularly on their reverse, and the palest have a darker stain in their throats. A colony of several individuals planted a foot or so apart will show this range of color in fascinating variety.

Seekers after fragrance in the garden might note that both in its genus and its species name *A. moschatus* bears the designation "musk scented." The plant has long been grown in tropical countries, particularly in India, for its seeds, which are used in perfumery. No species of *Abelmoschus* gives off the slightest whiff of fragrance in the garden. But blossoms of *A. moschatus*, picked on a warm August morning and laid in a room without being placed in water, may surprise the keen of nose with a faint perfume, dusty and sweet. To catch more of it there is no good plunging one's nose in the flowers. One must simply wait, while going about one's business, for a gentle tap of fragrance on one's shoulder.

Because both *A. manihot* and *A. moschatus* are slow to flower in cold gardens, one might think that a very early sowing of them indoors in late February or early March would hasten their bloom. They will germinate readily and will make sturdy plants when grown in warm conditions in full sun indoors. But north of Zone 6 they will sit and stare at one reproachfully when transplanted into the garden, hardly budging with a new leaf. They are therefore best started late in places where early June can be cold and drizzly. Late March or early April is soon enough. Because mallows resent root disturbance, it is best to sow their seeds two or three to a peat pot, clipping out all but the strongest seedlings, and planting the pot directly in the garden. Good results may also be achieved by sowing the seeds in the garden at about the time one would seed tender vegetables such as squash or corn, which is to say a week after the apple blossoms have shed their petals. Plants so seeded will often catch up with and even surpass plants sown too early indoors and transplanted into the garden.

In addition to the outdoor warmth that is beyond the control of gardeners, species of *Abelmoschus* require deep, fertile, well-tilled soil, abundant moisture at the roots while they are growing, and a light dressing of granular vegetable garden fertilizer when their growth accelerates in early July. *Abelmoschus manihot* is suitable anywhere in the garden that its tall stature, broad tropical leaves, and striking lemony flowers would be an asset. It is particularly fine at the back of a perennial border, where its boldness gives welcome relief from the sameness of texture that often occurs there. Because of its stateliness, it would be particularly attractive planted alone at the entrance to a barn or against a weathered board fence. *Abelmoschus*

Though sometimes sparing with its flowers, the hibiscuslike two-inch-wide blossoms of Abelmoschus moscheutos *glow, jewellike, against its fine dark foliage.*

moschatus, being a so much smaller plant with such delicately shaded flowers, requires a placement where it can be studied. It might look best in a sunny bay of quiet green leaves, perennial or shrubby. Because it relishes the heat, it could well achieve its best in a large pot filled with humus-rich earth, kept well watered and placed on a terrace or deck to revel in the reflected heat of high summer. Grown this way, it could be brought indoors when frost threatened its late-summer luxuriance of flower. On a sunny windowsill it might be expected to continue blooming well into the early part of December.

FAMILY: *Malvaceae*

COMMON NAME: *None*

FULL SUN; MODERATELY EASY; TENDER ANNUAL

AMARANTHUS CAUDATUS

Strange and somewhat giddy-looking are the flowers of Amaranthus caudatus, *beloved by flower arrangers. Though the more familiar plant produces streamers the color and texture of Victorian plush, the all-green form called 'Viridis' is easier to combine with other colors in the garden.*

Botanical names are often mystifying to gardeners, either because they are totally unpronounceable, or because they do not seem to apply, or most often because, just as one has gotten them to flow smoothly off one's tongue, the rules of "nomenclutter" require a change. Popular names are generally easier, though often they can be just as treacherous and sometimes just as mystifying. One sometimes cannot figure out why in the world a pretty plant has been given such an odd name. There are many examples; probably the best is the one the late English gardener Margery Fish recorded for *Sedum acris*, which was "Welcome home Father be ye ever so drunk."

Amaranthus caudatus could never top that, though for odd popular names it ranks high. Some poor soul chose to call it "love-lies-bleeding," and of all the labels it might have borne, that one has stuck most firmly. "Kiss me over the garden gate" is also current, as is "nun's scourge," which cannot strike anyone as cheerful. "Chenille plant" seems to most people both more descriptive and more pleasant, though, alas, not to me. For I vividly remember the consequences of a boring nap time when I was five years old, during which I systematically picked off all the puffs from my grandmother's best bedspread and arranged them into neat little piles. So on the whole, *Amaranthus caudatus*

Not typical of Amaranthus caudatus *but very beautiful is this form with shorter tassels collected by Marco Polo Stufano at Wave Hill in the Bronx. Like the more familiar form, its faded purple velvet gains beauty from being associated with weathered wood.*

seems to me the best that can be done to name a very exciting plant.

Amaranthus caudatus is for various reasons not an easy plant to place in the garden. It is tall, to five feet, and its thick, self-supporting woody stems branch freely and need lots of space. Its leaves are coarse, reddish in color, and often not in good condition. Florists, who value the plant highly, often strip away its foliage, though for obvious reasons such a practice cannot be followed in the garden. In high summer, however, *A. caudatus* redeems all its less attractive features by producing from each leaf axil long, ropey, down-hanging tassels that remain on the plant until autumn. In the typical form, they are a dark reddish-purple, though a

green form, 'Viridis', also exists. They resemble nothing so much as the plush valued in Victorian drawing rooms as chair covers, and the feel of the blossoms, at once faintly raspy and also soft, strengthens the impression.

It is perhaps the association with Victorian things that has caused *A. caudatus* to be so little valued in modern gardens. In the right place, however, it can be a stunning accent, both dignified and slightly giddy, looking like nothing else in the summer garden. It is the sort of plant one only wants a few of. It should be planted not only with plenty of room to display itself, but also in a position that will emphasize its arresting form.

Amaranthus caudatus comes very easily from seed, though success in the garden depends on careful timing. *Amaranthus caudatus* is a hot-weather plant that flowers most freely when days and nights are of equal length; thus seed should be sown indoors in sandy, free-draining, sterile soil about six to eight weeks before the last frost. The young seedlings must be grown in full sun and transplanted into three-inch pots. If they experience any check, from overcrowding or drying out or insufficient light, they will flower prematurely and never make good garden specimens. Though young, fast-growing plants readily accept transplanting, once they have formed their first flowers they cannot be moved. Gardeners who enjoy three or four frost-free months will have the best success by sowing seed in the open ground in late April. The young plants should be thinned to stand two feet apart. Any soil is suitable for *A. caudatus* if it is well drained, though giants are produced by a light dressing of granular vegetable fertilizer when the plants are about eight inches high.

FAMILY: *Amaranthaceae*

COMMON NAMES: *Love-lies-bleeding; chenille plant*

FULL SUN; EASY; HALF-HARDY ANNUAL

AMMI MAJUS

The delicate, chalk-white umbels of Ammi majus *can be encouraged to thread through stouter perennials or annuals, doubling its own beauty and that of its companion. Here it has been allowed to weave its way through the marine-blue cups of the perennial balloon flower (*Platycodon grandiflorus*).*

The name Queen Anne's lace is commonly applied to *Daucus carota*, a biennial native to Europe but widely naturalized and much loved throughout North America. Called also wild carrot, it is the progenitor, in its variety *sativus*, of the cultivated carrot. Though a beautiful plant that can glorify the wild garden or rough meadow with its wheels of lacy, chalk-white flower, it does not slip easily into the cultivated flower garden. Its long white taproot cannot be transplanted and if it is to be had at all, it must be sown in place to produce rank masses of carrotlike foliage followed the second year (if the mice allow) by abundant sprays of flower.

Still, it might be worth the space and trouble were it not for the annual *Ammi majus*, native to North Africa, which produces much the same effect with half the time and bother. *Ammi majus* comes very easily from seed, sown either indoors in early April or outdoors about two weeks before the last frost. The little plants are fibrous rooted, transplant with ease, and need little space. They can be placed here and there among larger established perennials, looking as if they had seeded in. However, the plants look best when they are planted mid-border in long elliptical drifts behind, and sometimes a little into, shorter, stockier annuals or perennials. By midsummer they will produce thin two-foot stems, much branched and topped with umbels of lace that repay close study. At the top of each stem is a ruff of trident leaves, thin as the finest grass and of the same color. Out of it radiate 30 to 50 tensile stems, varying in length from one to three inches. The longest are arranged around the outside and the shortest toward the middle. Each stem terminates in a perfect miniature of the whole, a little flat half-inch umbel packed with minute pure-white flowers. It is a challenge for children, or for anyone, to see whether the larger umbels can be held without causing them to tremble, for even the slightest touch will set all the tiny flowers dancing. Picked when fully open, the flowers add an incomparable grace and delicacy to summer arrangements.

FAMILY: *Apiaceae*

COMMON NAMES: *Queen Anne's lace; bishop's flower*

FULL SUN; EASY; HALF-HARDY ANNUAL

AMMOBIUM ALATUM

*From late June until frost, pearly everlasting (*Ammobium alatum*) produces its papery yellow-centered daisies atop curious winged stems. It is one of several annual plants that will lean upon a stouter companion, offering extra beauty and sometimes concealing dull or unsightly foliage. Support here is provided by the irislike leaves of the satin iris (*Sisyrinchium striatum*).*

There are gardeners who would never dream of making a dried arrangement. For them, the point of flowers is their living beauty. They strive to brighten the dark months of winter with flowering houseplants, forced branches, and pots of bulbs, and when all else fails, with sprays of persisting berries and brightly colored twigs. Gardeners of this persuasion often overlook the "everlasting" flowers, assuming that since their main virtue is a capacity to exist unchanging, they have no other charms.

A case in point is *Ammobium alatum*, which has been treasured chiefly because its two-foot-long winged stems topped with papery-white yellow-centered daisies can be harvested in summer and hung in a dark attic to dry, seeming to preserve their freshness down to the tiniest white-clasped unopened buds. It is, however, a charming plant in life as well as death, with a look unlike any other in the summer border and worth the attention of those who would never consider hanging it to dry.

Ammobium alatum begins its life in the garden as a loose rosette of ragged narrow leaves, about eight inches wide and looking like a chewed-on dandelion. By mid-June, however, the first flower stem emerges from the center of the rosette, clad in four continuous rippled wings. Here and there along the stem are branches and tiny secondary flower buds, signaled by a funny spur-shaped vestigial leaf where they depart from the main stem. At the top of the stem is the first flower bud, initially a little pearl and later a sempervivum cut from white paper. It unfolds gradually to surround a circle of hundreds of egg-yolk-yellow flowers. They mature, from the outside in, over a long period of time, eventually turning to rusty brown but keeping their snow-white ruff forever. Gardeners who are minded to dry the flowers should take whole branches, buds and all, before the yellow fades. Other stems will quickly come from the base to replace those cut, the whole summer long. As the flowers mature, they weigh down the stems, which twine among themselves, producing secondary up-facing blossoms all in a tangle. A great joy of *Ammobium alatum* is that its little daisies, when taken in hand and rubbed lightly with the thumb, emit a clear rasping sound, rather like the song of grasshoppers.

The name *Ammobium* comes from *ammos*, meaning sand, and *bios*, life, signifying the fact that the plant grows best on dry, free-draining soils. The seed, which is sown indoors in mid-April, should be sprinkled on a sandy potting mix, pressed in lightly, and never overwatered. As soon as true leaves appear, the plants should be pricked out into rich sterile soil lightened by half with sand, and grown on in sun. They may be transplanted into the garden about eight inches apart as soon as the soil warms. In warm regions the seed can be sown directly in the garden about the same time as indoor sowing occurs.

Ammobium alatum is so clear and fresh of flower that it conflicts with no perennial or annual of a stronger color. Its stems tend to be lax, however, and so it might be planted rather closely together to fall upon itself or on low-growing perennials that will not obscure its oddly crafted form, which is half the beauty of the plant.

FAMILY: *Asteraceae: Inula Tribe*

COMMON NAME: *Winged everlasting*

FULL SUN; EASY; TENDER PERENNIAL GROWN AS A HALF-HARDY ANNUAL

ARGEMONE SPECIES

The fragile flowers of Argemone grandiflora *secure protection from their fiercely spiny but beautiful sea-green leaves. Blooming from June to heavy frost, the season of this plant is much longer than that of most members of the poppy clan. Once established, it will reappear as random seedlings for many years.*

It is the birthright of all poppies to bear flowers of ephemeral beauty, as fragile as the finest silk. In the case of the argemones, however, fragility stops there, for all species arm themselves to greater or lesser degree with fierce-looking spines and bristles on the undersides and tips of their leaves, on unopened blossoms and seed capsules, and often on their stems. They may hardly be said to be friendly plants ("devil's fig" is a popular name for *A. mexicana*) but they are very beautiful, suggesting the stylized acanthus foliage on the capitals of Corinthian columns. Their leaves are deeply lobed, blue-green or sea-green, depending on the species.

All are marked along the veins with a tracery of pale glaucous gray. These leaves are richly produced on sprawling plants from one to three feet high; however, they branch freely along the stems where they topple over, creating graceful and sturdy bushes. They are never so fine as when they can grow in a poor, free-draining alkaline soil, reminding us that all are native to arid, desertlike places.

Though the connoisseur of foliage or the admirer of nature's ways of protecting her own might grow argemones only for their leaves, it is their flowers that will win them a place in most gardens. They are six-petaled chalices from two to four inches across, so delicate that one can see through their pleated and crinkled texture. In the center of each flower is a boss of yellow stamens, stained purple at their base and so rich in pollen that sometimes as many as a dozen bees will cluster inside a single flower, causing it to tremble with their energy. In only two days the flowers shed their petals, leaving behind a lime-green seed capsule topped with a little cap of mulberry red. No matter how many seeds are produced, however, the plant continues to bear fresh flowers from late June until September, providing a fine late feast for the last butterflies.

Of the 30 or so known species of argemone, four seem to be in general cultivation, and they are so similar in appearance that only a trained botanist can distinguish among them. *Argemone grandiflora* is an annual or short-lived perennial native to Mexico. Its flowers are generally white, though a pale-yellow form is listed. *Argemone hispida* is a perennial from the Rocky Mountains, white-flowered with fiercely prickled seed capsules. *Argemone mexicana* is an annual native to Central America and naturalized in Florida, with very glaucous leaves beautifully marked along the veins with a light-blue wash. Its flowers are yellow, though a white form ('Alba') and an orange ('Sanguinea') also exist. *Argemone polyanthus*, native to the western plains from South Dakota and eastern Wyoming south to Texas, is a biennial that in open soils can produce a taproot three or even four feet long. It is the least prickly of the four, and bears white flowers up to five inches across.

Whether annual, biennial, or perennial, all four species will produce flowers freely from a late April sowing in open ground. The small round seed should be lightly scratched in; after the first true leaves appear, the plants should be thinned to stand about a foot apart. Though all thrive best on relatively barren free-draining soil, a light dressing of granular fertilizer high in phosphorus and potassium but low in nitrogen will produce thriftier and more floriferous

Several forms of argemone occur in yellow as well as white. Argemone mexicana, *the Mexican prickle poppy, is typically a clear primrose yellow, though its tints can deepen even to orange and red. Its leaves are also dramatically marked with blue along the veins.*

plants. Grown in a spot that suits them, argemones will often reappear from self-sown seedlings in following years. With luck they will sprout just where they are wanted.

Because of the boldness and beauty of their foliage, argemones look best when grown with free space about them, in the rock garden or perhaps at the edge of a gravel drive or terrace. They find pleasant companions in other "architectural" plants, especially some of the noble perennial grasses like *Miscanthus sinensis,* 'Gracillimus' or *Calamagrostis* × *acutiflora* 'Karl Forester.' But they demand all the sun and fresh air possible, and will both look and be wretched when crowded closely among other bedding plants.

FAMILY: *Papaveraceae*

COMMON NAME: *Prickly poppy*

FULL SUN; EASY; PERENNIALS OR BIENNIALS TREATED AS HARDY ANNUALS

BRIZA MAXIMA

Even gardeners who think of grass as something to be weeded out of flower beds might be taken by quaking grass (Briza maxima). Its fine flowers, and later its seeds, are like catches of tiny green fish on a line, and the slightest breeze will set them in motion. Once established in the garden, quaking grass will reappear from year to year as self-sown seedlings.

A few years ago, having succumbed with all the gardening world to the neglected charm of ornamental perennial grasses, I ordered a selection from Kurt Bluemel's wonderful mail-order nursery and set them here and there about the garden. Shortly thereafter, I was showing a friend around, a great vegetable gardener and a nonstop talker. As she went, admiring this and that, she stooped down, yanked one of my new treasures out of the ground by its hair, gave it a few systemic thwacks and tossed it into the shrubbery. There was never a pause in the flow of her conversation, or any doubt in her mind that she was doing my garden a service.

It is still true for many gardeners that a grass, and particularly a self-sowing annual grass, is something to be weeded, not admired. Grass belongs in the lawn or in meadows, and flowers belong in beds, and no compromise is possible between the two. If you are still of this persuasion, then the charms of *Briza maxima* may pass you by, for it is emphatically, uncompromisingly grasslike. From an early germination in late March, it produces clean tufts of narrow-bladed foliage, gracefully outfacing in a small green fountain. By late June, the stems elongate from the center until they reach about a foot and a half, when they produce panicles of fat oatlike half-inch green buds on secondary stems, so hairlike fine that all hang down and the smallest breeze sets them trembling. Each bud is made up of overlapping scales like diminutive pale-green fish on a line. By late summer, the buds begin to flower (quite unobtrusively) and when they have finished, the panicles turn straw-colored, holding on up to a month after the seed has ripened. At this stage *B. maxima* is perhaps at its best, for it is strongly suggestive of fields of ripening grain. It carries this feeling in harvest arrangements indoors and in bouquets of dried flowers throughout the winter.

The chaffy seed of *B. maxima* should be rubbed lightly between the hands and sown, chaff and all, where it is to grow in the garden or on pots of sterile potting mix in late March. Usually enough young seedlings will appear the following spring for any garden. Once one has learned to distinguish their compact little tufts from the grasses one does not desire they may be left in place, if they are in the right place, or transplanted where they will look best. The most attractive plants are produced by spacing them about six inches apart.

Briza maxima always looks well planted along a path or in company with any stonework, and it adds a necessary lightness when it is threaded in and around the somber foliage of peonies after their great scented globes have been cut away. It transplants readily at any stage, especially if the work is done in showery weather; if not, then the plants should be well watered in after they have been moved. A diminutive grain field of *B. maxima* could be a wonderful surprise in a very formal garden, particularly if it is framed by clipped hedges of box or by stone coping. (In such a garden, the seedlings could be transplanted from a nursery bed, replacing an earlier display of bulbs.) I have always thought as well that it would be the best plant for a large pot so splendid that it needed no enhancement from flowers.

FAMILY: *Gramineae*

COMMON NAMES: *Quaking grass; annual Job's tears*

FULL SUN; EASY; HARDY ANNUAL

CANNA SPECIES

The leaves of all cannas are dramatic, but Canna × generalis *'Striata' is a gilded lily, ornamenting its foliage with stripes of butter yellow, above which even its burning orange flowers seem an afterthought.*

If plants could smile, cannas would be grinning all over at their new status in gardens. For almost 50 years, planting them was tantamount to confessing some low taste, such as a fondness for Hostess Twinkies or frozen potpies. Still, there was a sort of underground canna society, whose membership consisted of the very sophisticated and the very simple, but never of those who must wait for public approval to find out what they should be growing. For public approval has been strongly against cannas until quite recently. All the excellent virtues of these plants—their quick and easy growth, their splendid tropical leaves, their rich and abundant flowers, brassy, sometimes, it is true, but sometimes also surprisingly refined, their relish

for the hottest dull days of August—were passed over.

Meanwhile, the underground canna society continued to search out species and old varieties of uncertain parentage among the garbage cans and back alleys of the Deep South, to scour the cheaper, tabloid-type seed catalogs for new forms, and to trade roots back and forth, swapping a blue-leaved spidery-flowered yellow variety for a tall purple-leaved one with orange flowers. In this way, many fine forms have been saved, ready now to satisfy a renewed public interest.

There are 60 species of *Canna*, all native to the tropics and subtropics of America and Asia. All produce thick, self-supporting stems that grow from jointed underground rhizomes, each stem clad from its emergence out of the ground with clasping oval leaves that may, as the stem elongates, become quite large, to as much as two feet in length and half that or more in breadth. Those who think of the prototypical canna as a lowly plant with wads of orange or hot pink untidily lodged in its top will be startled at some of these species, for they possess great elegance and refinement. *Canna glauca*, for example, produces thin stems and grayish-blue leaves that give way at five feet or so to delicate rods of narrow-petaled flowers of a clear yellow. *Canna warscewiczii* is equally tall, but of more robust growth, with leaves and stems suffused with purple or reddish-brown and three-inch flowers of clear crimson. *Canna iridiflora* is considered the aristocrat of the clan, with ten-foot canes of huge bluish-green leaves and delicate racemes of soft rosy-pink two-inch flowers.

None of these species stood in particular need of improvement, and gardeners still wary of the genus will find in them beautiful and distinctive plants. But their blood, with that of other species, has been crossed and recrossed into a bewildering array of hybrids ranging from plants hardly 12 inches tall to 15 feet. Sporting leaves that are green or blue or bronzy red, or even striped, they bear flowers in every shade from white to deep red, excluding (so far) only blue and purple, and often displaying streaks or splotches of darker hues on a lighter ground. Botanically, these hybrids are listed as *C.* ×*generalis* (sometimes in older books as *C.* ×*hortensis*) and are further subdivided into "orchid-flowered" and "gladiolus-flowered" types, according to whether their petals are thin and curved somewhat backward or broad and flat-faced. It is the gladiolus type that many gardeners shun and the orchid type they seek, but recent work in canna breeding has created so many beautiful plants that are intermediate between the two that the old distinction appears to be breaking down.

Canna 'Le Roi Humbert' has been grown in gardens for over 50 years. Its purple leaves and scarlet flowers can hardly be overlooked in any planting scheme, especially as it can reach 10 feet with good culture. Those not faint of heart can have it with orange flowers as well.

All cannas are of very easy culture, even in cold short-season gardens. Seed, however, requires a trick or two. It consists of a shiny round black capsule, about a third the size of a marble, and is so hard as to have given the popular name "Indian shot" to the genus, for it was used by pre-Columbian Central American natives as ammunition. Before it can germinate, it must soak for as long as a week in water, or be nicked with a file. Even with such treatment, germination is uneven, a few seeds sprouting within a week and the rest taking as long as two months. Because they are so erratic, they are best germinated by placing them, well soaked or notched, in a plastic bag of moistened peat or sterile soilless compost in a place that can be kept quite warm, such as the top of a furnace or a hot-water heater. As the vigorous, ivory-colored shoots appear, surprisingly large even for so large a seed, they may be pricked out and planted carefully in small pots in a rich potting medium without disturbing those yet to germinate. If started in early February, the first seedlings to germinate will flower by midsummer, though tardier ones may make only leaves and rhizomes the first year. They will then flower the following year.

Only the botanically curious or those in search of particular species will bother with growing cannas from seed. A far quicker way is to procure dormant rhizomes, which may be ordered from several companies that specialize in bulbs or often bought at local nurseries and even hardware stores. The rhizomes should be firm, without soft spots, and possessed of one or more pointed growing shoots. In late February or early March, each rhizome should be potted singly in sandy, free-draining soil in a pot just large enough to hold it, watered sparingly, and held at about 75 degrees until evidence of life appears. Pots should then be brought into a sunny place, kept well watered, and fertilized with half-strength liquid fertilizer once a week to encourage vigorous growth. After all danger of frost is past, plants may be established in the garden, spaced from 12 inches to three feet apart, depending on their eventual height, or used, as is often best with cannas, as single plants at the end or toward the back of the perennial border or wherever a bold accent is required. All cannas are excellent in tubs and large pots that may be stood on a terrace or deck; used that way their somewhat startling tropical magnificence is easier to blend into most gardens. Because they are portable, they can be shifted around to provide emphasis

to dull spots, and even tried out by being placed in the border or shrubbery.

Once one has procured forms of canna that one likes, they can easily be carried over from year to year. As soon as the frost has withered the plants, they should be cut back to about three inches from the ground and the rhizomes dug with as much soil clinging about them as is convenient. Whole "stools"—the old-fashioned gardener's term for a knot of dormant rhizomes or roots—should be stored entire, as attempts to separate them or cut them apart in autumn may result in unhealed tissue that will invite rot or other fungus diseases over the winter. The stools should be placed in large boxes or plastic nursery cans, covered with barely damp peat or sand, and stored in a cool, frost-free place. In mid- to late February, the stools should be lifted out, shaken free of their soil, and severed with a sharp knife into joints with one or two dormant shoots. The divisions should then be potted up and grown on in the same manner as newly acquired stock.

All cannas do best in humus-rich soil that has been deeply dug and well aerated. Most like soils that are not waterlogged but never really dry, and so extra irrigation may be required during the summer. The most magnificent plants will be produced also by liberal biweekly doses of liquid fertilizer at full strength, especially when they are grown in pots or tubs. *Canna glauca* and its many beautiful hybrids, which may be known by a steely blue sheen on the leaves, are adapted to grow in standing water, and those lucky enough to have a large pond should try them, among rushes and water iris, at the water's edge.

FAMILY: *Cannanaceae*

COMMON NAME: *Indian shot*

FULL SUN; EASY; RHIZOMATOUS PERENNIAL TREATED AS A TENDER ANNUAL

CIRSIUM JAPONICUM

Though Cirsium japonicum *looks as fierce as any thistle, its pretty leaves threaten more harm that they can do. They are the perfect foil for the lipstick-red flowers, about an inch wide when fully developed, but showing their vivid color almost from first formation.* Cirsium japonicum *is one of many self-seeding annuals that will show up here and there throughout the garden once they have been grown for a season. Never invasive, always shy and lovely, the foot-tall plants seem to know where they will look the best.*

Few gardeners, and fewer farmers, will have a good word to say about any thistle. It is true that of the 200 or so known species, many bear beautiful blossoms composed of a shaving brush of hundreds of tubular individual flowers, usually colored a rich purple or rosy red and held in tightly by a wonderfully crafted scaly bract. Admiration generally stops there, however, if it gets even that far. For the blossoms of most thistles are born on a candelabrum of stout stem furnished with acanthus-like leaves that might also in themselves be considered beautiful were they not armed heavily with

fierce spines. Two species, *Cirsium arvense*, the perennial Canada thistle, and *C. vulgare*, the biennial bull thistle, are among the worst and most ineradicable of pasture weeds, the first from the fact that it can regenerate itself endlessly from the tiniest root fragments, and the second because it bears clouds of fluffy airborne seeds, every one of which seems capable of germinating, even in the thick grass of mown lawns. Where the bull thistle occurs, barefoot children learn to step carefully.

It must be from a bad family name that *C. japonicum* is so seldom grown in gardens, for its beautiful flowers display such virtues as the clan possesses and it is free of all their vices. As with all thistles, its leaves are wonderfully shaped, usually about four inches long, deeply lobed, and sometimes veined with silver. Though they look fierce they are not; the spines, when they occur, are soft and harmless. From an early spring sowing, slender plants a foot and a half to two feet tall are produced, branching gracefully along the central stem, each branch terminating in a single flower bud. From tiny infancy, the buds are covered with little silver-rimmed overlapping scales that are half the charm of the flower. The other half is the brush of close-packed individual flowers, which appear from mature and immature buds all at once, differing only in size. When fully formed and ready for pollination, each composite flower is about an inch across and as long, half of its length being made up of the scaled bract. In color, the flowers of *C. japonicum* are a luminous deep pink, unmatched in the garden except perhaps by the fine perennial *Aster novae-angliae* called 'Andenken an Alma Pötschke'. And though *C. japonicum* can bloom as early as mid-July from overwintered plants or from early sowings in March, its full value occurs when it blooms late. For, like 'Alma Pötschke', it is most beautiful in the suffused light and among the russet shades of the autumn garden.

Cirsium japonicum is technically a biennial plant native to Japan, as its species name indicates. In warm gardens, it will often appear as a rosette of attractive thistly leaves from self-sowings that will persist over the winter to flower the following summer. Even in colder gardens it will reappear here and there, though its seedlings will tend to germinate and flower in one summer. *Cirsium japonicum* is never overabundant of progeny, and its young can be eliminated easily (and painlessly) where they are not wanted.

Where plants *are* wanted, seed should be sprinkled thinly on well-cultivated ground in mid-April and lightly scratched in. The young seedlings should be thinned to stand about nine inches apart. *Cirsium japonicum* appears to be indifferent about soil, accepting rich and poor alike as long as it has good drainage. It does require full sun. If the young plants appear thriftless, a single application of vegetable garden fertilizer will encourage them to develop into strong plants.

A drift of *C. japonicum* could be beautiful in an open patch of the perennial border, particularly if it is grown close to some deep-blue flower, such as the late-blooming double form of *Platycodon grandiflorus*. The strong pink of its blossoms also associates well with silver-leaved plants such as artemisias and dianthus. Those who practice the exacting art of meadow gardening would want to sow it in patches made by lifting the turf and cultivating the soil, for, like all its relatives, it seems at home in thin pasture. Probably, however, *C. japonicum* is at its best when it occurs here and there about the garden as spontaneous seedlings. Grown that way, it is particularly fine in the rock or herb garden, along a stone path, or in the pavers of a planted terrace.

FAMILY: *Asteraceae: Carduus Tribe*

COMMON NAME: *Rose thistle*

FULL SUN; EASY; BIENNIAL TREATED AS A HARDY ANNUAL

DATURA SPECIES

Cool in leaf and dramatic in flower, Datura metel *adds tropical splendor even to a cold garden in southern Vermont. Its foot-long trumpets open at twilight and fill the garden with exotic perfume. Though each lasts for only a single evening, by early August there is a continuous sequence of flowers until frost.*

In Nathaniel Hawthorne's tale "Rappaccini's Daughter," a jealous magician is so possessive of his beautiful only child that he encouraged her to cultivate poisonous flowers in her garden. Bit by bit she becomes so imbued with poison herself that she is deadly to the touch. She might well have cultivated *Datura metel*, not only because of its sinister, night-born beauty, but also because, like many other members of the nightshade family, it is saturated with deadly toxins.

Many annuals are so familiar, so gentle and homey in their beauty, that we forget they are exotics, denizens of remote mountain tops or steamy tropical jungles. With daturas, no such error is possible. Though they have been treasured in gardens for well over a century, particularly in the Deep South, and though they have naturalized over much of America as far north even as Boston, no one could ever take them for granted. Homey they certainly are not, for they produce lax, large-leaved, shrubby plants as much as five feet in length, clad in felty bluish-green leaves that give off a strange scent when bruised, not precisely pleasant but not unpleasant either. They look in youth a bit like lusty eggplants, one of their close relatives.

The first stout stem the plant produces divides when it is about a foot tall to make way for a tapered bud sheaf that splits to reveal a tightly furled incipient flower of a dull greenish tan. It gradually elongates to a length of eight to 10 inches, at which point, just at twilight, it unfurls (visibly to the very patient) into a single enormous trumpet six to eight inches across, with a throat almost a foot deep. Colors vary from pure white to white flushed with lavender, to cream and yellow, and even, it is said, to red. Many forms are intensely fragrant, with a smell close to that of *Lilium speciosum*. The flower lasts only for a night and a little into the cool of the next morning, turning to a sad limp mass by midday (though if they are picked when fully open but before they have been pollinated, they will last two or even three days indoors in water). After the first bloom one must then wait a week or two for the next flowers, which may be twins, born in the clefts of the second stem divisions. By midsummer, however, the plant has divided and redivided to produce so many developing buds that several opening flowers become nightly events.

Datura metel is actually a catchall category for several annual or perennial species of *Datura*, tangled together in seed catalogs and hopelessly confused in gardens. The shrubby, even treelike daturas are easy to distinguish, for they produce stout woody plants to 10 feet high, and their trumpets are generally downward-hanging. Classed now as brugmansias, they make beautiful plants for the large conservatory or when placed out in pots or tubs in the garden. The common jimson weed (*Datura stramonium*), a plant native to the southern United States, is recognizable by its smaller blossoms, from two to five inches long, and by its sharp-spined seed capsules. Widely naturalized throughout the world, it is less garden worthy than *D. metel*.

But there the confusion begins, for what is often offered as *Datura metel* may actually be *D. meteloides* (-oides being a suffix meaning "closely resembling"), and *D. meteloides* has itself been confused with *D. inoxia* and with two of its subspecies. Seed offered under any of these names will still make very beautiful plants.

Seeds of all forms are handled in the same way. They are sown indoors in pots of sterile potting mix and lightly covered with sifted soil about eight to 10 weeks before last frost, just about the time one would sow seeds of their relatives, the peppers and eggplants. Kept at about 60 degrees Fahrenheit, seed should germinate within two weeks, and the young plants should be pricked out and grown on in sun. Just as with peppers and eggplants, the aim is to produce sturdy plants about six inches high by last frost, when they may then be transplanted to the garden. Seedlings whose roots are disturbed often have difficulty recovering, and so each plant should be slipped carefully from its pot and planted as gently as possible. They may sit for a while in any case. As their felty leaves are sensitive to liquid fertilizers, it is best to encourage them with a light dressing

Datura meteloides *resembles* D. metel *in every way except for the unearthly flush of pale lavender on its trumpets. Though the blossoms of both last in the garden only for a night, they may be picked just when they unfurl and placed in water, where they will stay fresh for two or three days.*

of the kind of granular food used for vegetables. Daturas can also be carried over the winter as root cuttings. (See "Root Cuttings," page 189.)

Daturas grown in gardens may extend to five feet in length, but they do not *reach* five feet. It is the habit of most to sprawl under their own weight, creating a lax, tumbling plant that presents its up-facing trumpets near ground level. This habit can be useful in the perennial garden, where plants may be encouraged to flop over gaps left by oriental poppies or by other early-blooming perennials that are cut back in July. Daturas can form an interesting vertical accent as well, if supported on a tripod of bamboo stakes. They will then present their striking flowers for close study at almost eye level. This is an effective way of growing them in large pots or tubs, which can be placed on the terrace, or for any other part of the garden in which one lingers at twilight.

FAMILY: *Solanaceae*

COMMON NAME: *Angel's trumpet*

FULL SUN; EASY; HALF-HARDY ANNUALS; SOMETIMES TENDER PERENNIALS

DIGITALIS PURPUREA, D. FERRUGINEA

Though modern strains of foxglove produce bells evenly spaced around the stems, and have been bred into delicate pale pinks and whites, many gardeners continue to cultivate the simple, strong-colored form shown here. Though beautiful in mixed plantings of perennials and annuals, foxgloves gain great dignity by being grown alone, and the shabby phase they inevitably experience is not so distracting to the gardener.

Except perhaps for hollyhocks, no flowers are more suggestive of quiet old country gardens than foxgloves. Their tall stately spires blooming in dappled shade are redolent of fresh summer mornings with the promise of heat in the day; and no matter how early one is up, the honeybees and bumblebees will already be hard at work, slipping busily in and out of each thimble-size flower.

Foxgloves are so closely associated with large rural gardens for good reason. It is true their rods of flower, rising to five feet, will be perfectly produced in dank sour city soils and in the shade of overhanging street trees and neighboring buildings. In the small city garden, however, where everything must usually be kept trim and tidy, their long season of growth requires precious space. And it takes a deal of patience to put up with their gaunt ripening stems and to find room for the swarm of high-summer seedlings that must grow on throughout the autumn before being transplanted in early spring to the places where they are wanted. Still, for those who love them, they are worth any bother.

And it is not so much either, if one gives a

little thought to their management. In almost any garden there is an out-of-the-way shady place where they may be seeded. The young seedlings can be grown quite close together until ready for transplanting; a patch hardly twice the size of a pocket handkerchief will raise more than one can use. Nor are the young seedlings particular about the soil at this stage, seeming to accept willingly rather dry thin soil if better things lie in their future. They are easy to transplant at any size from tiny seedlings to plants with leaves six to eight inches long, though one would not think it, for when dug from their first home they will come up with only a thin carrot of a root and some tiny hairs dangling at the end. But if their roots are not allowed to dry out, if the work is done in overcast or showery weather, and if they are given a thorough watering after being transplanted, every one will catch. Transplanting may be done any time from high summer to late autumn, and even in early spring in cold gardens. Planted in moist, humus-rich soil, young plants quickly form rosettes of broad, slightly felty, sage-green leaves, attractive in their way. Autumn transplants should not be given fertilizer until spring; that would make them too fat and fine to endure the cold. But in spring, as early as the ground is workable, a liberal dose of granular vegetable garden fertilizer should be sprinkled in a circle about six inches from the growing crown of each plant. The results will be magnificent spires of flower in mid-June, as countrified, in the best sense of that word, as can be.

It is after they are past their first magnificence that the real problem with growing foxgloves in a small garden becomes apparent. The single blossoms open from the bottom up, and a spire of fully opened flowers at the base, grading evenly upward to colored but unopened ones in the center and tiny half-formed buds at the top, is a wonderfully architectural shape in the garden. Shortly after, however, one begins to form a different opinion. For the first flowers

ripen quickly into fat seed pods while the remaining ones develop, and the effect, eventually, is distinctly shabby. It is best then to call a halt to the show, pick the rods that still have flowers in good condition, strip off the already formed seed and cut the stems down to size for long-lasting bouquets indoors. This means, of course, that one is clearing off a whole seed population for next year's display. But one rod can be left, even sometimes bent down to ground or tucked into surrounding plants to ripen unobtrusively and produce thousands of dust-fine seeds. They can be harvested when ripe by cutting the rod into a paper bag and shaking out the seed, which can then be sprinkled back onto the incubating patch for next year's flowers.

Digitalis purpurea is the species most gardeners imagine when they think of foxgloves. It occurs naturally in thin dappled woodlands throughout northern Europe, but it has been treasured for so long that it has come to appear wherever people have gardened and is widely naturalized in cooler places around the globe. In its typical form it bears light- or dark-purple flowers, though pale-pink and white specimens naturally occur, often strongly marked with spots of brown in the throat of each blossom. English gardeners who roamed the woods as children or who knew the plant as a simple old cottage flower transplanted from the wild will tell you that there is only one form of foxglove worthy the name, the "natural" one in which all the bells are borne on one side of the stem and hang gracefully downward. But putting aside the considerable force of childhood acquaintance with a flower, modern forms of *D. purpurea* have been bred that are far lovelier than the wild prototype. About 40 years ago, a pure-white sport of the plant was discovered in North America that bore its bells straight out and evenly spaced around the stem. From it has been created the Excelsior strain, which preserves the form of the parent. This strain produces taller spires than the wild plant and bears flowers of softer and prettier colors, ranging from pure white and white speckled inside with brown to primrose yellow and pale pink. It has largely replaced the older form in gardens of all but the most sentimental, and it can be kept pure through many generations by selecting plants with the finest colors and form for seed, eliminating all the rest.

Though *D. purpurea* is the only foxglove for many gardeners, it is not the only member of its genus that is worthy of a place in gardens. Of the 18 or so other species that exist, most are cultivated, and the best, after *D. purpurea*, is *D. ferruginea*. It is a pity that it is so over-shadowed by its famous cousin, for it is a wonderful plant. In youth, it looks nothing like *D. purpurea*, producing a tidy rosette of narrow, black-green leaves each nine or so inches long, tongue-shaped and radiating outward to produce a sort of nest. From the center in late spring emerges a single spire, clad in ever-smaller leaves until they give way to the developing buds. Each spire may reach as tall as six feet by early July, but remains arrow straight until the flower buds begin to open. They are a third the size of those of *D. purpurea*, tiny funnels hardly half an inch long, but they are closely packed around the stem, and their color is a complex brownish yellow. Each single blossom is fringed around its lip with tiny hairs, like the first beard of a youth. At no time in its existence, from newly sprouted seedling to withered stem, can *D. ferruginea* ever be said to be unattractive. In full flower, with five or so individuals making minarets of bloom in the rose border or in a neglected bay of shrubbery, it is arrestingly beautiful.

From an initial planting it will reappear about the garden for years, always rather shyly, sometimes at the back of a shrubbery and sometimes hard against a path. But wherever it comes it should be left, for it is one of those plants that seem always to know best how to complete a garden picture.

FAMILY: *Scrophulariaceae*

COMMON NAME: *Foxglove*

PART SHADE TO FULL SUN; EASY; HARDY BIENNIAL

DIPOGON LABLAB

Dipogon lablab *is a magnificent tropical bean that may be grown as an annual. It is as beautiful for its fine dark foliage and its brilliant purple seedpods as for its panicles of lavender flowers.*

Though the hyacinth bean will seem exotic to many gardeners, I cannot remember a time when its twining, bean-leaved stems, its vivid-purple flowers, and fat seed pods of the same hue were not familiar. It was treasured in my grandmother's garden in Louisiana, where it was planted to scramble up strings across her front porch and volunteered among shrubs. In company with the rampant pink-flowered sweetheart vine (*Antigonon leptopus*), it spread a glorifying mantle each summer across the derelict board fences along the railroad tracks from Shreveport to New Orleans, adding glamor to the unpainted cabins one glimpsed from the train speeding past. "It's not to eat," my grandmother would admonish. "It's only for show."

In this she might have been wrong, for Dipogon lablab (syn. *Dolichos lablab, Lablab purpureus)*, native to Egypt, was widely circulated throughout the ancient world as fodder for cattle, and when its protein-rich beans were boiled in several changes of water to rid them of bitterness, they were a valuable food to the poor. The superceded genus name *Dolichos* is ancient Greek for a form of pea, and the curious word *lablab* is the common name of the plant throughout much of Africa.

Where summers are long and hot, *D. lablab* is easy to grow. The beans are planted in spring where they are to mature with the "eye" facing downward, three or four inches apart. They will sprout in a week or two, depending on the weather, and should then be thinned to stand eight inches apart. (From a single seeding, some plants will come with violet-suffused stems and leaves, and some will be all green. Eliminate the green ones, for they will bear whitish or pale-lavender flowers, and are much less interesting than the purple form.) Growth is very rapid, and the first flowers will be produced by early summer on upward-growing stems five to eight inches long, soon to be followed by showy dark-purple pods.

In colder climates, hyacinth beans must be started indoors, four to six weeks before the last anticipated frost. Like all legumes, they are impatient of transplanting, and so should be sown three to a peat pot, leaving the strongest (and purplest) one to be transplanted into the garden when all danger of frost is past. Because hyacinth beans are able to create their own nitrogen, moderately fertile soil suits them best. They may be grown on a trellis or at the base of an arbor, or trained up sturdy posts and tied in for a vertical accent in the perennial garden.

Hyacinth beans are also wonderful when planted so that they scramble over and through established shrubs, throwing their purple flowers, cottage-garden fashion, all about. A few beans might be reserved to plant in pots in late summer for growing on a sunny windowsill throughout the winter. They will produce luxuriant, summery foliage and a few gorgeous flowers, with maybe a pod or two. By late winter, when the gardener's thoughts have returned to the out of doors, the plants will have become shabby and should be discarded.

FAMILY: *Fabaceae*

COMMON NAMES: *Hyacinth bean; bonavist; Egyptian bean*

FULL SUN; EASY TO DIFFICULT, DEPENDING ON LOCATION; PERENNIAL VINE GROWN AS A HALF-HARDY ANNUAL

ERYNGIUM GIGANTEUM

The pale silver-veined ruffs of Eryngium giganteum *always seem to catch the light. It is called 'Miss Willmott's Ghost' from the habit that great English gardener had of sprinkling seed of it in other people's gardens. Like most silver-leaved plants, it is invaluable for its capacity to brighten the tints of flowers grown around it.*

The names that plants bear, both botanical and popular, often become part of their charm and a reminder that all plants have histories to tell, of where they came from, who grew them and sometimes how or why they were grown at all. *Eryngium giganteum*, a biennial sea holly, would be a beautiful and treasured plant under any name; that it is called Miss Willmott's ghost, however, adds significantly to its value.

It came by that name because Ellen Willmott,

a legendary gardener of the end of the last century and the first three decades of this, is said to have had a few seeds of it always in her pocket. As she visited the gardens of others she would secretly scatter them about. Some months later, a strange silvery growth would appear, eventually to be surmounted by a branched stem bearing jagged ruffs of white leaves and two-inch-tall cobs of pale blue. Any gardener might legitimately consider this practice of Ellen Willmott's to be aggressive behavior, but as she *was* Miss Willmott, as the plant is very beautiful, and as her sowing hand could be counted on to know exactly the best place to sprinkle it, her work was left to stand. And the name Miss Willmott's ghost has become firmly attached to the plant as her best memorial.

The first year, from a late autumn or early spring sowing, *Eryngium giganteum* will produce a handsome rosette of basal heart-shaped leaves, each about four inches long, on petioles of equal length, of a pale grayish green, netted across the surface with veins that are almost white. The second year, in late spring or early summer, the "ghost" emerges, a tall branched stem that can reach six feet but is most often three or four. Wherever it branches, three overlapping bracts occur. They are cut jaggedly into spiny points like a holly leaf, heavily veined and of a green as close to white as green could get. At the end of each stem, terminal or lateral, the bracts increase to between seven and ten, surrounding each cob of flower with a prickly ruff about three inches across. The cobs are upstanding, prickly, and of a darker or a bluish green. In midsummer, when they become fertile, they are covered with bees. By late summer they have done their work and turned brown, but the architecture of the plant is so strong and so finely crafted that they are still very attractive. Usually enough seed will fall from the plant for a crop of new rosettes the following year, or they can be scattered elsewhere, in one's own or perhaps even in someone else's garden. Seed may also be sown outdoors in pots in autumn and early spring, pricked out, and grown on until the soil is workable and the young plants may be put into their permanent

places. Because *E. giganteum* is a quite hardy plant, little is gained by an early start indoors. Young plants can be bought from several mail-order nurseries.

Eryngium giganteum requires full sun, but is not particular as to soil, accepting poor gravelly clay as readily as good garden loam. The best plants, well branched and capable of supporting themselves, are grown in soils that are not over-rich. However, a side dressing of vegetable garden fertilizer in early spring of the second year is beneficial. In soils that are rich in nitrogen, the plants may topple over. They can then either be staked at ground level or allowed to lie among and weave through their neighbors, presenting their green-silver bracts and flowers as an unexpected surprise among other foliage.

Eryngium giganteum is always a little startling in the garden, and rather fierce and prickly-looking even when one does not touch it. Those who love it, however, find it valuable among other plants precisely because of its eccentricity. Planted in groups of three, its stark clear form can bring relief to the tedious sameness of texture that can easily occur in the perennial border. Like other plants of strong shape, it consorts well with stone or brick beside the terrace or in the formal herb garden or the edges of the rock garden. Wherever it is used, however, it should be planted so that it may be studied closely. It is always wonderful in a vase, alone or in combination with other, softer flower shapes.

FAMILY: *Apiaceae*

COMMON NAME: *Miss Willmott's ghost*

FULL SUN; EASY; HARDY BIENNIAL

EUPHORBIA LATHYRIS

Euphorbia lathyris, *called the gopher plant, has the reputation of discouraging those irritating underground creatures. But with its rigid dignity of form and its handsome, narrow blue-green leaves, each marked with a vein of silver, it deserves a place in gardens where gophers never venture.*

The genus name of this plant commemorates Euphorbus, physician to King Juba of Mauritania, and the common name, "spurge," is derived from the Latin verb *expurgare*, to purge. The problems must have been serious to justify such a remedy, for the sap of many euphorbias, when ingested, can bring on acute nausea and vomiting, and adding the sap to streams and ponds can stun or even kill fish.

Though these facts have been no impediment to the thousands upon thousands of Christmas poinsettias that are brought into homes each December, one annual species, *E. lathyris*, has gained recent attention just because of its poisonous properties. It is reputed to be a repel-

lant, or perhaps an exterminant, of moles, voles, and gophers. Whether they sniff it and pack off or ingest it and die dreadfully, no one can say and few must care. If it works, it is a treasure, for nothing is more annoying to gardeners than seeing a lawn disfigured by tunneling creatures, or sadder than watching a choice perennial languish, only to discover that its roots are dangling in the air of a subterranean highway.

But even if *E. lathyris* is not efficacious in eliminating small underground mammals, it is still worth growing. It is a rigid plant that even at the three feet it normally reaches might be called stately. Its thick stems are clad with lance-shaped five-inch-long leaves, arranged in fours evenly so that each leaf is neatly aligned with the one above and the one below. They are all of a cool blue-green, though with the first frosts they burnish into shades of copper and dull red. Even in very cold gardens plants resist the heavy frosts of November, standing up bravely when all the other tender things have been cleared off to the compost heap. Where they overwinter, the plants will produce small, yellow-green flowers at the top of each stem the following year, and a swarm of little seedlings that can be easily transplanted. Otherwise, seed is easy to start indoors in early April in the same manner as *E. marginata*.

If one's main interest in *E. lathyris* is as a deterrent to rodents, then little plants should be inserted just where mounded burrows are apparent, the riled soil pressed firmly about their roots. So planted, their strict military-looking order will convey a reassuring sense, at least, that they are doing their job. Because of its architectural beauty, however, *E. lathyris* might well be used at the entrance to a path, or next to a stone post as a strong vertical mark in the landscape. In such spots, two or three planted in the same hole, to give the effect of a clump, are always more interesting than the same number evenly spaced in a marching brigade.

FAMILY: *Euphorbiaceae*

COMMON NAMES: *Gopher spurge; mole plant*

FULL SUN TO PART SHADE; EASY; BIENNIAL TREATED AS A HALF-HARDY ANNUAL

EUPHORBIA MARGINATA

*Though snow-on-the-mountain (*Euphorbia marginata*) is grown for its white and sea-green bracts, the tiny flowers that nestle among them are also very beautiful, at least to the keen of sight. Wherever the plant is grown, it has the effect of cooling down everything around it, as here, planted with a sulfur-yellow* Achillea filipendulina, *a true perennial.*

The euphorbias are a vast clan of about 283 genera and over 7,000 species that can take almost as many forms as their numbers, ranging from lowly undistinguished weeds through shrubs and even trees. Many are glorious for the vividly colored bracts with which they surround their small, often obscure flowers. Perhaps the best known euphorbia is *E. pulcherrima*, the poinsettia, though the clan includes other wonderful house plants, such as the cunningly crafted *E. obesa*, called the baseball spurge for its roundness and the little lines of stitching that run up its sides. Gardeners in warm places can grow outdoors many beautiful euphorbias, the

best of which is perhaps *E. characias* subspecies *wulfenii*, which clothes its abundant five-foot stems with fresh lanceolate blue-green leaves and surmounts them with a five-inch whorl of chartreuse boat-shaped bracts, each chocolate-colored in the center. Where it grows well, it is almost always called noble. And in cold gardens, the perennial *E. polychroma* is indispensable for its mound of daffodil-yellow bracts in spring and its trim cushion of cool-green leaves throughout the summer.

But gardeners everywhere can easily grow at least one of the annual euphorbias, *E. marginata*. Widely naturalized in the Deep South, it volunteers each year in old-fashioned gardens, and is prized by those who have had to master the fine art of keeping cool. Shivery cool it certainly is, not only in its popular name, snow in summer, but in its appearance as well. Though its efforts in early spring are not much to comment on, being only modest growths of rounded gray-green leaves, by late summer it can produce an almost shrublike, much-branched plant three feet high. Then, the gray leaves all across the top variegate into margins of icy white, cool and suave against the violent colors and dust of late summer.

Though *E. marginata* will often sow itself just where it looks the best, or can be sown in place about two weeks before last anticipated frosts, early effects can be achieved by sowing it indoors in the first two weeks of April. The seed is large enough for children to handle easily; buried in a sterile potting mix to its own depth and kept warm on a sunny windowsill, seed will germinate in one to three weeks. The little plants should be pricked out when the first true leaves appear and grown on until after frost. They may then be planted out in the garden about a foot apart. Moderately fertile loam suits them best; an over-rich soil or frequent fertilizing can cause the plants to outgrow their space and become so heavy as to require staking.

Euphorbia marginata is useful for quieting the hot yellow and orange tempers of the late summer garden. But as with all peacemakers, it has its own distinction, and never looks more lovely than when planted in a sunny spot among dark-leaved shrubs or hostas. It is also wonderful against the tall spears of *Iris siberica* or *I. pseudacorus.*

Like all euphorbias, *E. marginata* exudes a thick, milky sap wherever it is bruised or cut. In contact with the skin of some people, this sap can cause a severe dermatitis, in effect rather like poison ivy. Extreme susceptibility is rare, but gloves are a sensible precaution when handling all euphorbias.

FAMILY: *Euphorbiaceae*

COMMON NAMES: *Snow-in-summer; ghost plant*

FULL SUN; EASY; HARDY ANNUAL

EUSTOMA GRANDIFLORUM

The native American Eustoma grandiflorum *was unknown to most gardeners until about ten years ago. Chiefly through the work of Japanese breeders, it now comes in gorgeous colors, including rich purple, shell pink, and pure white. Unless planted in generous drifts and rather thickly, as here, it can look stiff and artificial, for all its beauty.*

If there can be an annual of the decade, then it must be *Eustoma grandiflorum*. A magnificent native American wildflower with a natural range from Nebraska to Colorado and south to Texas, it was virtually unknown in gardens until about 10 years ago. (It is still largely unknown under its proper name, for it is very often listed as *Lisianthus russellianus*, a close cousin in the gentian family but a different and less showy plant.) Even with so short a history of general cultivation, it is not surprising that the eustoma has become so popular, for it is a great beauty, almost irresistible to those who see it.

But growing *E. grandiflorum* can be quite a different matter. It is a difficult plant, tedious to germinate and grow on, touchy about transplanting, exacting in its soil requirements, and so uncompromising in its shape and in the gorgeousness of its flowers that placing it in the garden requires great tact. It is the obverse of most annuals, which are in the main compliant and easygoing. Indeed, *E. grandiflorum* might be called a prima donna, (which is, ironically, the name Thompson & Morgan has given to their beautiful soft-pink double form).

Where it is well grown, however, *E. grandiflorum* is incomparable, a beauty to struggle for. Its thick stems are clad in bluish-green leaves with a waxen gloss, arranged alternately by pairs. Each stem is surmounted by three-inch flowers (at first only one at a time, the better to show themselves off) that open from cunningly furled buds. They are five-petaled cups, possessing the *art nouveau* grace that some tulips and many poppies have, with the same silken sheen, as if they were cut from satin or molded of wax. No annual comes in more beautiful colors, from pure and cream white to silvery pink and a rich purple-blue, often with a stain of deeper color at the base of each petal. The flowers last on the plant an unusually long time, often for two or even three weeks. Those gardeners who grow enough to cut say that they will also last as long, or even longer, in a vase.

Because it is actually a biennial, *E. grandiflorum* must be sown as early as December or January for summer bloom. The fine seed should be sparingly sprinkled over pots of evenly moist, sterile potting soil. Each pot then needs to be enclosed in plastic bags and stood on a bright but not sunny windowsill. Germination should occur in two to three weeks, at which point the plastic should be removed. When they have produced their third set of true leaves, the tiny seedlings should be pricked out and grown on in the sun. At every stage of its life *E. grandiflorum* is intolerant of poorly drained soil, so the potting medium should be liberally laced with sand, and watering should occur only when the pots seem moderately dry.

Like all gentians, growth at first will be very slow; do not attempt to hasten it by the application of liquid fertilizer, for the roots are sensitive to overfeeding and can be easily damaged. As the days lengthen, growth should accelerate, and the seedlings should be pinched back two or three times to encourage branching. By early June, plants should be large enough to place in the garden.

More than other annuals, *E. grandiflorum* seems to need a frame, a bay of shrubs, a large stone, the prominence of a gate or doorway or the edge of a terrace, to set it off, for in a garden where one mass of plants or flowers blends harmoniously into another, *E. grandiflorum* will always call attention to itself. Though plants are often seen placed at equal distance one from another, they are far more attractive when planted in clumps of two or three, as if they had sprung from the same root. And though all the colors are beautiful and the seed often comes in mixes, *E. grandiflorum* seems much more natural if colors are segregated, each shade given its own place. Because of its great distinction, *E. grandiflorum* probably never looks so well as when grown in a pot.

FAMILY: *Gentianaceae*

COMMON NAME: *Prairie gentian*

FULL SUN; CHALLENGING; BIENNIAL TREATED AS A HALF-HARDY ANNUAL

GAURA LINDHEIMERI

Gaura lindheimeri, *a perennial native to the American Southeast and hardy only to USDA Zone 7, can be grown by northern gardeners from an early seeding in late February. Its veil of tiny roses and white flowers will be produced from mid-July to quite heavy frosts.*

The appearance of *Gaura lindheimeri* in gardens was an event long overdue. A native of the more arid parts of Louisiana and east Texas, the plant is very beautiful, and it has what one might call virtues. The chief of them perhaps is that it flowers from early June until heavy frost, and is utterly undeterred, even encouraged, by temperatures that soar near 100 degrees Fahrenheit. It has as well a look like no other plant in the summer border. From a thick, carrotlike root, several thin wands emerge, branching here and there as they go, and furnished with narrow, toothed, willowlike leaves about three inches long. The stems may reach four feet eventually, and the leaves give way in the top half to tiny rose-pink buds that open into light spanglings of white, inch-wide, four-petaled flowers. They are always compared to butterflies, for they are scattered unevenly on the stems and look not so much as if they had grown there, but had settled briefly for a rest. As summer progresses, the thin flower spikes bend gracefully, more from their own fragility than from the weight of the blossoms. The very last of them, produced well into September, are burnished by frosts into a beautiful pale rose.

Gardeners who live in USDA Zones 6 to 10 can grow *Gaura lindheimeri* as a perennial, even as a long-lived perennial, though experience with it is still limited. But once established in well-drained soil, it should continue to appear for many years and will never need division or resetting. From Zone 5 north, however, it must be treated as an annual. There it will never produce the graceful thicket of flowering spikes it does in warmer gardens; three or four will represent its best effort, and there will never be clouds and clouds of butterflies, but only a precious sprinkling. Still, it comes very readily from seed, and plants begin flowering when quite young. So even the shy display it produces in colder gardens is well worth the effort.

Because it is a true perennial, *G. lindheimeri* should be started from seed early, in late February or early March, to produce flowers the first year. Seed should be sown on sterile, free-draining soil, and kept warm and humid by enclosing the seed pots in clear plastic bags or covering them with a sheet of glass and standing them in a warm place until germination occurs. The pots should then be uncovered, and stood on a sunny windowsill until the young plants are about two inches high, when they may be pricked out. Each plant will have a tiny white carrot for a root, and care must be taken to lift and reestablish the seedling without breaking it. At all times in its life *G. lindheimeri* requires excellent drainage, and so the potting soil into which young plants are transplanted should be liberally laced with sharp sand. Care

in watering is also required, as infant plants will rot if kept too moist. Seedings should be grown on in as much sun as possible, and hardened off for transplanting in the garden when all danger of frost is past. Sturdy young plants of *G. lindheimeri* may also be bought from several mail-order nurseries, and even, sometimes, as established, southern-grown, year-old plants in gallon cans. They are worth the money, even if they live only for a season in the garden, for they will flower continuously and in greater abundance than home-started seedlings.

Because of its fragile and windblown charm and its lovely pale color, there is almost no place in the garden that *G. lindheimeri* would not look well. It is often also best planted a little forward at the edge of a border, so its pale flowers and diaphanous form can be studied closely. But it would be an injustice to plant it next to brash, hot-colored annuals or perennials. It is an aristocrat, and not one of those pale or white-flowered plants of peace-keeping blandness. It would look most wonderful combined with other pale-pink or white flowers, using its subtle color to establish the whole scheme. Probably it could not be better used than among porcelain-pink, white, and cream-colored lilies, their large trumpets a contrast to its soft form. Their season would be briefer by far than that of *G. lindheimeri,* but when they departed, there would still be something wonderful to look at.

FAMILY: *Onagraceae*

COMMON NAMES: *None*

FULL SUN; EASY FROM STARTED PLANTS; MODERATELY DIFFICULT FROM SEED; TENDER PERENNIAL TREATED AS A HALF-HARDY ANNUAL

GOMPHRENA GLOBOSA

Most gardeners know Gomphrena globosa *in strident magenta, a color difficult to use well in the garden but splendid for drying. The plant now is available in other colors, the best of which are the soft old rose of this cultivar, 'Lavender Lady', and the burning scarlet of 'Strawberry Fields'. Gomphrena flowers tirelessly from early June to heavy frost.*

"Grand" was a favorite adjective of my east Texas grandmother's. By it she never meant anything exalted or pretentious. ("Uppity" was the word for that.) Grand simply designated anything that was gorgeous and bold, and in her garden it was the impression she aimed for. She loved an abundance of bloom in the most vivid colors, and her plantings would make a sophisticated garden colorist shriek. A favorite combination was *Gomphrena globosa*, in its most uncompromising magenta form, planted thickly among self-seeded lantanas in orange and yellow. She called gomphrena "life-in-death," a name perhaps of her own invention, born of her fondness for Baptist revivals, or perhaps from a dim memory of shreds of "classical" learning picked up during her time at the Carthage Normal School for Young Women. (We are told in Homer that the body of Achilles was covered with a blanket of gomphrena to signify his immortality.) From her plantings of gomphrena, she would harvest sheaves of bloom to hang upside down in the attic until they were dry, cramming them later into odd vases and receptacles for winter decoration. As a child, I agreed with her that the effect of gomphrena, in the garden and after, was grand indeed.

In the form I knew it as a child, *G. globosa* is a sturdy, much-branched, bushy annual to 12 inches, bearing hundreds of cloverlike blossoms in the typical magenta, and also in white and pale bluish-pink. Actually, the showy part of the flower is a tightly packed sphere of papery bracts, within which the starry yellow true flowers appear over a long period of time. It is the bracts that are dried for winter arrangements by cutting branches of them when they are well colored and hanging them upside down in a dark airy place. Unlike many everlasting flowers, their stems are stiff and thus easy to insert into a dried bouquet without breaking. Though the magenta form might still have its place in gardens, perhaps in the wilder parts with lots of grass to soften its bold color, it is for drying that this form is most treasured. In the dead of winter, in an arrangement of silvery dried artemisia and tawny ornamental grass, its color is very beautiful. Gardeners who like it for that often grow a row of it in the vegetable garden, and for them it needs no improvement.

But *G. globosa* has now been bred into beautiful colors that come true from seed, including a clear white and a soft lavender-mauve. There is also a shorter, more compact strain called 'Buddy' that makes tidy little bushes six to eight inches tall, no good for drying but useful for planting at the edge of the border. The most exciting breakthrough in the breeding of *G. globosa* is the vivid orange-red cultivar nicely named 'Strawberry Fields'. It is a lanky plant to 15 inches, but its long stems make it perfect for drying, and its burning flower bracts are stunning woven among clear-yellow–flowered perennials such as *Coreopsis verticillata* 'Moonbeam' or daisy-flowered *Anthemis tinctoria*.

Gomphrena globosa is native to India, and except in the hottest gardens it is slow to germinate when sown in the open ground, and very slow to develop until the arrival of summer's heat. It is therefore best started indoors, six to eight weeks before the last frost. Germination may be speeded by soaking the cottony seed masses for two or three days, or by bathing them in boiling water for a minute or two. The seed should then be spread out over sterile potting mix and pressed in lightly. Kept at about 70 degrees Fahrenheit, seeds should germinate in two or three weeks. The little seedlings may be pricked out when they are large enough to handle, and grown on in sun and warmth until after frost, when they may be transplanted into their permanent homes. Nothing at all is gained by too early a start. The little plants will just sit still and sulk until really warm weather arrives. First blooms should appear in late June when the young plants are hardly four inches tall and

Pure red can be one of the most difficult of garden colors to use well. Scarlet, however, has the happy effect of clarifying other colors and intensifying the beauty of green. Gardeners who know Gomphrena globosa *only in rose, white, or uncompromising magenta, will be surprised by the lovely new color of 'Strawberry Fields'. A little looser in growth than the traditional forms, it is invaluable as a color accent and as an addition to dried winter bouquets.*

will continue until frost, becoming more and more abundant as the heat of summer increases. Whole branches with many flowers may be cut for drying, or, if they are grown in the vegetable garden, entire plants may be harvested when bloom is at its peak.

Gomphrena globosa is so associated with high summer that few will think of it as a greenhouse or windowsill plant for display in late winter or early spring. Nevertheless, it can be very successfully grown in pots during the bright cold months of the turning year. Seed should be sown in December or early January, and pricked out singly into five-inch pots, to be grown on in the sunniest and warmest place one has. Flowering will begin in early March and will continue until late spring. Probably the compact 'Buddy' strain is best for pot growing, and no one seems to object when a well-grown specimen, even in the most vivid magenta, brings a hint of summer's warmth to blustery March and drizzly April. Stood on a table in a mossy clay pot with the magical smell of the greenhouse on it, it can look very grand.

FAMILY: *Amaranthaceae*

COMMON NAMES: *Globe amaranth; bachelor's buttons*

FULL SUN; EASY; TENDER ANNUAL

HELIANTHUS ANNUUS

Far from the heavy-headed sunflower most gardeners know is this delicate ivory-flowered form called 'Italian White'. Growing to a height of about four feet, it is easy to combine with other annuals and with perennials.

Any man's home is his castle, and so I had to tread lightly, and with many a warning cough, to collect the seed of my favorite *Helianthus annuus*. It grew luxuriantly in a rubble-filled vacant lot in south Philadelphia, next to an old mattress put out for sunning and a hut built of cardboard and other street-found oddments. The owner of the hut—and by right of natural possession, of the sunflower—was away for the day. So I took a few ripe seed heads, and left some money on the mattress. They were worth

the money, and worth the risk of being found trespassing, for the simple pure species of *H. annuus* is hard to come by through seed catalogs, though it has naturalized plentifully in sour vacant lots and neglected waste places of inner cities from Nashville to New York and from Baltimore to Kansas City. Residents of the plains states know it, in more salubrious environments, as a common roadside weed, and it is, of course, the state flower of Kansas.

It is a very beautiful plant, fast growing and

free branching to six feet or more, clad in raspy green leaves about seven inches long and half as wide, and producing, from mid- to late summer, a profusion of three-inch-wide golden daisies centered with disks of blackish brown. Its seeds are tiny, hardly twice the size of a grain of rice, and only a few will be produced by each flower. So it is, agriculturally speaking, pretty much no-'count, and the Incas, who first bred the sunflower into a productive plant, would have rogued out my favorite without a second thought. But its flowers are wonderful for picking, and the look of the plant, in its entirety, is quite simply the look of summer.

H. annus as most people now know it is far from what we might call the "vacant lot" or "roadside" sunflower. The most familiar of cultivated annual sunflowers is a great gawky giant called 'Mammoth Russian', which grows very quickly to 12 feet or so, and produces at the top of its stout stem a single giant head as much as a foot across. The solitary flower nods downward as if in shyness at its outrageous size, but actually from the sheer weight of the seeds packed within it. It is these seeds, arranged with fantastic mathematical symmetry (a phenomenon called *phyllotaxy* by botanists) that gives the plant its tremendous economic value, for they contain as much as 30 percent their weight in oil, which is very easy to extract, and very healthy for human, beast, and bird. The giant sunflower is also very easy to grow, being not much more particular about soil than the "vacant lot" sunflower, its remote ancestor. From land too poor for corn or other cereals, as much as 200 bushels of seed can be produced from a sowing of about three quarts. And the seed is delicious, raw or roasted, and provides a favorite food for many stock animals and for poultry and wild birds, and, of course, for the witty gray squirrels. Only other plants will fail to thrive on the seed of the giant sunflower or its husks, for they possess a quality known as phytotoxicity, which inhibits the growth or prevents the germination of any other vegetation.

It is for this reason that even lawn grass will fail to grow beneath a bird feeder stocked with sunflower seed for the winter.

Though it has great economic use, whether the giant sunflower has ornamental garden uses depends on one's sense of humor. For a great fat flower on a straight-up pole is a funny-looking thing. At the edge of a vegetable garden, or perhaps marching in a straight embarrassed line along a board fence, heads all down-hanging, they could be fun. Children love to grow them, for the seed is large and easy to plant, germination is quick, growth is rapid, and it is deeply satisfying to think that one's own small efforts have produced a plant four times one's own height and with a head twice as big. It is always important to remember, however, that some children are already gardeners, and such children might prefer plants that were genuinely pretty, which the giant sunflower never is, being simply very big and very odd.

Those who do not wish to wade into intimidating inner-city lots for the species form of *H. annuus*, and who do not particularly fancy being stared at all summer by the brown-faced giants of 'Russian Mammoth', will still find, even in seed catalogs, a wealth of sunflowers to grow. In 1910, a chestnut-red form of *H. annuus* (or perhaps of *H. debilis*, another annual species, or perhaps of a cross between the two) appeared in a field in California. From it have been bred a fascinating race of sunflowers, marked with zones of rust or mahogany or chestnut on a ground of yellow, and sometimes chocolate or wine-red all over. Double forms have also been bred, one so furry and cute on its three-foot stems that it has been named 'Teddy Bear'. Less winsome, though more useful for general garden schemes, are "chrysanthemum-flowered" forms with neat, full domes of petal in yellow, orange, rust, and copper-red. And through crosses with *H. debilis*, a race of miniature sunflowers has been produced, the best of which is 'Stella', a pale primrose-yellow with a black center, reselected into an even

*The annual sunflower (*Helianthus annuus*) has been bred into many sizes and shapes, from tiny stars an inch across to heavy circles with a diameter of a foot or more. The typical sunny yellow has been muted down almost to white, and tints of bronze and mahogany have been added as well. All sunflowers make excellent cut flowers, and when several forms are combined, the result, as here, is a fresh country morning bouquet.*

paler ivory called 'Italian White'. These miniature forms grow from 18 inches to three feet in height, and are excellent as drifts in the middle ground of the border.

As will be clear from the large naturalized stands of *H. annuus* in decayed inner cities, no plant could be easier to grow. Seed is sown on the open ground just as all danger of frost is past, and lightly raked in. Because even the smaller horticultural forms and the species produce seed that is still relatively large, the seeds can also be put in place one by one, and pressed into the soil to twice their own width, which is a more satisfying process for children than broadcast sowing and raking in. The seed will germinate in seven to 14 days, depending on soil warmth. Young seedlings should be thinned when they have reached about eight

inches in height, and spacing depends on the variety and the purpose for which they are grown. But two nice things may be said for *H. annuus* here: It accepts the close companionship of its kind better than most tall plants, so that even five- to six-foot branching forms may be grown as close as two feet from one another; and any unwanted seedlings can be very easily transplanted, when about six inches high, with a little ball of earth, elsewhere in the garden or into the garden of a friend. Plants will be gratefully surprised by a sprinkling of good vegetable garden fertilizer when they are about eight inches high, and though they do not positively need it, they will grow the stronger and flower the more freely for the attention.

One hopes that one would have noticed, without the famous instruction of Van Gogh, that *H. annuus* makes a wonderful cut flower. Barry Ferguson, a gifted flower designer who lives in Oyster Bay, Long Island, likes to take flowers of all forms, including the great staring Russians, the pale-yellow Italians and the brick-red and chocolate ones bred in America and in England, and combine them all together into a single arrangement. The effect, besides being very pretty, suggests some wonderful 19th-century botanical illustration, in which the various permutations of a plant family or familiar agricultural crop were spread out on the page "in variety." But in the matter of sunflowers, the child and the connoisseur, the simple and the sophisticated, join together. They are flowers at once so naive and so wonderful that a fistful of them, gathered casually and crammed into a mason jar, cannot be anything but beautiful.

FAMILY: *Asteraceae: Helianthus Tribe*

COMMON NAME: *Sunflower*

FULL SUN; EASY; HARDY ANNUAL

HIBISCUS TRIONUM

Once most gardeners have grown Hibiscus trionum, *they find they never want to be without it. Its delicate two-inch flowers, of the purest pale primrose yellow, are set off by hearts of a burgundy so deep as to be almost black. They appear throughout the summer, and are never so numerous as when August weather turns humid and sultry.*

It usually takes some time for *Hibiscus trionum* to work its modest way into the hearts of gardeners. For one thing, it has not been helped by its popular name, "flower of an hour" (though the flowers of most hibiscus are transitory, lasting but a day or a day and a half). Furthermore, it has been overshadowed by other members of its race, which include the tropical shrub *H. rosa-sinensis*, with its six- to eight-inch-wide blossoms of cream, yellow, hot pink, or scarlet. Another close cousin is the hardy, treelike *H. syriacus*, the old-fashioned rose of Sharon that enlivens the August slump with its five-inch-wide hollyhock flowers, single or double, in shades of white and pale to dark blue. *Hibiscus trionum* must contend as well with *H. moscheutos*, the marsh mallow, a hardy perennial that produces huge flat-faced Frisbees of white, rose, blood-red, or maroon, the largest flowers of any hardy plant grown in temperate gardens. Against such vivid competition, *H. trionum* can hardly be expected to take a prize.

Still, *H. trionum* has been grown in gardens for a long time and loved by gardeners, for though it lacks the flamboyant splendor of its near relations, it is a beautiful little plant with its own winning graces. A late-winter or early-spring sowing will produce small sturdy plants clad in three-fingered deeply lobed leaves of a green so dark as to be almost black. At first the plants form a single stem, surmounted by a cluster of podded buds, each consisting of five hairy leaflike structures, pleated and striped with dull maroon and forming a calyx that protects the infant flower. Even before the weather settles and it is safe to transplant the seedlings to the garden, one or two of these flowers may appear, the tightly furled maroon cones opening on a sunny day to five-petaled cups of pale primrose yellow about an inch and a half across and as deep. Each petal is marked on the reverse with a smear of maroon from when it was a bud, always on the left side, for the flowers unfurl that way. At the base of each petal inside the cup is a stain of purple shading to black, creating a zone against which the orange pollen-laden stamens and the turkey-red pistil glow. If, even at this point, one is not caught by the beauty of *H. trionum*, a place should still be found for it in the garden, for its steady production of little pale dark-centered cups from first transplanting until frost and its gradual thickening from the base into a many-branched shrub to two feet tall may yet work a magic on the gardener's heart.

One would suppose that being a mallow, *H. trionum* would demand a deeply cultivated soil, rich with humus and constantly moist. In fact, however, it seems utterly indifferent to soil conditions, asking only full sun, which it requires to open its flowers. In the garden, it can never be expected to produce a splash of color, and when asked to hold its own in a bedding scheme against brighter, more abundantly flowered plants, it will always look inadequate and faintly embarrassed. But it will shine if placed off by itself, in a sunny bay of the shrubbery or in an otherwise neglected corner, where its shy beauty can be studied like an antique botanical drawing. Three or five plants might be established together in such a spot, spaced about a foot apart, to interlace into a mass and to increase, for the gardener's delight, the number of flowers they produce.

Hibiscus trionum should be sown in early to mid-March in sterile compost. (In warmer, long-season gardens they may be sown directly in the soil and in the places they are to grow when the weather has settled.) Kept at a temperature of about 70 degrees Fahrenheit, the seeds will germinate in one to three weeks. Young plants should be pricked out and grown on in sun until all danger of frost is past, when they may be transplanted into the garden. Like all mallows, they resent root disturbance, so they should be tapped gently out of their pots, transplanted with care, and never riled about the roots. At transplanting time, the first stem they have produced can be clipped half away to produce bushier plants. Cuttings from side growth may be taken in midsummer and rooted for plants that will flower on a hot sunny windowsill indoors throughout the winter and into early spring.

FAMILY: *Malvaceae*

COMMON NAME: *Flower of an hour*

FULL SUN; EASY; TENDER SUBSHRUB TREATED AS A HALF-HARDY ANNUAL

HYMENOSTEMMA PALUDOSUM

The fresh, inch-wide daisies of Hymenostemma paludosum *perfectly reflect what daisy lovers expect from their favorite flower. Borne in great profusion on foot-high bushes all summer, there is almost no bedding scheme that would not be improved by their simple charm.*

For those who love a daisy more than any other flower there is no substitute. Even among daisies, those that are pink or blue or all yellow, or that are gathered into tight cobs of bloom, will not entirely serve. A daisy, a *proper* daisy, should possess a circle of snow-white ray petals around a furry bright-yellow disk. It should be borne on its own single stem, and should look as if it could tell whether love is true (even if one is past the time to put it to the test). On first opening, it should claim all the freshness of summer, though it might have leave to close in cloudy weather, reminding us that its name, "day's eye," is a metaphor for the sun.

To the connoisseur of true daisies, *Hymenostemma paludosum* (formerly known as *Chrysanthemum paludosom*) will not be a disappointment. It is a little plant, hardly a foot high and twice as wide at maturity, branched at the base into many stems, each of which is thickly clad with inch-long narrow toothed leaves. All across the top of the plant are hosts of little half-inch-wide daisies, with ray petals white as can be and disks of the proper egg-yolk yellow. Petals vary in number from as few as 12 to as many as 20, that number being by far the most frequent, so that if one begins with "she loves me," one is in for a letdown. Each individual flower lasts a long time, as daisies generally do. The effect from early summer to frost is of a sheet of perky white and yellow.

Hymenostemma paludosum is very hardy, producing its first flower on three-inch-high plants and continuing until heavy frost. It may be sown in a sunny site in any moderately rich garden loam in late April or early May. Young plants should be thinned to stand nine to 12 inches apart, and can be fattened up by weekly applications of liquid plant food at half the strength recommended on the package until they touch. Thereafter, the occasional removal of spent flowers is all that is required for a long season of bloom.

Hymenostemma paludosum is pleasant any-where in the garden that shows off its smallness of stature. It is useful at the front of the border, and is always charming along the stepping stones of a path. Like most chrysanthemums, it transplants with great ease, even when plants are fully mature and covered with bloom. A row of sturdy plants might therefore be kept in re-serve, perhaps in the vegetable garden, to fill gaps left after daffodil foliage has withered or the early summer show of forget-me-nots is past. Choose a dull day with a promise of show-ers, and transplant with a generous ball of earth. If the plants are watered in well and lightly wetted with liquid fertilizer at half strength, they will accept the move.

FAMILY: *Asteraceae: Anthemis Tribe*

COMMON NAME: *Baby marguerite*

FULL SUN; EASY; HARDY ANNUAL

IMPATIENS GLANDULIFERA

Reaching eight feet from seed in a single month, Impatiens glandulifera *is a dramatic plant for the moist shady parts of the garden. Its two-inch-wide curiously crafted flowers are typically either clear purple or pale pink, though a white form also exists.* Impatiens glandulifera *is an aggressive self-seeder, even in quite cold gardens, but unwanted seedlings are easy to eliminate.*

Every garden throughout the world seems to have its own worst weed. For some it is the little clover-leafed oxalis that sprouts in the cracks of paving or in any other place difficult to reach. For others, it is *Plantago major*, the common plantain descriptively called "white man's footprint" or sometimes "cart-track plant" from its relentless enthusiasm in following the agricultural improvements wrought by European settlers on the New World. The bane of all rock gardeners is any one of several species of *Saginia*, the pearlworts, which can find their canny way into the heart of the most precious kabschia saxifrage and slowly strangle it to

death. And many a casual gardener has found that patches of thin lawn or dry uncultivated sections of the border that he hoped could pass muster with a thin coat of woodchips has been vigorously colonized, just from one weekend to another, with crabgrass.

For me *Impatiens capensis*, our native eastern jewelweed, bears off the prize, without contest, for sheer noxiousness. It is in fact a very pretty plant, with healthy glaucous foliage, pale watery stems, and half-inch glowing flowers that can be orange or orange-yellow or sometimes even red. Along the damp shady woodland lanes and dirt roads it loves, it can be beautiful in its thick, four-foot-high shrubby masses. Still, it is a horrible pest. Shady sections of my garden given over to shrubs are heavily mulched, and though that practice discourages almost all weeds, it is bliss to jewelweed. It comes up initially like a groundcover and rapidly burgeons into a strangling green wave. It can turn boggy sections of the garden where good candelabra primroses grow into a persistent nightmare. Where it all comes from I cannot guess, though I know that it can shoot its abundant seed, pea-shooter fashion, for great distances, giving rise to another name, noli-me-tangere, or touch-me-not.

Given this experience, I hesitate to recommend *Impatiens glandulifera* (syn. *Impatiens roylei*), a close relative of *I. capensis*. *I. glandulifera* is a magnificent tropical-looking plant that can tower to eight feet on a hollow, succulent stem as much as eight inches in circumference. Clear-green lance-shaped leaves up to a foot long are produced gracefully as it grows, and from their axils appear secondary stems with smaller leaves. In early July, buds are produced at the top. They open midmonth into curious inch-wide flowers that look like a flattened snapdragon and are subtended by a spurred pouch almost as wide. These first flowers are soon followed by opening buds on the secondary stems, producing a display that lasts well into late August. Flowers may be clear pink or mulberry red (there is always a nice blend of the two) and sometimes glistening white. The first year one has it one vows never to be without it. The second year one might have other thoughts, though, for it is as promiscuous as *I. capensis*. Of all the seedlings produced we leave behind perhaps three percent, in a quite large planting. Still, those who see it here in late summer beg the seed. Despite my warnings, they do not depart happily until I have taken a large paper bag and forced a few seed pods to shoot noisily into its bottom. As with so many wonderful garden plants, it is a case of *caveat emptor*.

For all its tropical magnificence, *I. glandulifera* is a quite hardy plant, and seed will not germinate successfully until it has endured the rigors of winter. The seeds should therefore be sown in the garden in place, or in a nursery row, since young plants a foot or less high transplant easily. Alternatively, they may be chilled in the refrigerator for a month, and sown on sterile compost. Seed will germinate in early April, is able to endure some frost, and will grow rapidly with the onset of warm weather. Seedlings should be rigorously thinned to stand about two feet apart. Closer growing may cause them to topple over in a late-summer thunderstorm. *Impatiens glandulifera* will accept any good garden soil, provided it is moist or well watered. Fertilizing is seldom necessary, but anemic-looking plants can be encouraged with a drenching of liquid food. *Impatiens glandulifera* will accept full sun, but being very succulent, the vast plants tend to wilt depressingly at midday under such conditions, and bloom period will be shortened. Its best use is perhaps as a hedge on the shaded side of a patio, or in the wilder sections of the woodland garden. It relishes those shaded boggy conditions where few other annuals will thrive.

FAMILY: *Balsaminaceae*

COMMON NAME: *Himalayan jewelweed*

FULL SUN; EASY; HARDY ANNUAL

LAVATERA TRIMESTRIS

When well grown, Lavatera trimestris *assumes the character of a woody shrub, and smothers itself with an unending sequence of flowers from early July until quite heavy frosts. 'Grandiflora' is the variety pictured here, planted among antique roses, a combination that is always successful.*

To keep a garden in full flower throughout the summer requires a great deal of hard work and careful planning. Particularly in mid- to late August, the gardener's common apology to arriving visitors, that the garden has been and will be magnificent, is all too true. It is then that many annuals come into their own, since many originate from warm, long-season climates and relish that weather ruefully announced by the morning weather forecaster as "hot, hazy, and humid."

Among the many annuals that keep the garden going under such conditions, none are more wonderful than members of the Malvaceae, the mallow clan. Its 95 genera include cotton and okra and a host of excellent flowering plants, among which are hollyhocks, hibiscus, abutilons, abelmoschus, and anisodonteas. All bear cup- or bell-shaped or flattened flowers of refreshing simplicity, five-petaled usually (when they have not been doubled) and ranging from tiny half-inch stars to huge flat disks as much as a foot across. For sheer abundance of bloom, none is surpassed by the lavateras, particularly *Lavatera trimestris.* Where nights are cooler than the days by 15 degrees or so, it will produce sturdy shrublike bushes to three feet tall and almost as much across, amply furnished with dark-green wedge-shaped leaves. The flowers are four-inch-wide chalices of dusky old rose, pale pink, or glistening white, depending on the form one sows. Each flower is interesting in itself, being a perfectly formed miniature hibiscus of five flared and overlapping petals with the characteristic column of a pistil and many fluffy fused stamens in the center. The cultivar called 'Grandiflora' bears flowers of vibrant rose veined with mulberry. 'Silver Cups' is colored that invaluable shade known to gardeners as "silver pink," and 'Mont Blanc' is a pristine white with gossamer-thin petals of satiny sheen. However, *L. trimestris* is treasured not so much for the beauty of the single blossoms, but for their abundance. Flowers are born in such numbers from late July until frost that the sturdy plants are smothered with them. The air of clean good health carried by each plant is never spoiled by spent flowers, as they drop off like little furled umbrellas when the work of pollination has been done. Whole stems of *L. trimestris* may also be picked in early morning and gathered tightly together in a vase, where the flowers and the good green leaves combine together for a wonderful bouquet.

Lavatera trimestris is classed as a hardy annual, which means that it is somewhat frost resistant and may be sown in the open ground where it is to bloom. That is a good thing, for like many mallows, it resents root disturbance and is difficult to establish in the garden from small transplants. This can be done, by sowing the seed three to a peat pot in a sterile potting mix in mid-March and growing on the young seedlings until they have developed three or four sets of leaves, when all but the strongest should be decapitated at soil level with scissors. The remaining survivor should be encouraged to enjoy its good luck by weekly doses of half-strength liquid fertilizer until frost is out of the garden, when it may be planted, peat pot and all. Seeds sown in the garden about two weeks before the last frost date will usually catch up with transplants, however, and will produce healthier and more floriferous plants. The seeds should be sown in fertile well-drained soil and thinned to stand about 12 inches apart. A side-dressing of granular vegetable garden fertilizer applied when the young plants are six to eight inches tall and have begun to branch will assist in their development, though they will not really burgeon until the arrival of the warm days of early July; then their growth is surprisingly rapid and luxuriant. The first flowers will be produced by the beginning of August, while the last will appear well into September. The species name, *trimestris*, refers to the three-month-long blooming period of which the plant is capable, and though gardeners in short-season parts of the country will not get quite that much from it, what they do get will come just when it is needed most.

It is a poor thing to say of any annual that it is "perennial-like" or "shrublike," as if to be "annual-like" were a negative quality. It is true of *L. trimestris*, however, that its dense, three-foot-tall bushes, well furnished with both healthy leaves and beautiful flowers, create the effect of an attractive shrub in the garden. It is therefore very useful in sturdy substantial masses of three or more plants to lend weight in the perennial or annual border among more fiddling neighbors, and a single specimen is portly enough to stand alone. The best use of *L. trimestris* may be in the rose border, where its healthy green foliage can effectively mask the shanks of shrub or tea roses when they are not a garden asset, and where its beautiful flowers, planted in rich drifts of deep rose, pale pink, and white, can add beauty to a spot in the garden that could otherwise most charitably be described as resting.

FAMILY: *Malvaceae*

COMMON NAMES: *Tree mallow; rose mallow*

FULL SUN; MODERATELY EASY; HARDY ANNUAL

LINARIA MAROCCANA

Curious of name, and curious in flower is the toad flax, Linaria maroccana. *Though never showy, its gentle beauty is suitable for the edge of a path or the front of a border. In those places, its amusing flower form, like a tiny snapdragon, can be studied closely. It may be seeded directly over spring bulbs to take their place in summer, and it is lovely growing among the pavers of a planted terrace.*

The family *Scrophulariaceae* comprises about 120 separate genera and more than 3,000 species, many of which are much-loved garden plants, not only for their beauty but also for their perky whimsicality. This family characteristic is reflected in the droll popular names they bear, such as monkey flower (*Mimulus*), foxglove (*Digitalis*), clown flower and wishbone flower (*Torenia*), snapdragon (*Antirrhinum*) and toadflax, which is the common name given to *Linaria maroccana*.

Though the leaves of *L. maroccana* look like those of the true flax (*Linum*), it is a little hard to know how the toad part applies. Toads don't spin, one supposes, or wear linen shirts, except perhaps when they revert to princes. Perhaps the tiny faces of its flowers, hardly ever more than a quarter of an inch across, looked to someone like the face of that comical amphibian. Or perhaps toads were observed squatting among its thick tufts of grasslike leaves, waiting expectantly for the swarms of insects drawn to its nectar-laden flowers. However it came to be, the name toadflax has stuck, and it is not the least of *L. maroccana*'s charms.

Linaria maroccana is a small plant, hardly more than eight to 10 inches tall. It produces from a single woody stem many branches, thickly congested and facing upward as the plant creeps for a foot or so along the ground. The branches are dense with grassy leaves, an inch or so long where they sprout from the main stem but decreasing in size on secondary branches to little blades of less than half an inch. Each branch terminates in many wiry stems, close-packed with tiny flowers so that the whole effect is of a cushion of bloom. The flowers themselves are like minute snapdragons, with two flared upper lobes and a pursed lower lip flanked by two more lobes that look like the cheeks of a chubby little face. The color may be anything from white, yellow, pink, red, blue, lavender, or purple, but in all except the palest shades there is a smudge of yellow where the lip puckers outward. Though the individual flowers are extremely small, on a well-grown plant they are produced in such numbers that they offer strong patches of color, a garden value enhanced by their distinct charm when one takes a toad's-eye view of them.

Linaria maroccana originated in North Africa, as its species name indicates, but it has become naturalized in many places in New England, particularly along roadsides and in thin meadows where the competition from grasses is not too intense. Its choice of a foster home indicates its cultural preferences. It relishes a cool wet spring, and it flowers best where night temperatures drop 15 or so degrees below daytime highs. Under such conditions it will begin flowering in mid-June and continue through the summer, taking a small vacation in August and blooming again when the nights cool off. In warmer gardens it is transitory, flowering abundantly in early summer and burning off in the heat of late July.

Because it is a hardy annual, *L. maroccana* may be sown outdoors in late autumn or in very early spring, even on the partially thawed snow. Alternatively, it may be sown indoors about six weeks before the last frost date and transplanted into the garden where it is wanted after danger of frost has past. Seedlings should be thinned or young transplants established so that they stand about six to eight inches apart. They will quickly interweave into one mass, and flowering should begin about eight weeks after germination.

Linaria maroccana has many uses in the garden. Its low tufted growth immediately suggests it as a "facing-down" plant in front of taller annuals or perennials, but as its foliage is grasslike in effect, it should not be blurred by conjunction with lawn turf. It looks far better when it may tumble against some hard edge, a path or terrace or large boulders in the rock garden, or perhaps the top course of a stone retaining wall. The best use I ever saw for it was in a large fieldstone terrace, where it had liberally seeded among the cracks of the pavers. Over the years frost had heaved the stones into a less than level surface, and rather than undertake the labor and expense of relaying the stones, the owner had established mosses and low-growing tufted perennials among them and seeded in, for summer interest, several quick-growing annuals. Happiest among them, both in growth and in effect, were sheets of *L. maroccana* interspersed with white alyssum, all interwoven but kept separate, here and there, by the larger masses of pavement. The little faces of the toadflax shone against such a frame. For those who have such a spot it was an effect to emulate.

FAMILY: *Scrophulariaceae*

COMMON NAME: *Toadflax*

FULL SUN; EASY; HARDY ANNUAL

LOBULARIA MARITIMA

Lobularia maritima is invaluable for seeding among spring bulbs, to cover gaps when they are gone. Its gentle unobtrusive beauty also makes it an effective softener of harsher and more pronounced flower colors and shapes.

In southern Vermont, there is a time, usually in the last week or two of August, when a cold front moves in, sweeping away overnight the thick hazy humid weather, bane alike to the garden and the gardener. One knows it has come when one wakes in the night to the welcome sound of rain, and realizes sleepily that the covering of a thin sheet is not enough, that a blanket or two is needed. The next morning one wakes, for the first time in weeks it seems, refreshed. Everything sparkles in the cold morning air. The light slants differently across the leaves, more silver than gold. Tired foliage is freshened. The ground, yesterday powdery and gray, now looks rich and dark. A faint promise of heat in the day tells that summer's lease is not all spent, that hot days and drought and restless nights are still to occur. But for the time one's mood, the garden, and its plants all rejoice in the promise of the year turning toward autumn. It is just precisely on such a morning that I remember how much I like *Lobularia maritima*.

Long known to gardeners as sweet alyssum, the plant must now travel under that clumsy and unfamiliar name because, as *Hortus Third* notes, it is "lacking stellate hairs." For all that lack, about which the gardener can hardly care, it ought to be known as sweet alyssum still, for the name is as pretty as the plant. It designates the lovely fragrance of the tiny flowers that is always there, but that releases itself in honey-scented clouds on an occasional cool day in late summer and throughout the autumn, well past the first frosts. Alyssum, too, is a fine word, meaning "without rage." There could be nothing softer looking or more peaceful than its cushions of flowers borne in whorls so thick as to hide the little half-inch blade-shaped leaves. It will spread about the garden in any neglected place, never surprising one with its charms but rather creeping, bit by bit, into notice.

It has been a long time since I remember planting sweet alyssum in the garden. In addition to the white, however, I must have planted also some deep purples and perhaps some mulberry pinks, for the seeds that come up now, though faded from those shades, show a blend of white with pale lavender and the faintest old rose, like sun-faded chintz. As with many plants that may be counted on to self-seed in the garden for years after an initial planting, sweet alyssum seems to have an instinct for coming up where it looks best. It now appears in gentle sheets along the edges of the stone paths and in the crevices of the large pavers of the terraces. Though it must be there in summer, and contribute much to the general mass of flower then, it is in autumn, after frost has carried off many of the tender annuals, that it is the one flower one most notices. And smells.

Lobularia maritima may be seeded indoors in early April for early flower if one wants it. The tiny seeds germinate quickly when sown on sterile potting mix, left uncovered, and kept at about 60 degrees Fahrenheit. The infant plants are tiny at first, however, and they do not easily accept root disturbance. Old gardeners often sowed two or three seeds in half an egg shell filled with soil, growing them on without disturbance and planting them, shell and all, outdoors in the garden in late May. Results as good can be had by sowing them into the cells of thin-walled plastic six-packs, growing on two or three seedlings per cell until they may be gently eased out in a block and planted. Plants started indoors may begin to flower by early June, though they may bloom themselves out by midsummer. Then it is often worth shearing back their tips with scissors, removing only the spent blossoms and seed heads but not cutting hard back into the old stems. Drenched with liquid fertilizer, sheared plants often rally to bloom again.

Because *Lobularia maritima* comes so quickly and easily from seed, however, and because it is really most appreciated in late summer and autumn, it seems hardly worth seeding it indoors. Better to take a seed packet or two about the garden in late May and early June, tapping a few seeds along a path, at the foot of roses, perhaps in the brick or paving of the terrace, wherever they might seem to have come naturally. More than perhaps in any other place, they should be sprinkled lightly into the maturing foliage of clumps of daffodils, for they will grow happily among the withering foliage, and when it is quite gone, they will spread a soft clothing sheet across the ground above the dormant bulbs.

FAMILY: *Brassicaceae*

COMMON NAME: *Sweet alyssum*

FULL SUN OR LIGHT SHADE; EASY; HARDY ANNUAL

MELAMPODIUM PALUDOSUM

Five plants of Melampodium paludosum *were established in this old green sap bucket, and by late June they had grown to seem one full bush, studded with inch-wide daisies. Flowering continued until frost, providing cheerful (and portable) color throughout the summer. Like many annual composites,* M. pladopsum *sheds its spent flowers, saving the gardener the tedious work of dead-heading.*

The genus *Melampodium* belongs to the vast daisy clan, the composites, now designated as the Asteraceae by botanists. Like most members of its family, *M. paludosum* possesses an innate look of cheerful well-being. Hardly more than 12 inches tall at maturity, its inch-wide chrome-yellow daisies emerge on three-inch stems practically with the first true leaves. Wherever a flower sprouts, the stem divides, nestling two more buds beneath the mature flower. By early summer, the result is a fine green bush, well furnished with three-inch pale-green leaves, raspy to the touch, a sort of lilliputian sunflower. Abundant flowers are produced from

first setting out until frosts cut them down. Cuttings may be taken in midsummer for an additional stock of quick-maturing plants, or in late summer to flower over the winter in a sunny greenhouse or on a bright south-facing windowsill.

Though unknown in American gardens ten years ago, *M. paludosum* has already proven itself to be almost indispensable. It relishes a moderately fertile well-cultivated soil, and the heat and drought of July and August are what it likes the best. Overfeeding produces lush foliage at the expense of flowers, and a heavy damp soil will cause it to sulk, and encourage slugs. Its best uses in the garden are as clumps of from five to seven plants, spaced about eight inches apart in open areas of the perennial garden or along a path. They quickly grow together to form natural-seeming colonies. Though excellent with other yellow, orange, or red flowers in the "hot" border, the color of *M. paludosum* is clear enough and its leaves so fresh and abundant that it can offer an enlivening note of contrast to masses of blue, pale pink, or mauve.

Melampodium paludosum is also excellently suited to container culture. Its love of relative drought and abundant warmth brings it to perfection when other container plants have gone off. It can be used in pots and tubs or in window boxes with other annuals, but it is charming enough to be allowed exclusive use of its own space. It is a chatty sort of little plant that does best when it has plenty of conversation with its own kind.

Melampodium paludosum is simple to raise from seed. For the longest period of bloom it should be started under glass or on a sunny windowsill in sterile potting mix when even temperatures around 70 degrees Fahrenheit can be assured. Seedlings appear in about 10 days, and should be pricked out or thinned when the first true leaves appear. (As with many hairy-leaved plants, damping off from crowding or from poor air circulation is a threat.) Sturdy seedlings can then be planted out after all danger of frost is past.

FAMILY: *Asteraceae: Helianthus Tribe*

COMMON NAMES: NONE

FULL SUN; EASY; HALF-HARDY ANNUAL

MIMULUS SPECIES

*Many species of clown flower (*Mimulus*) have been crossed to produce the modern jewellike hybrids. Both in hybrid and in species forms, they are invaluable plants for the gardener with poorly drained soil, for they are among the very few annuals that grow best in permanently moist conditions. Cuttings taken in late summer or newly seeded plants will also flower quite happily indoors throughout the winter.*

Among the flowers that may be said to possess a sense of humor, species of *Mimulus* rank with pansies. The half-inch- to inch-wide mimulus flowers, though they sometimes come in vibrant single shades, are more often freaked and blotched, "splotted" one might say, with contrasts of color laid on any ground from clear yellow through red and purple to blue. The effect is always droll and witty, attested to by the genus name, from *mimus,* a clown, and by the popular name "monkey flower." They belong to the scrophularia family, and their flowers, two-lobed at the top and three-lobed at the bottom, somewhat resemble a flattened version of their close cousins in the clan, the snapdragons.

Of the 150 or so species in the genus, the botanically minded will find good garden value in almost all of them. *Mimulus aurantiacus* is a shrubby California native with handsome flowers that vary from tan to warm brown to mahogany red. It is very useful for summer bedding, though cuttings can also be taken in late summer to produce free-flowering plants in the greenhouse or on a sunny windowsill. *Mimulus luteus*, from Chile, is clear yellow in the species but spotted with red in some varieties. *Mimulus guttatus*, native from Alaska to

Mexico, is perhaps the best value for colder gardens, as it will often persist at the roots, and always seeds abundantly for plants the following year. Its chrome-yellow flowers are borne in great abundance in early summer, and the plant may be cut back for repeat blooming in August. Late-sprouting seedlings or cuttings can be taken indoors to provide flowers throughout the winter months. It will naturalize freely in any damp soil, and is fresh and lovely along the banks of a stream or the margins of a pond. Another range of color is offered by *M. lewisii*, a perennial native to British Columbia and California that occurs as far inland as the warmer parts of Utah. In late summer, its flowers appear in profusion and are typically rosy pink, though a fine white form, 'Albus', comes true from seed and is worth seeking.

One other species, *M. moschatus*, should be grown not only for its pretty clear-yellow flowers that occur all summer, but also in the hope of solving a great botanical mystery. Its first discoverers noted that it possessed a rich fragrance, and named it *moschatus*, meaning "musk-scented." For that fragrance it was grown for almost a hundred years, until suddenly it ceased to smell. Neither cultivated plants nor plants studied in the wild have since given off a whiff, and the puzzle over why it lost its fragrance has never been solved. There is always a chance that some single seedling will turn up sweet-smelling, and anxious gardeners worry it practically to death with their noses. But even scentless, it is well worth cultivating for its long and charming season of bloom.

Beside their flowers, species of *Mimulus* are worth growing for one other reason. It is rare among annuals to find one that will accept, and even relish, waterlogged soil. Most kinds of mimulus occur in the wild along stream sides, in ditches, and in bogs, and they are never so happy as when their roots are constantly bathed in moisture. They are thus excellent plants for wet gardens. So long as water at their fibrous roots is plentiful, they are not particular as to soil, accepting heavy clay and gooey muck as readily as good rich humus. They are most beautiful among the other denizens of wet places, such as ferns and true bog plants. They can extend the beauty of such spots in the garden into summer, long after the marsh marigolds have become rusty and the candelabra primroses have gone by.

The mimulus seed one buys from major seed houses is a complex blend of many species, bred for flowers of rich hue and often for the drollest splotting; the resulting plants are known as *Mimulus ×hybridus*. The dust-fine seed should be scattered over a sterile moist potting mix about eight weeks before last frost, pressed into the soil lightly, and covered with plastic wrap until germination occurs, usually in one to three weeks. The little seedlings should be pricked out when they are large enough to handle and grown on in bright light. At no point should they be allowed to dry out, and if they become leggy, they should be clipped off above the basal rosette of succulent leaves. Transplanting the seedlings into semi-shaded moist parts of the garden should occur when the weather settles and frost is not a threat. At all times of their life the species of *Mimulus* transplant easily, and quite large specimens can be moved with a ball of earth successfully if they are kept moist. All species can make showy houseplants, either in summer, or from late-summer cuttings or seedings as a winter display. There is probably no plant more satisfactory for window boxes or hanging baskets on dank, partially shaded city balconies.

FAMILY: *Scrophulariaceae*

COMMON NAMES: *Monkey flower; musk flower*

FULL SUN TO PART SHADE; EASY; ANNUALS, PERENNIALS, OR SUBSHRUBS TREATED AS HARDY OR HALF-HARDY ANNUALS

MIRABILIS JALAPA

*Four o'clocks (*Mirabilis jalapa*) are quaint old-fashioned annuals that are enjoying a return to modern gardens. The luminosity of their flowers occurs from the fact that thin membranes of one color are laid over another. Here, yellow overlies white, but from a single seed packet forms will occur with cerise over purple or scarlet over pink. Tubers of four o'clocks may be dug after frost, stored over the winter in barely damp sand or peat, and replanted the following spring for a new season of bloom.*

All gardeners know the anticipation of waiting for a flower to open. They make their rounds daily, peering into masses of foliage, parting it to observe the development of buds, saying to themselves "Well, maybe tomorrow . . . ." *Mirabilis jalapa* is slower with its gifts than many annuals, choosing not to flower until it has made a fat green bush and summer is spinning toward its end. But once it begins, it makes of anticipation a daily event, for it opens its flowers, first by shy ones and twos in early August, and then by dozens, with a surprising punctuality somewhere around four o'clock in the after-

noon. One cannot actually set one's watch by it, for it cannot tell time, or perhaps more accurately, it tells true time, as chickens do, independent of the arbitrary structuring of the hours we know by the clock. It is like those guests who choose to set themselves apart from slavish punctuality by attaching the suffix "-ish" to any designation of the hour. ("Expect us fourish.")

Around fourish, then, *M. jalapa* will open its little inch-long buds to reveal bright, sweetly scented, five-petaled flowers that remain open all night and into the next morning. They look like little umbrellas, and they stay open, as umbrellas should, all day long on cloudy and drizzly days. The plant was discovered in Peru by the conquistadors in the 16th century, and was given the name *mirabilis*, meaning "miraculous," from its habits of punctuality and also supposedly from its ability to produce on the same stem flowers of different colors, ranging from white and cream to pink, carmine, and red. Sometimes its blossoms will also be freaked or jetted with stripes of a contrasting color, most often yellow on red, or they may be overlaid with a darker color on a lighter ground—cerise on yellow or yellow on white—producing a curiously luminous effect. Each flower bears a drop of nectar at its tubular base, enough to send a late-foraging hummingbird contentedly to bed or to provide enticement to ghostly night moths.

Old-fashioned gardeners put a higher value on floral entertainment than modern ones seem to; a flower that was pretty was always valued, but a flower that *did* something, that opened in the evening and closed at daybreak, as four o'clocks, daturas, and moon vines do, that had curious unpredictable colors or that made odd decorative seeds, was always especially treasured. Modern gardens are not so rich in floral stuntmen, and for that reason four o'clocks should still be valued.

Mirabilis jalapa is of very easy culture. Seed should be started about four to six weeks before last frost date. Soaking it for a day in water assists germination. The soaked seed should be strewn thinly over pots of sterile potting mix, covered lightly, and the pots kept at about 60 degrees Fahrenheit. When germination occurs, place the pots on a sunny windowsill, and prick out the young plants when they are about two inches tall. They may be planted out into the garden after danger of frost has passed. Little is gained by rushing the young plants, as they will not really make strong growth until settled weather, and will not flower until late summer. In the warmer parts of Zone 7 and south, *M. jalapa* will often reappear, either from seed or

from the fleshy underground tubers the plant produces. In colder gardens, the tubers may be lifted and stored over the winter in barely moistened peat or sand. Planted out the following year, they will produce larger, more floriferous plants.

Mirabilis jalapa is not particular about soil, accepting sandy loam and heavy clay alike. The best plants, however, are grown in good garden soil, fertilized lightly with a granular fertilizer when they are first set out and given a wash of liquid foliar feed when they are about a foot tall and again just when the first flower buds appear. Plants that are afforded these luxuries grow lush and green, and also better resist insect damage. Since the foliage of *Mirabilis jalapa* is very handsome when well grown and constitutes a large part of the plant's effectiveness, the extra attention is worthwhile.

In old-fashioned southern gardens, *M. jalapa* always seemed to be grown in weedy waste places, or along the dank foundations of outbuildings. I remember as a child a splendid ribbon of it in a back alley a block or so long and interrupted only by garbage cans. The plant deserves better placement, however. It can create low shrublike masses in the perennial border or in a mixed planting of annuals, and its coarse dark-green leaves are an excellent foil for finer-textured foliage and for plants with more exuberant flowers. Always it is best in mixed colors, for then one can study and compare the endless jewellike hues of its blossoms. And not to plant it in a place one passes often at twilight or where one sits late in the afternoon seems to be missing a trick. Its quiet foliage, its brilliant though subtle flowers, and its fragrance make it magical in the evening.

FAMILY: *Nyctaginaceae*

COMMON NAMES: *Four o'clock*; *miracle of Peru*

FULL SUN TO PART SHADE; EASY; TENDER PERENNIAL TREATED AS A HARDY OR HALF-HARDY ANNUAL

MOLUCCELLA LAEVIS

*When well grown, bells of Ireland (*Moluccella laevis*) produces an effect in the summer garden like no other annual. Treasured by flower arrangers, the "bells" are actually enlarged calyxes, and the tiny pink flower within has given the plant the popular name of lady in the bathtub. Growing with it here is the richly colored grape purple form of* Salvia splendens.

For many people, and even for some gardeners, a green flower is a kind of pun. Flowers should be bright, pretty colors and *leaves* should be green. But there are gardeners who find a green flower fascinating, and who think that green ranks just below cerulean blue and close to white as one of the nicest colors a flower may be. Usually they are people blessed with very close powers of observation, and they perceive that green clarifies the fascinating forms of flowers much as a black-and-white photograph clarifies the beauty of a natural scene. They recognize that, of all colors, green is perhaps the one most subject to endless variation, from almost yellow to chartreuse to the color of limes or fresh grass or Russian emeralds, and from there into dusky shades that may be almost blue, purple, or even black.

Actually, among annuals, there are few that produce true flowers that are green. Notable among them are the tiny pendant green trumpets of *Nicotiana langsdorfii* and the magnificent all-green zinnia called 'Envy'. Mostly, however, what one perceives as a green "flower" is actually some other part of the floral anatomy, the calyx or a set of modified leaves or bracts that surrounds the true flower. So it is with *Bupleurum rotundifolium*, whose cool blue-green eucalyptus-like leaves give way in midsummer to numerous thin branches, each surmounted with a cluster of star-shaped bracts within which the tiny yellow flowers nestle.

Of all the plants that have modified their floral furniture into green "flowers," none is more beautiful or more finely crafted than *Moluccella laevis*. It has true flowers, of course, that begin as tiny pale-pink pearls nestled in the enlarged calyxes, and expand into funny two-part blossoms consisting of a pink arching hood and a twice-divided lip of a pink so pale as to be almost white. But what is showy about the plant is the large cup-shaped calyx that surrounds each flower. (This calyx is disproportionately large for the blossom it shields, giving rise to the popular name "lady in a bathtub.") At maturity, each calyx is about half an inch wide and as deep, slightly elliptical and outfacing. The calyxes are borne in fours all up and down the flowering stems, the largest at the bottom, grading upward to perfectly formed but somewhat squashed ones at the top. Their color is from a distance a bright clear green, whose luminosity may be seen up close to come from an overlay of fine, whitish-green veins on a yellow-green ground. Two or sometimes three paddle-shaped leaves on long petioles accompany each whorl of bracts. Florists clip them away to reveal the shape of the inflorescence, but in the garden they are part of the plant's charm.

Both botanical and popular names are often a tangle of confusion, but *M. laevis* may take the prize for poetic misunderstandings of its many names. It is called "bells of Ireland" not at all because it originated in that country (for it comes in fact from Asia Minor), but because its calyxes are as true an Irish green as could be found. Another popular name, "shell flower," refers to the resemblance of the calyxes to little clams. But the botanical name *Moluccella* has nothing to do with the phylum *Mollusca*, to which clams belong. It was applied from the mistaken notion that the plant originated in the Moluccas, the Spice Islands of the Malay Archipelago. And that idea came from the fact that the plant, a member of the large mint family, (*Lamiaceae*), can emit from all its parts a haunting fragrance, something like lavender growing near a pine woods. Hence comes yet another popular name, "balm of Molucca." "Lady in the bathtub," or less naughtily, "baby in the bath," are self-apparent.

Moluccella laevis is seldom seen in the full magnificence it can attain. It should be a symmetrically branched, almost shrublike plant three feet tall, with few leaves and many stems clothed in whorls of bells. Getting it to look that way requires that it be sown just where it is to grow as soon as the ground has dried and may be worked. One is frequently advised to start seed indoors six to eight weeks before the last frost date, and transplant the young seedlings into the garden after danger of frost is past. However, plants so treated will never be as good as those grown in place from the start. The ideal soil for *M. laevis* is good vegetable garden soil, which is to say soil that is humus-rich, deeply tilled, and inclined to dry out on the surface between rains. The young plants should be thinned to stand nine to 12 inches apart, and they should be staked when young. Supplementary feeding should occur just as for vegetables, with a side-dressing of granular food high in phosphorus and potassium.

Moluccella laevis is worth all this trouble, for a well-grown plant will produce many spires of bells 12 to 18 inches long that will last almost the whole summer and are splendid for picking. Florists know that anything may be done with stems of *M. laevis* by allowing them to wilt slightly, tying them to makeshift frames of canes or small sticks, and then plunging them into water. They will stiffen into the forms they have been given, and the frames may be removed. The plant is also treasured by those who love dried flowers, for if harvested when fully developed and hung in a dark airy place, the spires will keep their intriguing shape and turn a beautiful ivory-gold. Whatever use you choose for it, *M. laevis* deserves a place in the garden, for its gentle green is valuable against all colors, and the intricately crafted spires of bells are complementary to any other flower shape.

FAMILY: *Lamiaceae*

COMMON NAMES: *Bells of Ireland; shell flower*

FULL SUN; MODERATELY EASY; HALF-HARDY ANNUAL

Nicotiana

Among annuals a few return to the summer garden each year, and their absence would amount, almost, to no summer at all. Some are grown from sentiment, reminding us of gardens we knew at other times of our lives or of the people who tended them. Others are grown perhaps for these reasons also, but mostly because their value has come to seem simply incalculable. In this latter group no plants are more prominent than the nicotianas, for they seem to have everything. Even as tiny seedlings, their felty overlapping leaves, each pair larger than the ones before, possess great charm. Whether tall or short, all may be described as stately, with a single felty stem emerging from a basal rosette of rich-green puckered leaves, clad here and there with other, progressively smaller leaves, and branched gracefully halfway up. The first flowers occur while the plant still possesses its juvenile lissomeness; with summer's progress, something of that is lost, to be replaced by an abundance of bloom in a thick tangle of stem. In several species, the flowers open at twilight and remain open on cloudy days, emitting a fragrance of drenching sweetness. In others, the flowers are indifferent to time, beautiful even in the hot afternoon, but scentless, as if to remind us that much of life is an exchange of one good thing for another.

All nicotianas are easy to grow. Though they love full sun and will do their best in it, beautiful plants can be grown in half or even a third of a day of sun. About soil they are not particular though, like many other annuals, they appreciate a starting diet rich in phosphorus and potassium, best applied when they are established in the garden and have produced their fourth or fifth set of leaves. Their seed should be started early, in late February or early March, to produce blooming-size plants by midsummer. Scattered thinly over a sterile potting mix, seeds will germinate quickly. The young seedlings are tiny, and should be pricked out only after they have formed two or three sets of true leaves and may be handled easily. They are easy to grow on, developing well even on a windowsill that receives half a day of sun. Once established in individual pots, they appreciate a weekly dose of liquid fertilizer at half the strength recommended on the package. They may be transplanted into the garden after danger of frost is past. Unlike many other annuals, they relish a cool and drizzly late spring and will develop the better for it.

Once any nicotiana has been grown in the garden, even if it is a very cold one, self-sown seedlings will appear in subsequent years, sometimes charmingly placed along paths or in stonework where the gardener's weeding hand has not been overvigorous. Though self-sown seedlings will develop much more slowly than started plants, delaying their bloom until mid- or even late August, they are lusty and full of grace. And as all nicotianas are tolerant of light frost, they will provide an unlooked-for beauty to the late summer or early autumn garden. At the end of July, the smaller seedlings can also be potted up and grown on, to be brought indoors where, with weekly doses of weak liquid fertilizer, they will flourish on a sunny windowsill and produce flower well into December. The night-blossoming ones will remain open throughout the day in the dilute light one finds indoors and will be generous with their perfume.

Nicotianas are among several plants grown as annuals that may be carried over the winter as root cuttings (see "Root Cuttings," page 189) Because nicotianas are easy from seed, only the scientifically minded may wish to try this method, though when a particularly fine form occurs in the garden, it is useful to know that it can be carried over in this way.

NICOTIANA ALATA

Far lovelier than the modern "improved" forms of Nicotiana alata *is the species, which bears airier sprays of flower in pure white, and which preserves the rich exotic fragrance with which it was originally endowed. Though very beautiful in mixed plantings of other flowers, it gains in loveliness by being given a place all to itself, in a bay of shrubbery or surrounded by perennials grown for their leaves, such as hostas. Such a planting should always be contrived where one sits or strolls at twilight, when the fresh flowers open and are most fragrant.*

Among all the flowers that have suffered from the modern hybridist's work at "improving" them, none has been so mistreated as *Nicotiana alata* (syn. *N. affinis*). Gardeners 50 years ago valued it highly for its elegant, airy form, for its abundance of white, sweetly scented trumpets, and even for the fact that it opened at twilight and closed at midday, saving its rich fragrance for the evening hours only. It was planted next to porches, under parlor or bedroom windows, or wherever in the garden one lingered in evening. The conjunction of its ghostly flowers and its perfume contributed to the night garden charms finer than any it possessed under the vivid light of day. For those who linger in their gardens at all sorts of odd hours between twilight and dawn know that white is the only color for such hours and that flowers of that shade always bear the finest fragrance after the sun has set. Why so beautiful a plant required altering remains one of the minor mysteries of modern horticulture.

Altered, however, it certainly was, to the extent that the species form of *N. alata* and its hybrid progeny seem hardly the same plant. These modern descendants have been shrunk in size, from the four feet of the parent to two feet or even one. The rangy grace of the species has been compacted into little twiggy bushes, loaded, one may say, with flower. Color has been added to the original white, lots of it, in shades from cream and green to pale and dark pink, crimson-rose, and dark maroon. The fragrance of the original plant has got lost or essentially lost in the development of these new plants; but we are told, by way of compensation, that they remain open all day.

As with the progeny of many distinguished parents, the modern improvements of *N. alata* are not necessarily better, but other. For they are actually very pretty plants, and their abundance of flower and compactness of growth suits them for situations where lots of bloom and lots of color are desired. Looked at singly, the colors are also often very beautiful, particularly the pale pinks and dull rose-reds, in which the reverse of each tubular flower is a paler shade of its face. And for those who love a green flower, whether in the garden or in a vase, the form called 'Limelight', which comes true from seed, is wonderful. A nice thing happens, also, the year after one has grown these highly bred versions of *Nicotiana alata*. Their offspring, either from self-seeded plants or from plants raised from saved seed, will begin to revert, producing plants of strange pale shades, hardly tinctures of mulberry or rose or green on a white ground. Often there will be a star of white marked on the joined five petals of a flower, or its face will show one odd and almost indefinable color and its back another. Such glorious mongrels may also recapture something of the species' distinction in their fragrance, and they may even open at night. Fascinating though they are, however, it is doubtful whether they can replace the unadulterated species in distinction.

When well grown, *N. alata* produces a basal rosette of oval dark-green leaves, about 16 or so inches across. As the weather warms in mid- to late June, a central stem is produced by each rosette that develops with surprising rapidity to a height of about four feet. Secondary stems are produced along its length, candelabra fashion. These eventually elongate to about two feet, forming flower buds at intervals of an inch, more or less, as they develop. The first flowers open in late June and early July, and are three- to four-inch-long tubes that flare at the end into a crisp white star of five petals, an inch to an inch and a half across. The tube itself and reverse of each flower are a clear lime green, which perhaps accounts for the curious luminosity of the chalk-white face. Flowers open only in the evening, and they show up with startling and wonderful clarity in dim nocturnal light. It is then that they are fragrant, with a scent at once clean and strong, close to but not quite like the smell of jasmine, sweet but never cloying. Graceful sprays of flower picked in the evening or in early morning before they close will remain open in a vase indoors, and those with an acute sense of smell will pick up a lingering hint of fragrance. But there is some internal wisdom in the flower that causes it, even in a vase, to reserve its full richness until twilight, when even a few flowers will burst forth to scent an entire room.

Nicotiana alata is a plant of lax grace that throws its wiry stems about onto its neighbors. More than its nocturnal tendencies, it has been this easy attitude that caused it to be subjected to improvement. But though it bends beneath the weight of its opulent flowers, it is an untidy plant only in the eyes of those who require everything in the garden to be stiffly upright. The trick with it is to use it in bays of shrubbery or in a wide elliptical drift midway in the perennial border, in colonies of many plants spaced 10 to 12 inches apart. So treated, it will fall on and interlace with others of its kind, never requiring staking and always graceful, particularly at twilight when its fine large stars open all across the mass of stems arched one above another.

Nicotiana alata is grown in the same way as all nicotianas. The fine seed is sown on a sterile potting mix in late February or early March, pricked out as soon as the seedlings may be handled, and grown on in sun without a check. Young plants are moved to the garden after danger of frost is past, and side-dressed with granular vegetable garden fertilizer when they have become established and show signs of new growth. Bloom on plants can be prolonged well into autumn by selectively cutting away mature or almost mature stems just where they are clasped by a leaf. A new stem will emerge at that juncture to form more flowers, helped on perhaps by a drench of dilute liquid plant food. It is a good practice to remove a few rods of bloom weekly from July until the end of August in order to force the development of additional flower stems. Those who enjoy cut flowers indoors will have no difficulty with this regime, as the stems and blossoms of *N. alata* last well in water and are very beautiful, either alone or in combination with other summer flowers.

FAMILY: *Solanaceae*

COMMON NAMES: *Flowering tobacco; jasmine tobacco*

FULL SUN TO PART SHADE; EASY; TENDER PERENNIAL

NICOTIANA LANGSDORFII

For many gardeners, a green flower takes a little getting used to, but once one acquires a taste for green, it can become an addiction. One of the best green-flowered annuals is Nicotiana langsdorfii, *which grows to about three feet tall and produces airy sprays of flower from June until frost. The form pictured here is the one developed at Sissinghurst, with slightly larger, upturned flowers. It is backed by the somber purple hue of* Perilla frutescens.

Part of the fun always of discussing an unusual plant in one's garden with visitors is offering an account of how it came there. To the outsider, the chain of exchange ("I got it from . . . who had it from . . . who found it in the garden of . . .") may sound a bit like name dropping. However in truth it is a celebration of the connections that gardeners maintain with one another everywhere, which amounts to a firm highway traveled by good garden plants in their

progress around the globe. For many beautiful plants often must pass for a time among devoted gardeners before they become widely available through commercial sources. Sometimes the speed with which a plant travels through this network of exchange is surprising; within a dozen years, it may move from a status of great rarity to one of prominence in many gardens. Anyone minded to do the research might find it amusing to trace the path of one good plant in its pattern of dissemination. There would be dead ends, of course, when seed was too green to germinate, fell into the hands of the inexperienced, or was forgotten in its envelope on the shelf. But in the main, the history would spread out fantastically, like a chain letter or a family tree, comprising along the way gardening names of the first distinction and a good many "Aunt Ednas," amounting in itself almost to a history of gardening for that time.

There could not be a better candidate for such research than *Nicotiana langsdorfii*, which has been grown here and there in gardens for 50 years or more. It has burst its restraints in the last 10 years to appear almost wherever interesting plants are grown. It is certainly beautiful enough to justify this explosion into popularity, for its inch-long down-hanging bells are a wonderful vibrant lime green, of perhaps the strongest shade to be found among true green flowers. They are freely produced from mid-June until frost on sturdy but delicate much-branched plants that remain gracefully upright without staking. A single specimen can possess all the delicacy of a fine botanical drawing, and a large drift of individual plants spaced about a foot apart will interlace, producing an effect that may be described as frozen green rain. Hummingbirds adore the flowers, and a planting is never free for long from the whirr of wings and the flash of a similar but iridescent green and perhaps the fine contrast of a ruby throat. For flower arrangers, *N. langsdorfii* is a joy; its green bells are complementary to any other flower color, its graceful wiry stems are easy to insert as a finishing grace to a composition, and it lasts a week or more in water, opening its half-formed flowers in a vase.

Nicotiana langsdorfii is a plant that can attain, with good culture, a height of about three and a half feet. Each small pendent bell consists of a half-inch-long tube of polished green that swells into a little bulb before giving way to a cup of fused petals a third of an inch across. If one turns it upwards, one sees that the face of the blossom is a paler green, almost chartreuse, deepening down the tube where the color reflects on itself and gathering intensity from its four dull-blue stamens.

At three or four feet (or even five when well cultured) *N. langsdorfii* would seem to be a plant appropriate only to the back of the border, but its airy grace makes it suitable for many other places. In the perennial border, it can be brought forward to midrank, and is useful for filling gaps left by early-blooming plants that are cut back by the end of June. It is an excellent blender, softening the colors around it yet highly interesting in itself. It will often take the matter of placement quite into its own hands by seeding here and there in the nicest way once it has been introduced into the garden. Its self-supporting capacities allow one to use it along a path or in a foundation planting, where it is always nice in itself, and doubly nice for the fact that one can stand quite near the hummingbirds while they are busy over it. There is no color of flower against which its fine green bells are not pretty, though something magical occurs when they are segregated entirely from all other color in a bay of shrubbery as part of a symphony of green. Against the somber dignity of boxwood or the tropical luxuriance of hardy bamboo, *N. langsdorfii* is unforgettable.

FAMILY: *Solanaceae*

COMMON NAMES: *None*

FULL SUN TO PART SHADE; EASY; TENDER PERENNIAL

NICOTIANA SYLVESTRIS

For its huge leaves, its five-foot height and the quaintness of its down-hanging white flowers, Nicotiana sylvestris *would be a valuable addition to the garden in any month. But it reaches its greatest beauty squarely in the middle of the August slump, providing freshness, flowers and fragrance when they are most needed. Slightly shade tolerant, it can be grown at the back of a deep border where tall perennials and shrubs would discourage other annuals. It is also beautiful standing alone.*

Two common problems bedevil gardeners who maintain established perennial borders: Even at their peak when they are rich with flower, there is often a boring sameness in the qualities of leaf and stem texture; and though glorious with color in late June and July and again perhaps in early September, most are sadly deficient in any interest during what gardeners call the "August slump." *Nicotiana sylvestris* can offer a dramatic solution to both problems. From an early

spring seeding, by late June it develops large rosettes of grass-green leaves, each of which may be as much as two feet long and a foot across. One would think that something so vast would require a lot of space, but in fact the leaves, by facing upward where necessary, can tuck themselves against one another and into surprisingly small spaces of a foot or so without harming their neighbors. They are handsome in themselves in midborder, against the finer textures of phlox, platycodon, geranium, veronica, and other perennials treasured more for their flowers than for the interest of their leaves. And they are wonderfully bold at the back of the border, in the somewhat shady no-man's-land that results where large shrubs such as lilacs, beauty bushes, or mock oranges have been planted to provide a frame.

There would be reason enough to grow *N. sylvestris* for its splendid foliage alone. But to prove that it, too, can do something in the flower line, in midsummer it produces a single thick stalk from the center of its first basal leaves that rapidly extends to five or six feet, clad at intervals by more vast leaves, each of which cups a smaller-leaved side branch. The stems terminate in a cob of buds from which the flowers steadily emerge, beginning usually in mid-July and continuing until frost. Each flower is four or five inches long, down-hanging, consisting of a slender tube and a flared half-inch star of five joined petals at its end. From a single cob of buds there may be as many as 50 individual flowers at a time. They are chalk-white, glow in twilight, and are sweetly scented.

The plant itself is stately in height and power-ful in build. But its modest down-hanging flowers create on their long necks a somewhat foolish and giddy impression, like one of Dr. Seuss's fantastic bird-beasts, neither one thing nor the other. This humorous impression in no way detracts from the value of the plant, for those who perceive it like to smile at it, and those who do not, simply see a large white-flowered plant usefully filling up space.

Seed of *N. sylvestris* is treated in the same way as for any other nicotiana. It is sown quite early on a sterile potting mix, and the seedlings should then be pricked out when they are large enough to handle and grown on in sun, with generous weekly doses of half-strength liquid fertilizer. The young plants can be established in the garden once the danger of frost has passed. After young transplants have "caught," they benefit from a side-dressing of vegetable garden fertilizer.

FAMILY: *Solanaceae*

COMMON NAMES: *None*

FULL SUN TO HALF SHADE; EASY; TENDER PERENNIAL OR BIENNIAL TREATED AS A HALF-HARDY ANNUAL

NIGELLA DAMASCENA

*Love-in-a-mist (*Nigella damascena*) was treasured in old-fashioned gardens for its quaint form and its beautiful colors. It is due for a rediscovery, for it delicately weaves among other plants, and the clarity of its blossoms, whether blue, pink, or white, blends beautifully with other, stronger-hued flowers. Once established, it will self-seed for many years, but its slightness of form never crowds out other plants. Here it is grown with* Papaver commutatum, *a close relative of the more familiar corn poppy, for an effect as brilliant as medieval stained glass.*

Only two of the many common names for *Nigella damascena* are offered below, though between them they must encompass a good bit of the average human being's emotional history. *N. damascena*, treasured in gardens since at least the 16th century, has accumulated a number of other descriptive popular names. In French is is called *barbe-bleu* (Bluebeard), after Charles Perrault's tale (published in 1697) of the hideous *bête d'extermination* who murdered seven wives (and a few small boys) in quick succession. More gently, it is known as

cheveux de Vénus (the hair of Venus), presumably because of its finely cut hairlike leaves. In England, *N. damascena* was early known as Catherine's flower, from the supposed resemblance of its spoked blossoms to the fiery wheel on which Saint Catherine of Alexandria endured her martyrdom for refusing the solicitations of the emperor Maximinus. On the popular imagination, therefore, *N. damascena* has had a vivid, if not always a happy, effect.

Despite its sometimes grisly impression on those who grew it first, it is a very beautiful plant of old-fashioned charm, and sadly neglected in modern gardens. At the start, it has not much to show but symmetrically branched stems clad in green mist, for its two-inch-long leaves are divided and redivided into the finest filaments. At the top of each stem, however, they thicken into a soft green haze to surround the open flower, which is clear blue, purple, white, or sometimes rose. Each flower is about an inch across, with petals arranged in a shaggy wheel and centered with radiating green anthers in memory of the leaves out of which it grew (or perhaps of poor Saint Catherine's unfortunate end). There is a fine double form, with twice the number of petals, called 'Miss Jekyll', though the single one will do quite well enough.

Because of its hardiness, *N. damascena* is of very easy culture. Seed should be sown into cultivated soil in October, or, where winters are very cold, in early spring. Because the plant forms a long taproot, transplanting is usually unsuccessful, and in any case seed sown in place always produces the best plants. As soon as a strong crop has germinated and formed true leaves, the little plants should be thinned to stand about six inches apart. They will benefit from weekly or biweekly doses of water-soluble fertilizer, and the first flowers should begin to appear in mid-July. The period of bloom is short, about four to six weeks, but the flowers leave behind curious horned seedpods, rather sinister but harmless (presumably the devil in the bush). They are interesting if not precisely showy, and may be picked for dried arrangements. Any left behind will produce a crop of seedlings the following year; these should be ruthlessly thinned to encourage strong, free-flowering plants.

Nigella damascena also makes an interesting pot plant when grown in greenhouses or on a cool, sunny windowsill. Seed should be sown in September or early October, just about when they ripen on garden plants. Three or four should be sown to a five-inch pot, and all but the strongest eliminated when they are an inch or two high. They require good light, and watering must be done carefully, for too much will rot the young plants, and too little will cause unsightly yellowing of the foliage. Gardeners with patience will be rewarded in early March with fine-flowering plants, the more precious because they may be studied up close with few other floral distractions.

FAMILY: *Ranunculaceae*

COMMON NAMES: *Love-in-a-mist; devil-in-the-bush*

FULL SUN; EASY; HARDY ANNUAL

ONOPORDUM ACANTHIUM

*Though soft and woolly in appearance, the Scotch thistle (*Onopordum acanthium*) is as fiercely armed as any member of its family. It is a stately, architectural biennial that may reach as tall as 10 feet in its second summer. The first-maturing head of seed should be saved and sown at summer's end for plants the following summer, and the rest discarded, for a mature plant will become shabby and every seed that falls on open ground will germinate. No gardener will need that much* Onopordum acanthium.

If there were gardens on the moon, the ghostly *Onopordum acanthium* would surely grow there. And the moon, or any other place far away, is where some people might wish this plant, for it is frankly and fiercely a thistle, clad up and down, leaf tips, stem, and flower bud, with painfully sharp prickles. That is a lot of prickles, for the plant can grow to 10 feet when really happy, though five feet or six feet is usual. Despite its fearsome armor, however, it is a very beautiful plant in all its parts. From a basal rosette produced the first year it sprouts a giant stalk the second, with foot-long deeply crinkled acanthuslike leaves clustering at the base and occurring scantily up the main stem. Each stem, great or small, is wrapped in four continuous wings, irregularly toothed, with each tooth ending in a spine. Branches are produced from a foot off the ground to near the top, candelabra fashion, and furnished with leaves of the same shape that grow progressively smaller until they form a protective ruff around the flower bud. The spiny flower buds are perfectly round from their first appearance until they fold outward to reveal a shaving brush of bright purple flowers. Bloom is produced from early July until late August. All parts of the plant except the flowers are covered with white down. The effect is of a vast plant cunningly carved of silver, white at midday and spectral at twilight.

To say that *O. acanthium* is not particular as to soil is to understate the matter; it will grow easily anywhere there is sun and room for it to expand. Some might say it grows too easily, since it is an abundant self-seeder. From a single plant dozens of little seedlings will show up the following year, though always in the garden, for the seed must fall on open ground to germinate. Fortunately, the seedlings are easy to pull up. One may then leave one or two in place, if they are in the *right* place, or transplant them where they are wanted if they are not. They may be moved about the first year with great ease, though they make a single taproot, and when digging one should try to get it all.

From seedlings sown (or self-sown) in late April, handsome rosettes of foot-long leaves will be produced by midsummer, nice in themselves and very beautiful in late autumn when frost has carried off all the tender plants and most of the flowers. In the second year they will tower up, offering an arresting feature all summer long. By early autumn they will have become shabby and rusty, and they should then be cleared away, thus preventing the dispersal of too many seeds.

Onopordum acanthium always makes in the garden what landscape designers call a statement, and it should not be blurred by packing the plant in too closely among others. Full profit should be taken from its grand and startling appearance by planting it in a place that is a little surprising. If it is grown in the flower border, it might be placed rather more forward than its great height would suggest, surrounding it with low and modest plants. In a generous sunny pocket of shrubbery, backed by dark yews or sober-leaved deciduous shrubs, it could provide a summer's worth of interest. It is sometimes most wonderful when it looks as if it had chosen its own proper place to grow, as, for example, at the edge of a gravel drive, or in a scattered, spontaneous drift along an old fence. Its strong sense of architecture would make it stunning against a stark modern housefront, poised like living sculpture.

FAMILY: *Asteraceae*: *Carduus Tribe*

COMMON NAMES: *Cotton thistle; silver thistle; Scots thistle*

FULL SUN; EASY; HARDY BIENNIAL

OXYPETALUM CAERULEUM

Oxypetalum caeruleum, *a close relative of pasture milkweed, is so beautiful in flower that its relative lack of other virtues is easily forgiven. A lax plant to about two feet that could be called rangy, it still produces flowers of an unforgettable turquoise, rare in the temperate garden, and freckled over for good measure with dots of purple. Actually tender perennials, plants may be grown in pots and overwintered for many seasons of bloom.*

As plant families go, the Asclepiadaceae is a moderately large one, including about 130 genera and over 2,000 species of perennial herbs, shrubs, and vines. But it is poorly represented in gardens. Among the 30 species listed by *Hortus Third* as "in cultivation," three or four at the most might be recognized by knowledgeable gardeners. Among them, probably, will be two houseplants, hoya and stephanotis, both treasured since Victorian times as sturdy twining vines that flourish in overheated indoor conditions. Wildflower enthusiasts will pick out from the list *Asclepias tuberosa*, the butterfly weed

or Indian paint brush that glorifies thin sandy meadows from Massachusetts to Florida with its rich umbels of burning orange in high summer. And farmers might recognize one of several milkweeds that are a curse for their ability to colonize even thick, well-tended pasture, producing three-foot plants that are pretty in their fashion but inedible to the hungriest cow. In the remainder of the list, which includes names like *Caralluma, Cryptostegia, Edithcolea, Huerniopsis*, and *Stultitia*, few will recognize *Oxypetalum*, though it is among the prettiest of its race and very garden worthy.

For one thing, as the word *caeruleum* indicates, it is blue, and a blue flower in the garden is always to be treasured. But to call its inch-wide, strap-petaled flowers merely blue is only to hint at their charm. They are, when fully open, a color very rare among garden plants, a curious shade best described as turquoise and represented otherwise only by the winter-flowering bulb *Ixia viridiflora* and perhaps by the hearts of the blossoms of some delphiniums. They assume that odd and beautiful color only at one stage in their development; the buds are lavender-pink and, as they mature, they change to turquoise tinged with green and later to lavender, randomly freckled with small purple spots. In fully opened flowers there is always a tiny cup of fused petals of deep marine blue, surrounding a pointed pistil of white. It takes a long time for the individual flowers to complete their transition through many shades and colors. But after they are done, they drop off to give way to the development of a horned seedpod about two inches long at maturity, shaped like that of the familiar pasture milkweed and like it packed with many brown seeds, each possessing a silky parachute.

It is a good thing that *O. caeruleum* (syn. *Tweedia caerolea*) bears such curious and beautiful flowers, for even its greatest admirers would have to confess that it offers little else. Its stems are lax and scandent, trying as hard as they can but never quite succeeding in becoming vines. They grow to about three feet, and are clad in dark-green arrowhead-shaped leaves about two inches long. In the last foot of their growth the stems begin to produce loose umbels of two to four buds from every leaf axil; from a very early sowing indoors, they produce a profusion of long-lasting flowers from late June until frost. Each flower is so great a treasure, though, that one can forgive the plant its relative lack of other distinctions.

Like many tender perennials grown as annuals, *O. caeruleum* should be sown in late February or early March for the longest period of bloom. Seed should be sown sparingly on a sterile potting mix, pricked out when the seedlings are large enough to handle, and grown on in full sun. When the young plants are about six inches high, they should be pinched once to encourage several stems to a crown. After all danger of frost has passed, they may be transplanted into places that receive full sun. They relish a loose, well-tilled soil, but they tend to grow best where the earth becomes slightly dry between rains. They have no need of extra compost or nitrogen-rich fertilizer, which may cause them to become lank, floppy, and scant of flower.

In the garden, *O. caeruleum* should be treated as the aristocrat it is and not placed in close conjunction with other, more vividly colored flowers that would detract from its elegance. Three or so plants might be established at the edge of a border, and surrounded with silver-leaved plants against which the curious blues of its flowers would gain added value. Both its beauty and its tolerance for dry soils make it an excellent subject for pot culture, even established singly in six-inch clay pots. Grown that way, it can be cut back in late summer and carried indoors or into the greenhouse for late-winter flowering. It will thrive at temperatures of about 55 to 60 degrees Fahrenheit at night, with an increase of 10 or 15 degrees in the day. The pots should be free draining, and water should be applied only when the soil surface is dry to the touch. At winter's end, plants that have been carried over indoors should be cut back again and fed with dilute liquid fertilizer for another summer of bloom.

FAMILY: *Asclepiadaceae*

COMMON NAMES: *Blue milkweed; southern star*

FULL SUN; MODERATELY EASY; TENDER PERENNIAL TREATED AS A HALF-HARDY ANNUAL

PAPAVER NUDICAULE

Although all poppies seem to be children of light, none is more luminous than the Iceland poppy, Papaver nudicaule. *Its clear, vibrant colors of orange, yellow, scarlet, ivory and white are especially intense because the sun shines not so much on, but through, the gossamer petals.*

Firmly settled for life in USDA Zone 4 of southern Vermont, where winter lows dip to −20 degrees Fahrenheit and there are sometimes no more than 75 frost-free days in a summer, I wonder occasionally how much farther north the pleasures of gardening might be pursued. There are beautiful gardens, I know, in Zone 3, where winter temperatures of −35 degrees must be endured. And I suppose that even in Zone 2, with life-threatening winter lows of −50 degrees, the human passion for gardening still finds ample exercise. One plant at least must reach perfection there, for such a climate is the chosen home of *Papaver nudicaule*, the Iceland poppy. It originates in the subarctic

fields of Siberia, Eurasia, Iceland, northern Canada, and the high cold slopes of the Rocky Mountains. Occurring well into Zone 2, it flourishes in places with short cool summers where the sun hardly sets, and its chalices of burning orange and yellow must, as Celia Thaxter remarked in *An Island Garden*, "warm the wind." Even if it lacked any other distinctions (which it possesses in plenty) *P. nudicaule* would be remarkable for being among the most cold hardy of all plants commonly grown as annuals; and for its brief moment of splendor, a wide field of it could be almost garden enough.

All members of the family Papaveraceae have a birthright of great beauty, but within the clan,

P. nudicaule is precious for a quality of color and a poise of growth never quite matched by any of the others. From ferny, grayish-green rosettes emerge thin rods of stem, a foot and a half tall, as fine and strong as green wire. Each stem eventually is surmounted by a three-inch bowl of four gossamer-thin overlapping petals surrounding a symmetrically arranged fringe of stamens and the wheeled cap of the green ovary in the center. But the greatest distinction of these flowers is their curious quality of luminosity. There is a vibrancy to each flower, whether it is white, greenish white, ivory, coral, salmon, pink, or scarlet. Most probably this quality occurs from the overlay of one color on another in the thinnest wash. In one strain at least, 'Oregon Rainbows', this overlay has been broken into distinct streaks and fadings, green into white, salmon into yellow, or coral into pale pink. But flowers of every seedling of *P. nudicaule* will seem to glow from within, to a higher degree than any other poppies, all of which are children of light.

Despite its origins in the cold subarctic, *P. nudicaule* is a little more difficult to grow than other commonly cultivated poppies. In late autumn or in very early spring, the fine seed should be sown thinly on ground that has been well cultivated and raked smooth. Young plants should be thinned to stand about six to eight inches apart, and may be encouraged, once all danger of frost is past, with a light application of granular fertilizer high in phosphorus and potassium and low in nitrogen. The best development of the plant occurs in cool conditions, hovering around 50 to 60 degrees. Flowering should occur from an autumn or early spring seeding in mid-June and last for about a month. Gardeners who live in the Deep South, in southern California, or the cooler parts of the Southwest can buy *P. nudicaule* already well developed in six-packs or peat pots, to transplant into the garden for a display of flowers in late winter and very early spring. As with all poppies, *P. nudicaule* resents root disturbance, and so should be shifted into the ground with great care.

FAMILY: *Papaveraceae*

COMMON NAME: *Iceland poppy*

FULL SUN; MODERATELY EASY; HARDY BIENNIAL AND SOMETIMES PERENNIAL GROWN AS A HARDY ANNUAL

PAPAVER RHOEAS

*Three forms of annual poppy occur in this planting, the clear red form of Flanders poppy (*Papaver rhoeas*), the closely related* P. commutatum, *with a stain of black at the base of each petal, and the tall-growing opium poppy (*P. somniferum*), here in a fully double raspberry pink. Such profusion of forms can easily occur in the gardens of true poppy lovers, but each species is so lovely that it should have a place to itself.*

As a very small child, May 30 was always a special day for me. It was then called Decoration Day and was set aside to commemorate the dead of World War I. Later it became Memorial Day, expanded to remember the American dead of all wars. I could not have known much about that at the time. What made the day special for me was that I was always taken downtown and was given a bright scarlet, crinkled-petaled paper flower to wear for the day. It was the only flower a little boy *could* wear, and the wire stem of one, wrapped in sticky green tape, was twirled around the strap of my blue seersucker sunsuit, just at the level where my tongue could reach its funny, furry little green paper center. I could wear it for the whole day, just that day, and its gorgeousness to me was vaguely overlaid with a solemnity, reflected in John McCrae's sonorous lines, which I still remember, I hope accurately: "In Flanders fields the poppies blow / Between the crosses, row on row". That was an incantation, seriously repeated into the face of my flower, over and over.

The prototype of the Memorial Day poppy is *Papaver rhoeas*, called the corn poppy from the glorious way it colonizes European fields of ripening wheat, and sometimes still the Flanders poppy from its association with May 30. The great southern gardener Elizabeth Lawrence remarks somewhere that its stained-glass-red has spoiled many a garden scheme, and that is the only point of difference I have ever had with that excellent garden writer. For to me there is no garden picture that is not enhanced by its fragile blossoms, at once vivid and ephemeral. The French painter Corot agreed with me, for it was his favorite flower, and dozens of his beautiful and brooding canvases were made magical by its dots of scarlet.

No part of *P. rhoeas* is ugly, from its first ferny glaucous leaves to its downy stems, clad in fine silver-green fur, to its shy goose-necked unopened buds, casting off their twin calyxes on a bright June morning to shake out the crumpled petals, packed and folded within like the wings of a newly emerged butterfly. It is a hardy self-seeder, and on first recognition of its tiny fragile rosettes of new leaves, I always stay my weeding hand. The reward is many fine four-petaled inch-wide scarlet cups, whose individual life is short but whose demise is replaced by a succession of others if spent blossoms are plucked away, lasting from mid-June well into early August.

For those whose memory of the Memorial Day poppy is as strong as mine, there cannot be any other *P. rhoeas* as beautiful as the original red. A patch of it in the flower border, surrounded by plenty of green and white, conveys the freshness of summer itself. It is also almost an obligatory component of the annual wildflower meadow, companioned with its ancient associate in grain fields, the blue cornflower, *Centaurea cyanus*. But *P. rhoeas* has been bred into many wonderful strains, subtle of color and useful to those who do not enjoy clear red in the flower garden. The most famous is the Shirley poppy, bred by the Reverend W. Wilkes in his vicarage garden at Shirley, England. Around 1880, he noticed a single specimen of *P. rhoeas* that sported a fine band of white around each red petal and a zone of pale pinkish white in the center. He saved the seed of this plant, and the seed of its progeny, eventually creating a strain with fantastic and wonderful shadings of carmine red, coral, peach, and ivory, many preserving the band of white that had been his original discovery. Eventually a double form occurred, with all the grace of the single four-petaled one, but with eight petals overlapping in an upturned cup. From this mutation, fully double forms were created, with many petals held in a crinkled dome, called "begonia-flowered" and sometimes "peony-flowered," for "poppy-flowered" they are not. And though they may lack the essential elegance of the simple flower, they have a certain fin-de-siècle opulence, and come true from seed.

A further wonderful advance on the appearance of *P. rhoeas* was made by the late Sir Cedric Morris in his garden at Benton End in England. Working with the palest forms, he carefully selected only those plants that preserved a dusky, smoky color. His aim was eventually to create a lavender form, but he succeeded in producing a race that shows many strange and beautiful colors from brooding purple and dove-gray through palest mauve and lavender-white. Beth Chatto, who has carefully preserved and nurtured his strain at her garden and nursery at White Barn House near Colchester, calls them "thunder-cloud colors," and continues to select forms that exhibit the odd, pale shades Morris cultivated. American gardeners can come close to this strain by planting one of two seed selections called 'Fairy Wings' or 'Mother of Pearl'. And they can come closer still by eliminating the brasher, brighter colors before they scatter seed, for all strains of poppy commonly grown in gardens can, with patience, be selected over a few years to display just the colors the gardener wants.

Papaver rhoeas is one of the easiest of all garden annuals to grow. Indeed, once it has been established, it will reappear for many years, requiring only that the gardener recognize the tiny seedlings in early spring and thin them to stand six to eight inches apart. This will give them the room they need to become strong, well-flowered plants. Because, like most poppies, *P. rhoeas* resents root disturbance, little is gained by starting plants indoors. New plantings are established by sprinkling the seed onto well-tilled garden soil, having first mixed the very fine seed with sand to avoid overseeding. Seeding may be done either in late autumn or early spring, even, as some gardeners recommend, over the last crust of snow, to be washed in by its melt. *Papaver rhoeas* is very hardy, and the best results will always occur when the seed has germinated and begun to grow in quite cool, moist conditions. Flowers from autumn or early spring seedings should begin to occur by mid to late June, and will continue into August if the spent blossoms are picked away, leaving only a few to ripen seed for the following year.

As *P. rhoeas* is one of the most beautiful cut flowers of summer, the prevention of seed formation is more a pleasure than a chore. Blossoms should be cut, with all the stem they have, in early morning, just as the twin calyxes have split apart to reveal the crinkled petals within. Stem ends should be dipped as soon as possible in boiling water, or held for a second or two above a gas flame, and then plunged into barely tepid water. The flowers will open almost immediately, and so treated, will last for two or three days, longer, actually, than in the garden. So poised and graceful are they that it is almost impossible to arrange them clumsily.

FAMILY: *Papaveraceae*

COMMON NAMES: *Corn poppy; Flanders poppy*

FULL SUN; EASY; HARDY ANNUAL

PAPAVER SOMNIFERUM

Papaver somniferum, *the opium poppy, has been treasured in American gardens for more than two hundred years. Though for the first half of its life there is no summer plant more beautiful in all its parts—leaf, stem, flower and seed head—the last half is a trial to gardeners of the tidy persuasion. Fortunately, one or two cunningly crafted seed urns contain all the future poppies a garden is likely to need. The rest can be cleared away when the plants become yellowed and shabby.*

Most gardeners, and many garden writers, put firmly aside the ancient, baleful associations attached to *Papaver somniferum*. It is the irresistible beauty of its flowers, and not the fact that it is the source of opium, that recommends it in gardens. Those who take the time to do a bit of reading, either from curiosity or from anxiety at what the neighbors might think, will discover that acres of *P. somniferum* are required to produce an appreciable amount of opium, and that its successful extraction requires a great deal of patience and ingenuity and just the right climatic conditions. Others simply prefer to remain oblivious to all that, and cultivate happily their own carefully selected colors and forms, year after year, simply for their great beauty. They may prefer to call it lettuce poppy, from its broad, glaucous, succulent leaves, and they may even harvest a jar of its abundantly produced seed (which has little trace of the drug) to sprinkle over homemade breads and to make poppyseed cakes. So, when grown in gardens (as opposed, perhaps, to the whole back forty) the cultivation of *P. somniferum* is a case of *Honi soit qui mal y pense* ("Shame to him who thinks ill").

There is nothing illegal about selling the seed of *P. somniferum*, and several seed companies offer it. It can be had in a wide range of soft, sherbet colors—pale pink, rose, lavender, and grayish white—and in some stronger colors— vivid red and dark purple and wine. Flower shapes vary also, including elegant singles and semidoubles, some with fringed edges, full doubles packed with many petals, and "pen- wiper" sorts, in which all the petals have been modified into a soft furry ball. Whatever their shape, the size of individual flowers is about four inches across, and almost all show a stain at the base of each petal, black in the more vivid colors, faded to a beautiful slate-gray in the paler ones and to a faint lavender in the whites.

For about half its life, *P. somniferum* is one of the most beautiful flowers of the summer garden. From an autumn or early spring sowing directly in the garden, or from self-seeding once it has been grown, graceful rosettes of pale, bluish-green toothed leaves appear in April, all down-curved into reversed spoons. If thinned to stand a foot or so apart, the rosettes will steadily enlarge to touch, and from the cen- ter of each will emerge a stout stem, bearing the first bud. It will branch along the way, pro- ducing more buds, many of which will open together into a bush of glorious blossoms in late June. The life of each flower is short, hardly more than two days, though the show will con- tinue for two and sometimes three weeks as younger plants mature into bloom. After the petals have fallen, they leave behind neat little urns about an inch long and as much around, each surmounted by a pleated brown cap, curi- ously decorative in their way.

At this point, however, an ungraceful process of aging sets in. The handsome leaves begin to yellow, the ripening seedpods stand up gaunt and naked, and one wonders, for all their early summer magnificence, why one grows *P. som- niferum* in the first place. It is then that all but a few plants should be cleared away. And it is useful to know that in each of those urns are hundreds of seeds; they will scatter in midsum- mer breezes, pepper-shaker fashion, to clothe the ground come next spring with a thatch of progeny. Only a few pods need therefore be left to ripen for next year's flowers, and those should be of the best, the finest colors in what- ever range and shape the gardener fancies. By such selection over three or four years, won- derful color strains can be built up and kept pure, so long as one does not succumb to the temptation of sprinkling in seed admired in someone else's garden.

Papaver somniferum, like all poppies, re- quires full sun and a good, open, well-draining soil not too rich in nitrogen. Thinning is essen- tial, because the plants are large, to four feet or more when well grown, and need space to develop well. A light dressing of granular fertil- izer high in phosphorus and potassium and low in nitrogen, sprinkled lightly around each plant when the rosettes are about six inches across, will produce strong, free-flowering plants. Strains with heavy, fully double flowers may topple over from sheer weight after a summer shower, and it is worth the trouble to stake them individually just as the first blossoms open. If they are likely to topple, they will do so at the point where the stem emerges from the ground, and a single stake eight or so inches long and fastened to the plant with a single tie will prevent such a mischance.

FAMILY: *Papaveraceae*

COMMON NAMES: *Opium poppy; lettuce poppy*

FULL SUN; EASY; HARDY ANNUAL

PERILLA FRUTESCENS

Perilla frutescens *has a dark, brooding beauty that strongly appeals to some gardeners and is anathema to others. Here it is boldly paired with* Petunia violacea, *one of several species from which the familiar garden hybrids have been developed.*

For many children the first inklings of wealth must be the troves of small change collected from beneath the sofa pillows after grandfather had finished his nap. For me as a child, however, the sense of wealth, of something rich that one had plenty of and to spare, came with *Perilla frutescens*. Not for the first year, however, for I was given only a single small plant that I grew in a little bed I had made around a chinaberry tree in the backyard. The perilla grew impressively to three feet, a bushy, rank plant clothed in large dark-purple leaves that smelled odd when touched. It was the following year that I learned from my plant the meaning of wealth, for early in the second spring hundreds of tiny purple seedlings appeared, in my flower bed, in the grass beside it, and even in the cracks of the cement driveway nearby. It was all the perilla I could ever have wanted, an inexhaustible supply, and I think I transplanted every one to somewhere in the yard. That was my perilla summer, and the real beginning, I suspect, of the mad path that I have since pursued as a gardener.

The fortunes of *P. frutescens* in gardens have been rather up and down through the years. Its dusky-purple, sometimes almost funereal leaves were much treasured by the Victorians, who liked that sort of thing. Its quick growth, its full somber-tinted form, and its immunity to heat, drought, and disease made it invaluable as a bedding plant. But when elaborate bedding schemes fell out of fashion, *P. frutescens* largely went with them, descending to the status of what my grandmother used to call a "chicken-yard plant." Until fairly recently, one's only source for it was such shabby strongholds, and it was freely given for the asking, with a phrase such as, "Oh, that old thing? Take all you want. But be careful—it seeds!"

And seed it does, even in the coldest gardens. Where once it is grown, tiny purple stars will pepper the ground for years to come. They are easy to eradicate, though, and willingly will transplant where one wants them, if, indeed, one continues to want them at all. The problem, I suspect, is not so much in their abundance, and certainly not in the difficulty of eliminating them, for they can be brushed or hoed away without trouble. The problem is that almost no plant is more winning than *P. frutescens* when it first comes out of the ground. It is purple from the very beginning, and its first four leaves make a fat little cross, full of life and beauty. So what to do with them all may be the real difficulty.

Still, as many people seem recently to have rediscovered, it is a fine garden plant, easy and undemanding of culture, and its rich coloration lends it to many subtle uses. It accepts some shade, and so can be grouped around the bare shanks of tall-growing shrubs such as lilacs or old-fashioned roses. It can be very beautiful against silver-leaved plants such as *Artemisia* 'Powis Castle' or the old-fashioned *Artemisia ludoviciana*. Subtle colorists will like its dusky maroon leaves among pink-flowered annuals or

perennials, and the really bold might plant it with red and orange cannas and hot pink and orange zinnias and marigolds, as the Victorians did. But however it is used, it is best planted in groups of three, five, or more plants, to give full value to its coarse but beautiful texture.

The best source for *P. frutescens* may be any other gardener of one's acquaintance who has ever grown it. Seed companies have begun to offer it again, and it is making a hesitant showing in garden centers. It can also be bought from companies that specialize in Oriental vegetables, often under the name "Chinese basil," for its aromatic leaves are used in Asian cooking. If ordering from these sources, be sure to get *P. frutescens* var. *crispa* (or 'Nankinensis') for a less pungent weakly-purple or all-green form is sold for culinary purposes.

Perilla frutescens may be sown in the open ground as soon as it can be worked in early spring, thinned to stand about nine inches apart, the excess seedlings transplanted to other locations in the garden or given away. It is also easy to start indoors on a sunny windowsill. Seed should be sown on a sterile potting mix and kept moist until it germinates. After the first two sets of true leaves have formed, the seedlings should be pricked out and grown in sun until after danger of frost is past, when they may be transplanted into the garden.

FAMILY: *Lamiaceae*

COMMON NAME: *Beefsteak plant*

FULL SUN TO PART SHADE; EASY; HARDY ANNUAL

PHACELIA CAMPANULARIA

Though it may prove cranky in moist cool eastern gardens, the limpid blue flowers of Phaecelia campanularia *are so beautiful that they may be worth a little extra trouble or a second or third attempt. Soils that drain quickly after rains are one key to success.*

Phacelia campanularia, a native of western America from Colorado to the Mojave Desert, has all the charm of a rare rock garden plant, and for me, much of the difficulty. But blue, a perfectly clear limpid marine blue, is the most precious of garden colors, and gardeners who see its beautiful five-petaled cups of that color, each set off by starry up-turned anthers heavily dusted with pollen, can not rest until they have it. An inch across, the flowers nestle in loose cymes at the tips of thick watery stems, and even the leaves, twice their size and delicately notched into little fans, suggest something rare and to be treasured. (Those leaves, when crushed, are said to emit a delicate scent, but that is yet another charm *P. campanularia* withholds in our cold damp garden, for I can never pick up a whiff.)

Gardeners who live in regions where nights are cool and days are burning hot, and the soil is open to downright sandy, often have an easy time with phacelia. Those who grow it well brag that it produces sheets of its gentian-blue flowers, and they seem able to do with it what they will, even shearing it back for more bloom in autumn, or repeat-sowing it throughout the summer (for its season is short, six weeks or less). In Vermont, where the days often rival the nights for coolness, it is a cranky plant, easily passed over were it not for its great beauty. Like many annuals from California and the arid Southwest, it produces a thick taproot with few root hairs, and is both difficult to transplant and uncomfortable in heavy, water-retentive soils. As it is quick from seed and quick to flower, it is best to wait for settled weather before sowing it in place. It can also be started under glass, in a quick-draining medium composed at least half of sand, judiciously watered and transplanted with great care so as not to disturb its delicate roots. Our best success with it has been to sow it in place, in a dry sunny spot when we can count on a sequence of bright dry days, usually in mid-June. The plant is tolerant of frost, and relishes a long cool growing season before flowering, but it will not stand the prolonged rainy spells that are common with us in late spring. In such weather, slugs (which seem to love a blue-flowered plant as much as does the gardener) will also pack it quite away, running a race with rot for who gets the best of it.

Wherever phacelia is happiest is the place to grow it, for there is no color save the rankest magenta that would not look good with its clear blue. As with all flowers the color of the sky or sea, one could hardly have too much of it. It is a little plant, creeping about on stems hardly a foot long that weave amiably in and out of taller, more permanent plants. In the rock garden, it is a stunning replacement to the spring-flowered gentians, whose color it matches; and in window boxes or balcony pots, high above the slugs (which cannot fly, though it often seems they do) it is, for its brief time, a treasure. It is also wonderful seeded directly into the cracks of a well-drained terrace laid on gravel or sand.

FAMILY: *Hydrophyllaceae*

COMMON NAME: *California bluebell*

FULL SUN; CHALLENGING; HARDY ANNUAL

PHASEOLUS COCCINEUS

*The scarlet runner bean (*Phaseolus coccineus*) is so beautiful that it might well be liberated from the vegetable garden and grown among ornamental plantings. Its abundance of good green leaf and the clarity of its scarlet flowers blend easily with many bright-colored annuals and perennials.*

The present fashion for growing vegetables among flowers is not a new one. It really represents only a return to the practice common in old-fashioned country gardens, of growing flowers among the vegetables. A few bright-red zinnias or orange calendulas, some tall magenta cosmos, a rangy spider flower or two, were often considered as important a part of the vegetable garden, in their way, as beans and carrots. They dressed up the plot, made things cheerful-like. Often, too, they came of themselves from year to year, requiring only that one kept an eye out for the seedlings and moved them by when they were in the way of the vegetables. Many old vegetable gardeners went a step further, deliberately including a posy patch of simple flowers that could be picked to decorate the church when Sunday came around, or to carry along to family reunions with the fresh berry pie, or, as was always the custom in the

Deep South, to bring to May Workings in old family cemeteries, where they were placed before the graves after the tall grass was cut away.

Scarlet runner beans were always prominent in such plots. But whether they are vegetables or flowers appears open to debate. It seems to me that the last word on the subject was pronounced by an old Vermonter I knew who said, "Some plants is to feed man and beast, and some is for show, and some is wuthless. That posy bean is all three." People certainly have eaten them for a very long time, for it appears that *P. coccineus* was the bean that filled the granaries of the Aztecs. The first English colonists sent it home, where it rapidly became a popular table vegetable, and by the end of the 17th century had been bred into a form half-white and half-red called 'Painted Lady', which is rarely seen today. From England it crossed to Holland, where an all-white form called 'White Dutch Runner' or 'Dutch Case Knife Bean' was developed. To many English and European vegetable gardeners, *P. coccineus* is still the table bean of choice, eaten either steamed when the pods are less than three inches long, shredded when they have become a little longer but are still free of fibers, or shelled and boiled when they are mature.

In America, public favor passed over *P. coccineus* more than 50 years ago in favor of the climbing form of *P. vulgaris*, and particularly the cultivar called 'Kentucky Wonder'. This is, for most American gardeners, *the* pole bean. (Pole beans and runner beans both do the same thing, which is climb, but "pole" is American usage and "runner" is British.) Scarlet runner beans are still grown, however, for "show" in many old vegetable plots, and the display they make there is hardly wuthless. They are extraordinarily free-flowering, bearing, from late June until frost, quantities of eight-inch-long stems furnished with papery translucent bean flowers of an unusual clear scarlet. On each flowering stem a few beans are borne, and if not taken when they are quite small, at which point they

really are delicious, they will develop into monster pods, sometimes a foot and a half long, covered with fine silver fur and swollen where the mature seeds are forming. The vines are handsome in themselves, able to scale a 10-foot pole or tripod by high summer and richly dressed with eight-inch leaves, divided into three parts. Their fresh lettuce-green color is the perfect foil for the scarlet blossoms that protrude showily among them. In the formal vegetable garden of a friend I once made a tall gothic arch of saplings, which she then planted to scarlet runners. The effect, walking beneath their shade and looking up into the light-green leaves and vivid flowers, dappled with falling sun, was magical. And the thick pods hanging down within, though long past the point of edibility, still had the look of summer's abundance.

In old country gardens, the beauty of *P. coccineus* has always caused it to be liberated from the vegetable garden and brought closer to the house. It is often seen grown on strings against the weathered siding of a barn, planted on the supports of a sunny porch, or trained over split-rail or board fencing at the back of a perennial border. The recent fashionableness of vegetable plants as components of the ornamental garden has given it prominence even in very sophisticated urban garden designs. There, trained on tripods or on white-painted trelliswork, it brings to city gardens a strong note of rural charm, a sense of freshness and relaxation and an appropriate emphasis on good things, whether edible or not.

Phaseolus coccineus is no more difficult to grow than any other bean. Like all of them, it resents transplanting, and as its growth is so rapid, little is gained from starting it early indoors. The fat beans should be pressed into well-cultivated, humus-rich soil in late May or early June, at a depth of about three times their thickness, each an inch or so from the other. Such spacing is far too close for good growth, but not all the beans may germinate, and if they do, all but the strongest should be removed so that the young plants stand about eight inches apart. When they have formed their first true leaves, they will be grateful for a side-dressing of granular vegetable garden fertilizer, applied in a circle around each plant—far enough from its stem that no particles of fertilizer touch and burn it. Another application may be made when the vines have begun to climb.

A sturdy support should be in place when the seeds are planted, as it is difficult to put in once the vines begin to grow. Scarlet runners are traditionally grown on stout tripods of woodland saplings or on single poles about eight feet high. It is important not to underestimate the heft of a well-grown vine; drenched with summer dew or rain, it can pull down a flimsy contrivance of thin twine or topple a slender cane. Though supports may seem to loom at first, they will quickly be covered with vines and seem much less imposing. Young vines will need some training in the way that they are to go, and it is useful to know scarlet runners are unusual in twining *against* the motions of the sun, and so should be guided from right to left or they will not take hold. It is a good idea, as well, when training scarlet runners to a pole or tripod, to tie a generous length of garden twine to the top of each support and twirl it around the stem of the vine when it is halfway up, tying it in at the base. That way one can avoid the depressing experience of having the whole vine give way and slip down to the bottom of the support under its high-summer weight.

FAMILY: *Fabaceae*

COMMON NAME: *Scarlet runner bean*

FULL SUN; EASY; PERENNIAL VINE TREATED AS A
  HALF-HARDY ANNUAL

PORTULACA GRANDIFLORA

In its typical shades of magenta, cerise, orange, scarlet and yellow, Portulaca grandiflora *is as bright as a Mexican paper toy. It is now also available in softer shades, and even in an icy pure white. A lover of dry, gravelly soil and the heat of summer, it should always be seeded directly where it is to grow.*

My first acquaintance with *Portulaca grand-iflora* was on trips I made each summer with my grandmother to visit her childhood friend in east Texas. Her name was Miss Kate, and she had chosen to remain on her family land outside Carthage, living in relative poverty, after all her friends had moved to Shreveport during the Depression. She had had a husband and a son ("both no -'count," my grandmother would succinctly remark), but when I knew her she was a gaunt old country woman living alone, dressed always in faded flowered cotton and sporting (for the sun hurt her weak eyes) a green plastic visor such as gamblers wore.

Her style of gardening must have been unique to that area, for not a speck of grass was allowed to grow around her house. The yard was sprinkled and swept each morning until it was hard as a tennis court. The house was a pre–Civil War raised cottage, really two houses lifted on posts a storey above the ground, connected by a wide doorless breezeway and surrounded on all sides by a deep, balustraded porch. It was here that she grew her flowers, in unimaginable profusion. All sorts of old buckets and tubs were brim-full, often with strange night-blooming cactuses, delicate lavender achimenes, and huge-flowered tuberous begonias. Most she had gotten as slips or roots in trade from other gardeners through the market bulletin, or at the annual May Working, a sort of extended family reunion held in the cemetery on the first of May to smarten up the graves and cut the grass for the summer. Others had been on the place for as long as she could remember, notably some fine pink rain lilies (*Zephyranthes grandiflora*) and the moss roses (*Portulaca grandiflora*). She grew them together in a collection of old enameled dish pans with holes in the bottom, on the successful theory that as the rain lilies would always flower after a prolonged period of drought followed by watering, they were perfect companions to the portulaca, which loves dry soil. That soil was renewed only when the rain lilies required division, and the portulaca, a true annual, seeded across the top from year to year. It formed a cover of succulent little leaves and produced a splendor of inch-wide satiny flowers in yellow, hot orange, cerise, and red through which the larger pale-pink chalices of the rain lilies would occasionally appear.

Portulaca grandiflora is an excellent plant for gracing containers more elegant than the crazed and chipped dishpans I remember. It is also a good garden plant, easy to germinate and quick to flower, accepting dry barren soils even to the edges of gravel drives and cracks in pavement. Though never more than six inches high, it quickly forms mats of attractive, sedumlike succulent foliage, topping each stem with satin-textured "roses" in great profusion throughout the hottest part of the summer. As a child I knew it in its unimproved single form, and in colors as brash and vivid as a Mexican toy. It now comes with flowers that are double and larger, up to two inches wide, and strains have been developed that do not close at midday as did the old forms. Colors now are also more subtle, chiefly in shades of pale and peach-pink, apricot, cherry-red, and primrose-yellow, all

with a boss of stamens in dull orange. There is also a splendid double white form called 'Swan Lake' that comes true from seed.

Portulaca grandiflora grows best in very well drained, somewhat dry soils in full sun. As the plants flower quickly from seed, and as they do not achieve their best until the weather is warm and settled, little is gained by starting them early indoors. The best plants are produced when the fine seed is sown directly where the plants are to flower and the young seedlings thinned to stand four to six inches apart. Though they are extremely drought tolerant at maturity, young plants benefit from irrigation in dry weather and from a light dressing of granular vegetable garden fertilizer. Once flowering begins, however, they are entirely self-sufficient. *Portulaca grandiflora* will often self-seed in warm gardens, though not always in the finest forms. It may also be reproduced by cuttings rooted in damp sand, which may then be potted up in a free-draining sandy medium and carried through the winter on a sunny windowsill.

In the garden, *P. grandiflora* always seems prettiest when it is seeded spontaneously, in pavement, along paths, or perhaps in irregular patches among tea roses, so that it looks like a lovely weed that came of itself. Because of its tolerance for drought, it is an excellent choice for pots and window boxes, though it will not be happy or look good when crowded among other, lusher annuals. It needs plenty of sun and its own space to produce its bright flowers, which are worth admiring without other distractions.

FAMILY: *Portulacaceae*

COMMON NAME: *Moss rose*

FULL SUN; EASY; HARDY ANNUAL

RHODOCHITON ATROSANGUINEUM

Like many members of the family Scrophulariaceae, Rodochiton atrosanguineum *seems to have gone to extra trouble to make itself both beautiful and engaging. All along its twining vines that grow to six feet in a season, it produces fuchsia-colored calyxes from which emerge club-shaped flowers of deep violet, opening into waxy, four-petaled flowers. Gardeners who appreciate its wit train its stems laterally on wires, so that its down-hanging bells display themselves in a perfectly graded sequence from the older, fully opened ones to the tiniest bells.*

Outside of large botanical gardens in the most temperate areas and in the collections of those omnivorous gardeners who seek out and grow curious plants, *Rhodochiton atrosanguineum* is never seen. That is a pity, for it is a charming, one might say even a witty little vine, possessing in its funny small flowers a large measure of the whimsy that seems typical of most members of the family Scrophulariaceae.

But even in that droll clan it sets itself apart, for it is the only species in its genus, and it carries its distinctions so far as to forgo the tubular faces typical of most of its garden relatives—snapdragons, monkey flowers, and foxgloves—to produce inflorescences with quite something else in mind. Each hangs downward from the vine on a slender stem that may be three or four inches long and is as fine as a pack-thread. Dangling at the tip is a four-pointed calyx about an inch across at maturity, billowing outward like a parachute and colored a vibrant fuchsia red. Within is an inch-long tubular flower of a purple-red so deep as to be almost black. Each inflorescence is beautiful in itself, but in mid-July, when the vine begins to flower, they are borne in graduated sequence all along the stem, from the oldest and largest to tiny bells the size of a pea, as if each could sound a progressively smaller silver note when struck. Each calyx remains in good color and condition long after the tubular inner flower has given way to a fat spherical seed capsule, thus offering until summer's end an ever-increasing show of bells.

Rhodochiton atrosanguineum is a tender plant native to Mexico that will produce graceful ropes of light vines as tall as 15 feet where it is hardy, which is to say USDA Zones 9 and 10. There it will be perennial, returning each year with greater and greater strength but never so rampantly as to smother all around. In colder gardens it will be shyer, hardly reaching eight feet or so when started indoors early and transplanted after all danger of frost is past. Even without its striking flowers, which *will* come eventually and last a month or a month and a half before frost cuts them down, it is a pretty vine, bearing heart-shaped puckered leaves of thick texture with petioles that twirl themselves around anything they touch. The leaves are suffused with purple at their tips and on their undersides, and the petioles and stems show the same hue, deepening down sometimes to eggplant-purple.

Because it is actually perennial, gardeners who live in cold climates should start it early, in mid-February or thereabouts, for the longest season of growth and flower. The flat papery seeds should be sown in a sterile potting mix to which a scattering of sharp sand has been added for perfect drainage. The use of peat pots into which the seeds can be sown and grown on without disturbance is a good idea, to avoid even the slight check to growth that will result from pricking out. Seed germinates quickly when kept at about 70 degrees Fahrenheit, and when the young seedlings are about two inches high, all but the strongest should be clipped out. Young plants should be fed weekly with half-strength liquid fertilizer when they have produced four or five leaves, and grown on in full sun and in temperatures that hover around 70 degrees. When roots become apparent on the base or outside walls of the peat pots, the plants should be shifted, pot and all, into five-inch clay or plastic pots, taking care to firm fresh soil around the walls of the peat pot working from the bottom up.

Because *R. atrosanguineum* relishes the heat, young plants should be kept growing strongly indoors until all danger of frost is past, or even during the dank drizzly weather that can sometimes occur in late spring and early summer. They should then be planted carefully in the warmest parts of the garden, against south-facing walls or fences. A light grid of sturdy garden twine should be provided for their support, and stems should be trained laterally wherever possible. That way the evenly graded little bells will hang down all in a row, which is much of their charm.

FAMILY: *Scrophulariaceae*

COMMON NAME: *Purple bell vine*

FULL SUN; MODERATELY EASY; TENDER PERENNIAL VINE TREATED AS A TENDER ANNUAL

Salvia

Several years ago I showed an old Italian lady who spoke not one word of English through my garden. It was a difficult visit, not because she was determinedly unilingual, for we have had other non–English-speaking visitors with whom we could enthusiastically communicate through botanical Latin and, when that failed, through gestures of eyes, nose, fingers, hands, and shoulders. It was a difficult visit because the lady was on several fronts very sure of her due. She came of an ancient Florentine family, and she had borne 12 children successfully. They had in turn produced, apparently to her great credit, dozens and dozens of grandchildren. You got the impression, however, that it had been years since she had said anything nice to a human being older than four, for fear of giving them notions.

As she walked about with her companion, she would occasionally ask for a plant name with a frown on her face, as if she meant to record in her memory something *not* to grow. Very occasionally, when she saw a plant she could not but admire, the word *bella* would slip from between her tight lips like meager alms given to beggars at the church door. We continued in this way until we reached the end of a stone path where several plants of culinary sage are grown, not just for their aromatic leaves but also for their pretty flowers. At this point the old lady brightened a bit, and said, not to me but to her companion, "Ah, salvia, *sal*-vi-a! Un giardino senza salvia non è neanche un giardino!" This remark her companion rendered as, "Your garden would be nothing without this sage!" But I think the same remark could be more graciously translated as, "Every garden should have sage in it."

And this is so, proving once again that truth is truth, whatever its source. There are groups of closely related plants, often quite large, that seem to share by common birthright the same heritage of beauty. The salvias rank high in this gathering of noble families, for of the 750 or more species that bear the name salvia (early translated into English as "sage" from the medieval French *sauge*, meaning wise or healthful), very many are eminently garden worthy, more, perhaps, than even the largest garden can accommodate. They are shrubs, subshrubs, perennials, or annuals, but many flower the first year from seedlings or small cuttings. They produce their blossoms, in dense or loose corymbs and sometimes surrounded by showy bracts, either in one great month-long splash or often over a whole summer. Many are purely ornamental, though some have been grown as long as history itself for culinary or medicinal purposes, and even those are showy garden plants. So my difficult visitor was correct: "Every garden should have sage in it."

SALVIA FARINACEA

Salvia farinacea *is familiar to most gardeners in insensitive and rigid bedding schemes in front of filling stations and restaurants across North America. But its flowers, tirelessly produced over a long season, come in precious shades of rich blue and purple, invaluable for massing in the perennial border. A native of Texas, it is not winter hardy in northern gardens. Most gardeners are content to replace it each summer from plentiful supplies of young plants available in most garden centers.*

It is a sad thing for many annuals and plants treated as annuals that they are so easily grown, so free with bloom, so vivid of color, and so *available*, in six-packs at every garden center, that they become endlessly overused, causing experienced gardeners to turn away from them. *Salvia farinacea*, an excellent tender perennial, native to Texas, has suffered such abuse. Its three-foot spires of blue, pale or dark but always tempered by the white powder or "meal" on its bracts, are familiar enough in bedding schemes before filling stations, the better funeral parlors, and restaurants that specialize in

"Surf 'n' Turf." One might feel, observing it marching among orange marigolds and silver dusty miller, that enough is planted each year in America without adding to the numbers in one's own garden.

But *S. farinacea*, like many other annuals, is a plant that should be rethought. A true perennial that will overwinter in USDA Zone 8, it comes quickly and easily from seed, grows rapidly into several three-foot-tall spires from the base, and produces beautiful flowers—and *blue* flowers—from early summer until frost. They are borne in terminal spikes that contribute strong vertical accents to the perennial border, and that are excellent for picking. Like most salvias, *S. farinacea* is disease-free and tolerant of drought, once established, though the best plants are always produced in open, fertile loam that receives a sprinkling of vegetable garden fertilizer when the plants are about eight inches tall. A deep watering in prolonged dry spells will encourage the plants to continue producing abundant bloom through the dog days of August.

No one need be at pains to start *S. farinacea* from seed, for it is available in many shades of blue, dark purple, and white from garden centers. It is, however, easy to grow from seed. Started quite early, in late February or March, seed will produce early-blooming plants. It may be soaked for a day or two to speed germination, and then sprinkled over a sterile potting mix and barely covered. The pots should be kept warm, at about 75 degrees Fahrenheit, until germination occurs. Young seedlings should be pricked out when they are an inch or so tall and grown on in sun. They may be planted out in the garden after danger of frost is past. At summer's end, established plants in cold gardens may be cut back, potted up, and kept from frost until late March. They should then be brought into bright light to grow on; when the first growth appears, the plants may be divided into several rooted pieces, potted on, and placed in full sun.

The least satisfactory way to use *S. farinacea* is to throw it together in a bed of other annuals to provide the blue note. It should be treated with the same dignity one would accord any other desirable perennial. Looking always a little lonely and embarrassed when planted singly, it becomes splendid in drifts. They might occur midway in the perennial border, perhaps around the trying gaps that are left when the hardy geraniums go off in late June. Its upright form, which never requires staking, qualifies it for planting a little more forward than one would normally place a three-foot plant. So treated, it will break up the storied ranks of other perennials, fracturing that feeling that the border has been trimmed on a slant with shears. And *S. farinacea* is so easy of culture and so accepting of neglect that it can be wonderfully used in large spontaneous drifts, in front of an old barn or split-rail fence or as a large pool of blue in a grassy meadow.

FAMILY: *Lamiaceae*

COMMON NAME: *Mealy-cup sage*

FULL SUN; EASY; TENDER PERENNIAL

SALVIA GREGGII

Salvia greggii *is a native of Texas and New Mexico, tender in all but the warmest gardens. But from seed or from rooted cuttings it makes a tidy two-foot bush by midsummer, surmounted with small vivid flowers of deep pink, scarlet, or peach that continue to frost. Then cuttings should be taken, particularly of those plants whose colors most please the gardener, for overwintering indoors and for a fresh supply of plants to enliven the next summer's garden.*

It is of course not true, as Oscar Wilde once remarked, that nature follows art, for the purposes of the natural world have far different ends than those consciously contrived by painters and sculptors. It *is* true, however, that artists teach us to perceive in nature effects that we learn to see as beautiful, and see the more for having been so taught. For gardeners, the vast world of painting is a perpetual stimulation, offering possibilities that we may translate into our gardens with something of the painter's original perception and often in imitation of his genius. The paintings of Corot are a case in point, for their somber greens and grays are often lifted to sublimity by dots of scarlet red. Gardeners will recognize those burning hints of flower as *Papaver rhoeas,* the European corn poppy. From Corot's canvases we can learn to use red in a way that will reproduce the sense he captures of enlivenment. Red, as Corot uses it, is at once assertive and ephemeral; it spangles the gloom with reflected light but never dominates the dim hues that lie around it.

The practical question for gardeners is how to come by plants that will achieve just that effect. For flowers of true scarlet are scarce.

Among annuals and plants treated as annuals several are red-flowered, though almost all of these flowers tend to be stuck onto themselves, producing assertive wads of scarlet rather than an airy ephemeral effect. So it is, sadly, with *Salvia splendens*, the scarlet sage, and with red bedding geraniums, which always look better in a pot than in the garden. So the choice, for the connoisseur of summer-blooming plants, might well settle on *Salvia greggii*, a plant rare in gardens until the recent vogue for all salvias lifted it into prominence.

Salvia greggii is in fact a native American species, occurring in natural stands in southern Texas and into Mexico. It is a woody, persistent plant to four feet tall, well branched with many wiry and graceful stems from the base upward, clad in arrowhead-shaped leaves of a fresh dark green that smell when crushed of underripe peaches. Each stem is surmounted by a loose panicle of inch-long tubular flowers in two parts, a sickle-shaped upper hood and a flaring underlobe. There are never many flowers on one stem at a time, but the color is so vivid that they are always enough.

Naturally occurring stands of *S. greggii* show some variation in flower color from the typical clear scarlet to peach and to a rich dark velvet-red that is almost maroon. A white form ('Alba') also occurs in the wild. But of them all, the scarlet is best. (From a seed packet it is that typical form that one will mostly get.) It is a curiously luminous color, produced by the red being evenly laid over a ground of yellow. This causes its flowers to seem to glow with reflected light.

The common name autumn sage is apt only for the plant in the wild, for early sowings in February or March will produce plants that will flower in late June and continue until frost, with greater and greater abundance as the plant branches and develops. Seed should be sown indoors on a sterile potting mix, and kept at about 60 degrees Fahrenheit until germination occurs. When about an inch or so tall, the young plants should be pricked out and grown on in full sun until danger of frost is past, when they may be planted in the garden. Alternatively, young plants, often grown from cuttings, can be bought from several mail-order nurseries, in selected color forms if one wants them, or in the typical scarlet. Whether from seed or cuttings, however, the plants will seem at first rather angular and unpromising, consisting only of a single leafy stem. They may be cut back to four inches from the base to encourage branching, or the single stem may be bent to the ground and pinned down (old gardeners used an old-fashioned hairpin for such purposes), in which case they will branch freely all along the stem and root at the tip. Plants should be spaced about 12 inches apart; by midsummer they will have interlaced into a single shrubby mass. Cuttings may be taken at any time and rooted in damp sand, either for additional plants in the late-summer garden or to overwinter under glass. In late autumn, after frost has withered the foliage but not killed the stems, *S. greggii* may also be cut back hard, to within four inches of the base, potted up, and carried over in a cool, frost-free place. In March the potted plants should be brought into the light and grown on in sun for large, free-flowering summer plants. As *S. greggii* is reliably hardy only to USDA Zone 8, seedlings, cuttings, or overwintered plants are the northern gardener's only way of producing its magical effects.

FAMILY: *Lamiaceae*

COMMON NAME: *Autumn sage*

FULL SUN; EASY; TENDER SUBSHRUB

SALVIA OFFICINALIS

*The culinary sages (*Salvia officinalis*) come in many beautiful leaf forms, from the sea-green of the typical plant through purple, and purple splashed with pink and cream. One of the prettiest is the gold-leafed cultivar called 'Icterina', which makes a low mounded bush a foot or so across in a single season. It is more tender than the plant usually grown for seasoning, and so cuttings or rooted stems should be potted up each autumn and grown on a sunny windowsill for the winter. In addition to preserving the stock for the following summer, these plants will accept an occasional snip of a leaf or growing tip to flavor winter stews and omelettes.*

Among all the beautiful sages one might grow, room must first be found for *Salvia officinalis*, the culinary sage. It has been cultivated since Roman times as a seasoning, and it makes its most familiar appearance as a dry woolly powder, smelling of dust and pungence, when it is time to prepare the stuffing for the Thanksgiving turkey. Good cooks know, however, that the pungent leaves, taken fresh from the garden, have other uses. They are wonderful when laid, sprigged stems and all, inside the cavities of

brook trout, over a stuffing of good bread crumbs moistened with stock and butter. And shredded fine, mixed with hot olive oil in which garlic has been fried until it is barely golden and then minced to a paste, they can be added to freshly cooked pasta with a little good hard Italian cheese for an elegant lunch.

It may have been the culinary value of the plant, and not its great beauty, that aroused the single response of enthusiasm from my Italian visitor. But in fact culinary sage is a splendid plant, to two feet tall, clad in narrow, five-inch-long puckered leaves of grayish green ("sage green," one would say), from top to bottom. From an indoor seeding in April or from young plants bought from the local garden center, it will make fine bushes by early spring that grow fatter for being picked to use in the kitchen, though whole sprigs and not just leaves should be taken. It is a quite hardy plant, actually a true shrub and not an annual, and the second year of its life it will produce loose panicles of purple-blue flowers above its fine leaves so long as it is not cut back hard in spring. (After flowering, for longevity, it is well to shear back the whole plant to within six inches of the base; it will quickly reclothe itself, though there will be no more flowers.) *Salvia officinalis* occurs not only in the fine purple-flowered form, but also in a pristine white ('Albiflora'), and in a diminutive form called 'Compacta', which has tiny, three-inch-long leaves and grows into a fat bush only eight inches high. All three forms can be trained, with patience, into little single-stemmed trees surmounted by a mop of foliage. (See "Standards," page 198.)

There are several other forms of *S. officinalis* that are beautiful in gardens, though all must be grown as annuals in much of the country, for they have given up some hardiness in favor of richly colored foliage. Best of them, perhaps, is *S. officinalis* 'Icterina'. It produces leaves more tongue- than blade-shaped, each of which has a flame of sage-green in the center and is beautifully margined with chartreuse-yellow. It develops into a low, flat-topped clump about eight inches high, with many upturned stems thickly furnished with overlapping leaves. Each stem roots where it touches the ground, producing a colony about two feet wide by summer's end. The name 'icterina' has a pretty sound, until one learns that it is a medical term for "jaundiced," signifying the yellow mottling of the leaves. That is one of many cases in which one would have something to say to the plant's namer. It is perhaps the very best

yellow-variegated tender plant for sites in the garden or for bedding schemes that require that brightness.

Much more somber, even moody, is the cultivar called 'Purpurea', in which the leaves are all a dark rich purple. It, too, is shorter than the standard green-leaved sage, though it forms tufted bushes that are more often dome-shaped than flat across the top. It is also much more tender than the species, and so is best treated as an annual. The same is true of the most baroque member of this group, *S. officinalis* 'Tricolor', which is low of growth as well, never topping nine inches, but which clothes itself with leaves that are dark purple in the center, shading outward to pale pink and then to a pink so faint as to be almost white. It sounds in description rather lurid, and can be so in the garden; however, its substance and its distinctly "herbish" character make it seem somehow less anomalous in garden schemes than coleus. Used in just the right place it is very beautiful.

All three vividly colored forms of *S. officinalis* are as pungently scented in leaf as is the green form (and are as excellent for culinary use, though they lose their bright colors when cooked). As all these cultivars are rather tender, hardy only to USDA Zone 8 and south, they will never produce flowers, which are borne on second-year wood; they must be started anew each year (from young plants purchased each spring) or from cuttings taken in autumn and pot-grown throughout the winter on a sunny windowsill. It is an easy process, as many rooted stems may be found at the base of each plant, and cuttings taken in late summer root quickly in damp sand.

Plants grown on a sunny windowsill may become shabby in late winter (either from indoor conditions or from frequent "harvests" for winter soups and stews) but their woody bases will quickly regenerate lush foliage when planted out in good garden soil in spring, after danger of frost is past. The white-flowered and dwarf forms must also be carried over in this way or purchased anew in spring. The tall green, blue-flowered form is easy to start from seed, eight to 10 weeks before last frost. Seed is sown on a sterile potting mix to which one-third sharp builder's sand has been added by volume. The seedlings are pricked out into a similar mix when they are an inch or so tall, and grown on in sun, to be planted out after danger of frost is over. In the garden, *S. officinalis* asks only fertile, well-cultivated soil and plenty of sunshine. To produce the best plants fertilize with granular food about the roots. Like many pungent-leaved herbs, they will suffer by being kept overmoist, enjoying a little drying out at the roots between waterings.

In all its forms *S. officinalis* is an excellent plant for the flower border. The cool-green leaves of the species, at once light and substantial, make it valuable in almost any flower scheme, loud or quiet, annual or perennial. The pretty blue flowers arc a bonus always. The forms with colored foliage lend themselves to many special garden uses. 'Icterina' brings sunshine with it wherever it is grown, and its color is soft enough to blend with any other, whether hot orange and red or cool blue, violet, and mauve. 'Purpurescens' might well be used for dark contrast against pink or white, or even as a somber intensifier to red. 'Tricolor' is perhaps the hardest of all *S. officinalis* cultivars to use well, and seems to look best in isolation, in a pot or weathered wooden bucket or on the sunny fringe of a shrubbery. All forms of *S. officinalis*, whether from ancient association or simply because of something in them, seem at their best in close conjunction with stonework or with antique brick, and all combine beautifully with silver-leaved "herbish" plants such as artemisias and dianthus. And if one should achieve a splendid standard tree from any of them, one cannot do better by it than to acquire a pot of Italian terra-cotta for it to grow in, standing such an elegant accent in the garden wherever its distinction shows best.

FAMILY: *Lamiaceae*

COMMON NAME: *Culinary sage*

FULL SUN; EASY; HARDY SHRUB TREATED AS A HALF-HARDY ANNUAL

SALVIA SPLENDENS

Like a sort of vegetable bonfire, Salvia splendens *can offer a startling beauty to the summer garden. Insensitively used, it can also be visually indigestible, "bidding the rash gazer wink his eye." It is best used in complete isolation from other flower colors, in quiet bays of shrubbery with green leaves only for a foil. Then it can be splendid indeed. In addition to the typical flaming red,* S. splendens *can also be had in ivory white, salmon pink, or a fine dark purple.*

Salvia splendens is perhaps the most familiar of all garden sages grown in America. Like most members of its family, it is actually a subshrub, capable in climates that resemble its Brazilian homeland of producing sturdy, persistent plants up to 8 feet tall. Many gardeners, however, will feel relief when frost takes it quite away, for the vivid-red bracts it typically sports are among the most difficult of all flowers to combine sensitively in the garden. Proof exists in front of almost any filling station or in ribbon beds throughout North America, where its bunchy form and screaming scarlet color vie with dwarf orange marigolds.

Still, *S. splendens* must have its garden uses. So far I have found them only in fantasy, though I imagine that the color might be exquisite in a scheme devoted all to red and white, like a giant valentine. I can see it also as isolated clumps of three or so plants scattered through an herb garden in which there was no other flower color, but only the quiet grayish-greens of sage, the silver of artemisias, and the fine dark-green dignity of parsley. It could be wonderful, too, dotted among the ripening grasses of a newly plowed meadow, perhaps even intermixed with gloriosa daisies in just the shades of orange that make it so visually indigestible in front of gas stations. Distance and the always quieting effect of grass might make for it just the place it deserves.

Beyond its brash scarlet, *S. splendens* now comes in other shades, scarcely less assertive in their way but perhaps easier to combine with other plants. There is a striking grape-blue form, a wavering pink, and a greenish-white. 'Carabiniere Purple' has dull garnet-red bracts, an interesting contrast to the scarlet flowers it has preserved from the species. Sadly, all these forms remain as bunched and stocky as their parent, which suggests that the real difficulty with *S. splendens* is not its color but its habit. Someone, someday, may breed the plant into a looser, more free-branching shape, and then we can think to plant it in all sorts of places, as dots of airy scarlet or purple or pink woven through and softened by surrounding foliage.

Because of its popularity, no one should be at pains to start *S. splendens* from seed, for even in its less usual colors it is available in spring from most garden centers, in bloom as infants in the six-pack. Those who like to grow their own plants on principle, however, should know that it is slow from seed, requiring a thorough soaking for one or two days. It should be started on a sterile potting mix in late February or early March, and kept at about 70 degrees Fahrenheit until germination occurs. Young plants should be pricked out when the first true leaves appear, and grown on in full sun, kept moist, and well fertilized with soluble plant food to develop their strength. They should be planted out in the garden when all danger of frost is past. Cuttings may be taken in late summer from side shoots and rooted in damp sand, potted on, and grown for winter display in the greenhouse or on a sunny windowsill. Single plants, flourishing in five-inch clay pots, probably look more wonderful in February than at any other time, for even the brashest scarlet will be welcomed then, perhaps in conjunction with a pot of paperwhite narcissus. At all times, *S. splendens* requires rich, free-draining soil and plenty of fertilizer to develop well.

FAMILY: *Lamiaceae*

COMMON NAME: *Scarlet sage*

FULL SUN; EASY; HALF-HARDY ANNUAL

SALVIA VIRIDIS

It is a wonderful fact about annuals that they offer almost unlimited choices for experimentation. But out of each year's samplings, one or two will prove indispensable for future plantings. For summer-long beauty, compact growth and vividly colored bracts, Salvia horminum *is such a plant. It comes in a pretty mix of white, rose-pink and blue, but is also available separately. Here the blue form is planted as a ribbon in front of a foundation hedge of the rose-splashed* Berberis 'Ruby Glow'.

Though *Salvia viridis* (syn. *S. horminum*) has no culinary or medicinal use that I know of, it is one of the most garden-worthy of a large family. Within its clan, it possesses the distinction of being the only true annual that is generally cultivated, producing flowers from seed and seed from flowers in one short growing season of two months or less. All the other sages cultivated in gardens, though they may be capable of bearing flowers, even in abundance, from an early seeding, are in fact shrubs, sub-shrubs, or tender perennials. They are capable of going on from year to year in mild climates or when carried over the winter as rooted cuttings or dormant clumps. *Salvia viridis* gets the business of being a plant over with rather quickly, though for that it has no special claims, since many a weed can say the same for itself. It is the way it does it that matters; it produces vigorous, quick-growing, much-branched plants of many stems, each of which decides, about a foot above ground, to clothe its remaining foot or so of growth in vividly colored bracts. They are about an inch long, produced in threes at intervals of an inch or so along the stem, and they may be deep purple, purplish-blue, pink, or white, each clearly veined with a darker shade or, in the paler forms, with leaf-green. The tiny flowers borne below the bracts are of no value to the gardener (though they matter, of course, to the plant), being tiny quarter-inch inflorescences with a sickle-shaped hood of blue or pink and an underlip of white. Once pollinated, the flowers fall off, leaving behind a funnel-shaped green calyx that protects the fast-maturing seed. But the bracts on the upper parts of the stem remain, from their first appearance until the plant exhausts itself in early autumn, providing what can only be called a splash of color. These stems may be picked for summer bouquets, for they last a long time in water, and they preserve their strong colors when dried for winter arrangements.

Seed of *S. viridis* comes in mixed colors, and an interwoven planting of pale and dark purple, rose and white can be very beautiful. But the best effects are achieved by growing it in selections of one color, and I can think of no planting that would not be improved by the purple form. It is at once rich and luminous, complementary to any other shade in the garden from yellow and orange to pink and red. With a liberal mixture of silver leaves—from artemisias or mulleins, for example—its bracts can glow like the rarest stained glass.

Salvia viridis is of very easy culture. Impatient gardeners may start it about six to eight weeks before the last frost, sowing the seed on a sterile potting mix. Germination should occur in a week or two at temperatures around 60 degrees Fahrenheit, and the young seedlings should be pricked out and grown on in sun until frost is out of the garden, when they may be planted in place. However, seed sown directly in the ground about two weeks before the last frost will usually catch up with seedlings started indoors, and the plants will be stronger and more abundantly bracted. Once one has grown *S. viridis* in the garden, self-sown seedlings should appear from year to year, never as a nuisance, for the heavy seed falls near where the plant grew the year before, and young seedlings are easy to transplant. Any seedlings should be thinned to stand about eight inches apart. They will quickly weave into a mass of color, useful midway in the perennial border, as clumps of three to five plants in the herb garden, or as drifts in a wild meadow garden interwoven with low grass. Though, like most salvias, *S. viridis* is drought tolerant and accepts lean soils, the best and longest show of color is produced by fertilizing with a granular vegetable garden food when the plants are about six inches high and by keeping them well watered until the first bracts appear. Thereafter they will take care of themselves, though an occasional deep watering in very dry weather will help to prolong their display.

FAMILY: *Lamiaceae*

COMMON NAME: *Clary*

FULL SUN; EASY; HARDY TO HALF-HARDY ANNUAL

SCABIOSA ATROPURPUREA

Even in bud Scabiosa atropurpurea *possesses an engaging form. It is called the pincushion flower from the way its stamens are stuck all about in the tightly packed rounded two-inch flower. Pretty in the garden, it is even finer in a vase, where it will stay fresh for more than a week.*

The number of quaint popular names a plant has accumulated is often a good indication of the time it has spent in gardens. In its 300-year tenure as a cultivated plant, *Scabiosa atropurpurea* has picked up an impressive collection. A native of southern Europe, it was cultivated by the elder Tradescant for James I, and was early known as "mourning bride" for the somber reddish purple or even purplish black color of its flowers. In French it was called *fleur de veuve*, "widow's flower," and in English sometimes also "mourning widow." Cottage gardeners gave it the more cheerful name "pincushion flower," for the way the little white stamens in each floret stand above the tight-packed rounded mass of the bloom like pins in a cushion. It has also been known as "star flower" for the spangling of these stamens across the dark blooms like stars in a purple night. Among all its names, morbid, industrious, and puzzling, it has at least never been called in English "itch flower," though the Latin genus name reminds us that it was considered an excellent cure for scabies, a parasite-borne skin disease that plagued our sometimes not-well-washed ancestors.

In its original form *S. atropurpurea* presents some of the oddest, and certainly the darkest, colors offered by any annual. As a garden plant, it would have remained of interest chiefly to the adventurous colorist and the morbid of mind, were it not that the plant has been bred into many lovely and lighter-hearted shades, from white to pale and dark blue to rose, mauve, and clear purple. Grown well, it presents many long stems and few much-divided leaves, and can bear its pincushions, first by ones and twos in early June from a March sowing, and then by tens and twenties until heavy frost cuts it down in September. They are ideal for picking, because the stems are long and wiry, and the blossoms, usually about two inches across, last well in water and possess a form unique among cut flowers.

Like many flowers that sit midway in the continuum between true biennials and hardy annuals, *S. atropurpurea* benefits from a very early sowing, just in the place it is to grow. Gardeners north of USDA Zone 8 should sow it as soon as the ground is workable, usually in late March, thinning the young plants to stand about eight inches apart. South of Zone 8, magnificent plants may be had by sowing the seed in October, in a coldframe or in the garden, and protecting them from very frosty weather by a light mulch. Seed may also be sown in peat pots or plastic six-packs about four to six weeks before last frost in a well-draining sandy potting mix on a sunny windowsill. However it is grown, *S. atropurpurea* must be transplanted carefully, for it produces a long taproot. Plants may be moved when young, but they will never be as tall or as floriferous as plants grown in place or transplanted without root disturbance.

There is really not much to *S. atropurpurea*

but flower, and so it should be planted in the garden in sunny patches among or behind other stout perennials. They will hide its thin growth of leaf and stem and give some support to its wiry stems, which will otherwise flop about and even gooseneck into themselves. Even so planted, it is worth the trouble of inserting a bamboo stake or forest twig at the base of each plant and tying it in, since flopping occurs most frequently at ground level. Seed is usually sold in mixes, and they should be avoided. A single packet will produce funereal purples and sky blues, creating a muddled effect. Of all the shades available that come true from seed, I concentrate on the blues and bluish mauves, since those are colors always to be sought for the summer garden. Removing spent flowers will encourage a long period of bloom.

Scabiosa atropurpurea is one of many annuals that may be grown in pots for winter display. For this purpose, seed is sown in September, in a potting mix that is rich but well draining. The seedlings should be pricked out first into small pots, and then moved on to pots six inches in diameter. When the roots have filled these pots, a dilute liquid fertilizer should be applied weekly on bright sunny days. Young plants should be grown on in quite cool temperatures ranging from about 45 degrees Fahrenheit at night to 10 degrees higher by day. Plants should begin flowering in the bright days of February and will continue through April. A well-grown plant of *S. atropurpurea* brought into the house in its mossy clay pot is, to say the least, a stunning substitute for paperwhite narcissus or a lingering Christmas poinsettia.

FAMILY: *Dipsacaceae*

COMMON NAMES: *Sweet scabious; pincushion flower; mourning bride*

FULL SUN; EASY; BIENNIAL TREATED AS A HARDY ANNUAL

SOLANUM JASMINOIDES

Solanum jasminoides is an elegant first cousin of the common potato, and is popularly called potato vine. A native of Brazil, it is not winter hardy north of USDA Zone 9, but small cuttings produce seven-foot vines by midsummer, and flowering is abundant in August. Before heavy frost, it is worth the trouble of digging and potting young vines, and cutting them back to a central stem. Kept over winter on a sunny windowsill or in a home greenhouse, they may then be easily replanted in the garden when the weather is settled for another summer of bloom.

Solanum jasminoides belongs to a large family that also shelters members of great economic usefulness, including tomatoes, potatoes, peppers, and eggplants. Its relationship to the common potato becomes obvious as soon as it blooms, for it produces many down-hanging racemes of star-shaped white-petaled flowers that are highly fragrant and that very closely resemble those of that familiar vegetable. Hence the popular name, potato vine, about which some-one has commented that it is not a very glamorous name for so beautiful a plant. That person must never have stood in a field of potatoes in full flower or held a tightly packed bouquet of their blossoms, for they are magically sweet smelling.

Solanum jasminoides is actually a climbing perennial shrub native to Brazil and hardy to USDA Zone 9, which is to say central Florida, the lower third of Texas and Louisiana, and much of California. In these climates it can grow to 20 feet, producing a thicket of many up-reaching stems that cling to strings or trellises or anything else they touch. In northern gardens, it will make a beautiful plant, as well, though it is slow to get started and will not produce its clouds of scented flowers until well into August. Nor will it achieve its full height, six to eight feet being as much as it cares to do so far from home. But it stays in bloom throughout the dog days of August and continues well into September.

Solanum jasminoides may be obtained from several mail-order firms that specialize in greenhouse and indoor plants. It may also be grown from seed, which should be started quite early, in December or January, in order to achieve sizable plants for setting out in late spring. Seed is sown in a sterile potting mix, lightly covered and kept at about 60 degrees Fahrenheit until germination occurs. The young plants should be pricked out as soon as they have two or three true leaves and grown on in full sun. They may be transplanted into the garden at about the time one would transplant their close relatives, tomatoes. Growth will be slow until mid-July, though it may be hastened a bit with applications of dilute liquid fertilizer applied to the leaves and around the base of the plant. With the onset of warm weather, *S. jasminoides* will grow with surprising rapidity, producing the first scattered flowers by midsummer and clouds of them thereafter.

Once one has *S. jasminoides* in the garden, stock may be carried over by taking cuttings in late summer, rooting them in damp sand, and potting them into rich compost in five-inch pots. The first year or two, plants may also be dug just before killing frost, cut back hard, and potted to carry over in a greenhouse or on a sunny windowsill. Eventually, however, they will become too woody for such treatment, and new stock must be acquired from cuttings, seed, or started plants. Few blooms will be produced indoors, but their fresh, dark-green leaves are pleasant in the winter and easy to keep in good condition.

In the garden, *S. jasminoides* may be grown on trellises, arbors, or on strings attached to the side of a building. As it is a shrubby, free-branching vine with attractive foliage, its best use in the garden may be as a pillar plant, trained up and tied into an old weathered post for a vertical accent midway in the perennial border or by the entrance to a path. It is also wonderful grown in a large pot and trained on a bamboo tripod, to be stood on a terrace or deck. Its white flowers, which seem to glow in twilight, and its fresh sweet fragrance, gain added value when it is grown in this way.

FAMILY: *Solanaceae*

COMMON NAME: *Potato vine*

FULL SUN; MODERATELY EASY; TENDER SHRUBBY
  CLIMBER GROWN AS A HALF-HARDY ANNUAL

TAGETES SPECIES

Marigolds, in large "African" pompons or in bronzy "French" buttons, are familiar to gardeners everywhere in America. Less well known are the delicate, refined selections of Tagetes tenuifolia, *called "signet marigolds." Their delicate ferny foliage and their abundant half-inch flowers seem to settle more easily into garden schemes than some of their brassy cousins.*

For many years, with all his considerable authority among grass-roots American gardeners, David Burpee agitated for the adoption of the marigold as the official national flower. He lost out to the rose, but the marigold would not have been a bad choice, not just because of the ubiquity with which it colors the American landscape in summer, but also because no better emblem could have been found, perhaps, for a nation made up of so many diverse ethnic

groups. The plant was developed from species of *Tagetes* native to Mexico and Central America, is called "African" when it is large and "French" when it is small, and the nicest cultivar ever, to my thinking, bore the name 'Irish Lace'. And many gardeners will remember when Alice Vonk, from Sully, Iowa, captured in 1975 the prize (of $10,000) for finally achieving a white marigold. At the time the prize was awarded, Mrs. Vonk was largely celebrated as yet another instance of the triumph of the stick-to-itiveness of simple American ingenuity over big business and the impersonal forces of the world.

But to many American gardeners, these days, the planting of marigolds is an unthinkable act. Their hard, bright colors, their simplicity of cultivation, and most especially their vast overuse, have won them contempt in the end. Indeed, a critical opinion of marigolds has become one of many small attitudes that signal the "sophisticated gardener"; in most garden literature, the marigold has come to be *the* example of plants beyond the pale.

That is a great pity, for putting aside all the sterling values of the plant—the ease with which it may be raised; its acceptance of hostile conditions; the generosity with which it rewards the clumsiest handling, flowering almost nonstop from first setting out to heavy autumn frosts—there is still something about a marigold. That something is its fragrance, not of flower so much as of leaf, and not so much sweet as pungent and fresh. Without that smell, summer would be incomplete, and space in the garden must always be found for a few of them, if only in a pot. Still, the truest and funniest comment about marigolds was written by Henry Mitchell, garden columnist for the *Washington Post*: "Marigolds gain enormously in impact when used as sparingly as ultimatums."

All marigolds in gardens descend primarily from two species, *Tagetes erecta* and *T. patula*, both native to Mexico and Central America. It is from *T. erecta*, a stoutly upright plant to three feet with light-yellow to orange six-inch flowers, that most African marigolds have been developed. *Tagetes patula*, a lower-growing plant, a foot and half tall with single two-inch flowers in yellow, orange, brown-red, or sometimes particolored, has been the parent of the bushy French marigolds. But blood of other species has entered both races, to the general delight of modern hybridizers and often of gardeners alike. The Burpee catalog of 1991 listed over 40 varieties in every height, color, and flower shape possible, given the genetic makeup of the two principal species, and some until recently impossible, as in 'Snowbird' and 'Snowdrift', two ivory-white cultivars descended, one must presume, from Mrs. Vonk's victory. There are even, for some reason, two "scentless" forms, one oddly named 'Sweet n' Yellow' and one called with blunt directness 'Odorless Mixed'.

But to me, the prettiest marigolds are not those bred primarily from *T. erecta* and *T. patula*, but from another Central American species, *T. tenuifolia*. They are fey and wild looking, with fine lacy foliage and tiny half-inch single flowers with five ragged little petals borne profusely on foot-high bushes. As the Burpee catalog says about its two offerings in this group ('Golden Gem' and 'Lemon Gem'), they are "quite different from other marigolds; you'll love them in your garden." (Many gardeners might see something other than a non sequitur in the two clauses of that catalog recommendation.)

To the tenuifolia group, popularly called signet marigolds, must have belonged the cultivar 'Irish Lace', which I grew with great pleasure for several years. It was a slightly disheveled little plant about a foot tall, with fine, ferny leaves, and its flowers were a yellow getting as close to green as they could while still being yellow. I have lost sight of it, and I wish I had saved seed, for it probably was sufficiently unimproved to come true, or possibly better, almost true. And generally, gardeners impatient of overhybridized marigolds might still grow a few, particularly of the French sort, just to save the seed and breed backwards. For there is often a delicacy and a simplicity in the progeny much more to the gardener's taste and far from the wadded exuberance that has been inflicted on the marigold.

There can be no seed of commonly grown annuals easier to start than marigolds, and indeed, on opening the packet, most gardeners will have a rush of memory, for the narrow gray-brown seeds may be the first ones ever shook out into one's hand. About six weeks before last frost date the seed should be sprinkled thinly on a sterile potting mix to which a generous lacing of sharp sand has been added. Seeded pots should be evenly moist but not sopping, and covered with a pane of glass or a film of plastic until germination, which will occur usually within four or five days. The young seedlings should then be uncovered, placed in a sunny windowsill, and grown on until they have achieved four pairs of true leaves. They should then be pricked out into similarly free-draining soil, kept moist but never waterlogged, and grown on in sun until they may be hardened off for planting in the garden.

Because marigolds are quick from seed and quick to flower, they may also be seeded directly into the garden about the time the apple blossoms fade, and the seedlings thinned to stand from 10 inches to two feet apart, depending on the height of the variety. Open-seeded plants will bloom slightly later than those started indoors, but will often make stronger and healthier plants (if, indeed, any marigold given half a chance ever is unhealthy). Marigolds will often begin to bloom within eight weeks of seeding, and continue until frost. They are in fact surprisingly frost-hardy, and the last best blooms of tawny yellow, orange, or burnt red appear just when they look the best, among the autumn leaves that match them for vividness of hue.

Marigolds, being of easy and cheerful growth, are one of the best annuals for growing indoors during the winter. There is an old variety called 'Lieb's Winter Flowering' that might still be found. Most modern hybrids, though a little less willing to produce abundant bloom without strong light, will still flower shyly in late winter and profusely as the days lengthen toward spring. Because of their compactness and their generous flower production, however, French marigolds or those from the tenuifolia group will make the best indoor plants. Seed for winter-flowering marigolds is sown in mid-August; alternatively, cuttings, which root easily, may be taken from vigorous side growths in September. Young plants are potted on into five-inch pots and grown vigorously out of doors until the first frosts. The pots should then be brought into sunny indoor conditions, where they must be kept rather cool at night, around 50 to 55 degrees Fahrenheit, with daytime temperatures climbing into the low 70s. The soil in the pots should be allowed to dry out slightly between waterings, but never so much as to cause withering of the plants. When growth quickens in late winter, the plants will be grateful for a dilute drenching of water-soluble plant food, applied at half the strength and twice the frequency recommended. Plants grown for winter display can often be cut back and regrown for the summer, and cuttings are always easy to take. With a good or unusual form, such as the 'Irish Lace' I regret having lost, carrying plants over the winter would always be a bright idea.

FAMILY: *Asteraceae*

COMMON NAME: *Marigold*

FULL SUN; EASY; ANNUALS OR TENDER PERENNIALS TREATED AS HALF-HARDY ANNUALS

TITHONIA ROTUNDIFOLIA

Tithonia rotundifolia *is aptly called torch flower for the smoldering brilliance of its sunflowerlike blossoms. A tall, coarse-growing annual from Mexico, it looks best at the back of large border or perhaps isolated in front of an old weathered barn or silver-gray fence. Its three-inch daisies are freely produced from mid-July to frost, and are adored by bees, butterflies, and flower arrangers.*

Tithonia rotundifolia is one of three species of shrubby annuals or perennials that commemorate Tithonus, a mortal youth so adored by Eos, goddess of the dawn, that she petitioned the gods to grant him immortal life. She neglected, however, to ask for perpetual youth, and so she rose from her couch each morning, renewed in beauty, to see Tithonus shriveling into old age. Finally she was obliged to wrap the old man in swaddling clothes like a babe, though his voice *would* go on in unceasing complaint of his fate. Eventually, Zeus changed him into a grasshopper, the garrulous creature of an hour, in warning to all mortals to make use of their short day and not seek to extend it.

Nothing in the vigorous fiery splendor of *T. rotundifolia* suggests a parallel to this story. The species name *rotundifolia* is not accurately descriptive either, for the plant will bear, all up and down its hairy hollow stems, leaves that are trident- or broadly spear-shaped, but never round.

Putting its botanical name aside, however, *T. rotundifolia* is a magnificent plant, unrivaled for height and splendor in the summer garden except by its cousins, the annual sunflowers. It grows tall, anywhere from five to seven feet, depending on soil fertility. On its abundant branches it carries many vivid-orange blossoms, each three inches wide, the velvet-textured ray flowers overlapping and pleated at their bases where they join the disk. The effect is not unlike a single dahlia, though the stems, where they meet the flowers, flare out trumpetlike as if blowing a blast of scarlet sound. There are chrome-yellow forms as well, though a clear, untainted scarlet is almost as rare in the garden as pure blue, and so one must wonder why they come in any other color.

Tithonia rotundifolia is emphatically a flower for high summer, not only because of its color, but also because it relishes the hot weather of August. It is native to Mexico and Central America, and will not really hit its stride until the weather in more temperate gardens reminds it of home. The worst of the dog days will cause it to grow with renewed strength, and each flower will then be busy with honeybees and bumblebees, wasps, hummingbirds, and butterflies.

Tithonia rotundifolia may be started in peat pots on a hot windowsill about six weeks before last frost. The large seeds germinate quickly, within one or two weeks, and the young plants should be grown on without a check. They may then be planted two to four feet apart in the garden just about when it is safe to transplant tomatoes. But except in the coldest gardens, or perhaps if one is aiming at plants large enough to be slipped in among perennials without becoming overshaded, little will be gained from a very early start. Stronger, more steadily growing plants may be achieved by sowing seed where it is to grow, just about the time one would sow sweet corn. *Tithonia rotundifolia* is not particular about soil, though it does appreciate a dusting of vegetable fertilizer when it is established, and deep, thorough waterings in dry spells while it is busy achieving its great height. Any check in its growth, whether from transplanting too early or growing in impoverished soil or from drought, can stunt its growth and cause its shanks to become prematurely deciduous.

Tithonia rotundifolia is without compare at the back of a deep border, where its blood-red flowers will enliven the uniform yellow of the great summer-blooming perennial daisies, the inulas, rudbeckias, coreopsis, and helianthus, and where it will continue to fill a gap when they are past. It has enough mass and density to form a quick-growing summer hedge, and would be splendid planted to screen a deck near the bright light of the sea. The plant is never so wonderful, however, as when it is planted alone in clumps of three or five against a weathered barn or towering over rough-mown grass. A few seeds might also be planted at the ends of corn rows in the vegetable garden, as a visual part of a fine late-summer harvest.

FAMILY: *Asteraceae: Helianthus Tribe*

COMMON NAMES: *Mexican sunflower; torch flower*

FULL SUN; EASY; HALF-HARDY ANNUAL

TROPAEOLUM PEREGRINUM

All gardeners know Tropaeolum majus, *the common nasturtium. Less familiar is the canary vine (*T. peregrinum*), though it is just as easy to grow. By midsummer it will fling a delicate veil over somber evergreens or climb six feet or more up a trellis. Almost as pretty as its bright-yellow flowers, in which the fanciful see tiny canaries, are its graceful sage-green lobed leaves. Streamers of* T. peregrinum *make interesting additions to arrangements of summer flowers, and they will often root in the vase for a fresh supply of small plants.*

Many of the beautiful annual vines of summer, such as limpid-blue morning glories or spectacular night-opening moon vines, require a great deal of planning from the gardener. They must be started on the south-facing side of a building, a network of strings or a trellis must be provided, and they must be frequently "stopped" by pinching their growing tips during their determined ascent upwards. Otherwise, they will quickly reach the top of their support and tumble downward in an untidy tangle. Though canary vine will behave with a much nicer restraint, reaching a height of from eight to 10 feet when forced directly aloft, it requires no great help to go about its way. Its species name means "wandering," and it will thread happily in and out of the branches of other plants without further troubling the gardener. Indeed, it does best when planted at the base of a large shrub or randomly along a hedge. There it will produce lettuce-green succulent stems and leaves of the same lovely light color, cut cunningly into five-lobed hands that all turn upward. They are perfectly graded, also, like beads on a string, from the oldest two-inch-wide ones at the bottom to the tiniest new ones at the top, hardly the size of a pea but still perfect in shape.

The leaves alone would justify growing the plant, as they can delicately enliven a quince or forsythia long past its moment of glory or add grace to a somber yew hedge. But in midsummer, from the axil of each leaf, a little soft-yellow inch-long flower is produced with only two petals, five-lobed also in mirror of the foliage, held above the essential parts like the fluttering wings of a tiny bird. They are the delight of children, or of anyone else who sees clearly how one thing wonderfully resembles another.

Tropaeolum peregrinum is a first cousin to the familiar nasturtium, *T. majus*. Both possess seeds that are large, easy to handle, and quick to germinate. Though both species prefer to be planted just where they will grow, *T. peregrinum* may also be started in a peat pot or carefully transplanted from a plastic six-pack without disturbing its roots. That way, the seed can germinate happily in the warmth it requires, and the little vine can achieve enough length to be planted at the base of a shrub and threaded upward toward the light. There it will grow quickly and flower nonstop from the end of June until frost. Canary vine is also beautiful tumbling from a window box or planted in a pot with a tripod of bamboo stakes to climb on. Cuttings can be taken from side growths in late summer, rooted in damp sand, and potted on to grace a sunny windowsill in winter. And from such plants, new cuttings can be taken in early spring for replanting in the summer garden. Such perpetuity will be worth the little trouble it costs, just to have a canary vine all year long.

FAMILY: *Tropaeolaceae*

COMMON NAMES: *Canary-bird flower*;
  canary vine

FULL TO HALF-SUN; EASY; HALF-HARDY ANNUAL

VERBENA ×HYBRIDA

Even in its old-fashioned colors of bright pink, magenta, and scarlet, Verbena ×hybrida *is valuable in gardens for its low matting growth and its continuous show of flowers from June to heavy frost. It is now available in softer shades. Particularly beautiful are the pale-pink form called 'Silver Ann' and a soft-pink and ivory one released under the name 'Peaches and Cream'.*

There are flowers one knows from childhood that can never be forgotten or surpassed, however sophisticated one becomes as a gardener. The old-fashioned *Verbena ×hybrida*, called rose vervain or rose verbena, belongs to this class. The product of several related South American species, it is the one remembered from childhood, usually in bright pink or scarlet, picked on summer afternoons from hot dry beds in fistfuls while the grown-ups talked on the porch. Its capacity to bloom throughout the summer and its willingness to bloom again, in double abundance, wherever it was picked meant that one could take all one wanted. But better even than the bright unsubtle blossoms crammed into a mason jar was the way the older flowers in a single three-inch nosegay of bloom, the ones just around the edges, could be slipped from their calyx and held between new front teeth to extract the drops of nectar within, all up the tube in satisfying little crunches until one reached the petals themselves, which only tasted green.

Memory is a great reason for growing any plant, but in fact, the tolerance of *V. ×hybrida* for drought and baking weather, its capacity to produce unending flowers from May until frost, and the beautiful colors it now comes in—from white and cream to pale pink, rose, red, purple, and blue, often with a contrasting perky eye of white—make it almost indispensable in the summer garden. Its lax trailing growth and its preference for drying out a bit between waterings make it invaluable as a trailing plant in window boxes and in large tubs and urns. Single plants may be bedded in gaps among the perennials, where their scandent stems will root along the ground, helped a bit by piling earth on them wherever they are bare, quickly filling their allotted space.

Verbena ×hybrida may be grown from either seed or cuttings. Seed is available in selected colors, but even in expert hands it can be very cranky to germinate. It should be sown in a warm greenhouse or on a windowsill eight to 10 weeks before last frost and covered with cardboard until it germinates. Sprouts from about 50 percent of the little brown twigged seeds constitute a good return. Fortunately, however, unless one is seeking a scarce cultivar, this bother may be left to the commercial growers, who produce millions of healthy plants in lovely colors, often showing their first bloom in six-packs on the garden-center bench.

When one finds a particularly nice form, however, or acquires a named cultivar, it is worth the trouble to take cuttings, if trouble it may be called. Pieces of stem root with great ease in damp sand, and can be struck anytime from late spring to autumn, either for additional plants in the garden or to overwinter as stock plants for the following season. Indoor-grown plants or ones hung near the glass of a greenhouse will flower sparingly but preciously during the winter, and though they may become shabby and a bit of a trial by winter's end, they should not be cut back. Old rangy specimens may be planted in spring, an inch or two deeper than they grew in the pot, the shabby stems fanned out and buried with only the tips exposed. By this method, I have carried the beautiful English plant called 'Silver Ann' through three generations in our garden. It opens bright pink and fades quickly, apple-blossom fashion, to blended pinks and white, making, in two or three weeks, a sheet of color at the top of an old limestone wall.

FAMILY: *Verbenaceae*

COMMON NAME: *Vervain*

FULL SUN; EASY; TENDER PERENNIALS TREATED AS HALF-HARDY ANNUALS

VERBENA BONARIENSIS

Very different from Verbena ×hybrida *is the species* V. bonariensis. *Its pale-lilac flowers are borne on stems so slight that the plant seems almost transparent, but so strong that they never need staking. In southern and southwestern gardens it will self-seed once established, often with perfect tact, as here in the pavement of a Los Angeles garden. Elsewhere it must be started anew each year from seed, though an excellent use of it is to plant it here and there as if it had come of itself.*

Unlike *Verbena ×hybrida, V. bonariensis* cannot be said to produce sheets of bloom, or sheets of anything. It is a stiff, upright, branching plant to four feet, embarrassingly ill clad in a few five-inch-long narrow-toothed leaves. Indeed, given the sheer lack of photosynthesizing surface, one wonders how it lives to grow so lustily. And seeing its tiny corymb of first flower, borne at the top of a gawky stem, one might well ask what the bother was about.

The effect, at a quick glance, is hardly showy, and seems distinctly inclined to magenta. Nursery owners say it will not sell, and little wonder, for *V. bonariensis* is one of many growing things whose first presentation is not its best.

Nevertheless it is a wonderful plant, with a skeletal grace unmatched in the summer garden. The adjective "airy" suits it perfectly, and by a happy pun, that is what it is botanically called, since the species name *bonariensis* means "good air," from the city of Buenos Aires, where it was first found in 1726. If the first angular stem it produces is cut back to within three inches of the base, it will produce four or six new ones, to form a plant that branches and rebranches, each stem dividing many times and terminating in a flat, two-inch corymb packed with tiny flowers, hardly three times the size of a pinhead. To call those flowers in any way magenta is to be unobservant, for they are of the purest lavender, shaded at their bases into violet. Pick a few branched flowering stems and put them in a vase for close study. You will not harm the plant, for all its apparent fragility, since more branches and flowers will appear wherever you cut. And what you cut will last a long time in water, opening successive generations of minute flowers for a week or more. Once you have looked closely at their beauty, you will never pass the plant again without peering close, just to see.

Verbena bonariensis is almost unimaginably easy to grow. It is tolerant of a wide range of soils, from double-dug manure-enriched ones to sandy dry gravel. Seed germinates readily under glass, requiring only warmth, moisture, a sterilized potting mixture, and protection from light, in the form of sheets of newspaper or cardboard, until sprouting occurs. Young plants are easy to grow on along a sunny windowsill, and if they become lanky (as is their nature)

they can be cut back. This is in any case necessary before they are planted out. Unless you have all the plants you need, do not discard those cuttings. They may be severed into sections with two joints each, the leaves removed from the lower joint, and inserted in damp sand, where they will root within three weeks.

Verbena bonariensis has many uses in the garden, though none of them are quite predictable. It can be stunning planted in a large drift of 20 or 30 plants, close enough so that they all lace together into a shimmering curtain of violet. But its best use may be when placed here and there in sections of the perennial border or in the wilder parts of the garden, rather spontaneously, as if it had seeded in of itself. (Indeed, in warmer gardens than ours, it will do just that.) Its light, airy frame will never crowd other plants, and though it can quickly achieve four feet in height, it is delicate enough to place rather far forward in the border, breaking, for punctuation, the general rule of short, medium, and tall.

FAMILY: *Verbenaceae*

COMMON NAME: *None*

FULL SUN; EASY; TENDER PERENNIAL TREATED AS A HALF-HARDY ANNUAL

ZINNIA SPECIES

Gardeners who turn away with scorn from the brasher cultivars of Zinnia elegans *may well be captured by the all-green form nicely named 'Envy'. Here, among alliums, a lavender form of* Verbena × hybrida, *and a single self-seeded* Perilla fruticosa, *it strikes a note of great suavity.*

I knew an old woman once who all her life had been famous for the beauty of her flowers. With the advance of age, she was forced to abandon first one section of her beautiful garden and then another. Finally, she had a pretty little hedged room off her parlor tilled up, and in it she planted only zinnias, all in neat well-hoed rows. Those she could not forgo, and she left instructions that if she died in summer, only zinnias should be used to decorate her grave. And so it was.

All gardeners must have some one flower with which they hope to end their days. Most often, the choice must be of something simple and naive, easy of cultivation, full of lusty good health and carrying in its open flowers a memory of all the gardens one has known and loved, early and late. Though I am still far from the contractions downward to one single flower, I am not sure that in the end it will not be zinnias for me as well. Only marigolds would be a rival, and at the last I might bargain for a row or two of them also, for as a gardener I have always been willing to forgo sublime simplicity to greed. No two flowers can be more redolent of summer, or more vivid reminders of where one began as a gardener. As such, no matter how avidly one seeks the rare and unusual and even unknown, these two hold their place.

The most familiar of garden zinnias are all

Looking little like a zinnia, but one nonetheless, is Zinnia angustifolia, *a new addition to most American gardens. From June to frost its lax stems, clad in narrow clean green leaves, are surmounted by small single inch-wide daisies of glowing orange. Each flower takes two or more months to mature into seed, and so one seldom sees a spent or faded flower the whole summer long. In this planting,* Z. angustifolia *is paired with a great aristocrat,* Oxypetalum caeruleum, *which may also be brought to flower the first year from an early seeding indoors.*

bred from *Z. elegans*, a Mexican native that in old gardens carried the popular and very apt name of "youth in old age." The little round scaled buds appear in abundance with half-opened flowers and with those that are completing their life, still with beauty.

Zinnia elegans was once a rather gawky two-foot-tall perennial with coarse semidouble flowers in an unsubtle range of colors from dirty white through pink, red, orange, and scarlet. It has now been bred into many sizes, several flower shapes, and magnificent clear colors. It has been shrunk into tiny six-inch-tall bushes smothered in fully double flowers, and

stretched to long-stemmed three-foot-tall plants perfect for cutting. In between are compact, well-branched bedding types that grow to two feet and produce a steady succession of flowers from mid-July to early September. There are fully double forms that show a perfectly rounded mass of ray petals shingled one atop the other in exact symmetry, though old-fashioned semidoubles with a cob of disk flowers are also still available. There are cactus-flowered types, in which the petals are quilled into ragged mops, and scabious-flowered forms with a thick pincushion of modified petals in the center surrounded by a ruff of perfectly formed ray petals. The original hot colors have been purified into subtle shades from pure white through cream, soft pink, salmon, clear orange, and red, and an exciting lime-green form named 'Envy' has also been developed. To this range have been added forms that are mahogany red, some with contrasting petal tips of clear yellow, and others, called 'Peppermint Stick', that are freaked and spotted with cream on red, red on yellow, or yellow on orange. Best of all, modern strains of *Z. elegans* have been bred to resist mildew, once their scourge but now virtually eliminated.

Those who love *Z. elegans* will need no particular advice about where to grow it. All forms look better in masses, and unless one is growing a form with unusual flowers or aims at a particular color scheme, zinnias gain in beauty from being planted in mixed colors. The smallest forms can be used for edging, if one still feels one must edge, but lined up along the verge of a bed they can sometimes look rather smug and determined. They are better when planted in an ellipse, fairly broad in the middle and tapering at the ends, to form a bay of color. They are of course perfect for pots and tubs, and one plant, grown alone in a six-inch clay pot, can form an instant flower arrangement for the summer picnic table. Taller forms may be used midborder in natural drifts. The tallest may require staking, but it is useful to know that they can be bent to the ground and pinned down, under which treatment they will produce their large flowers in sheets from every leaf axil. It is a handy trick to know for covering gaps in the perennial border left by plants that go off in midsummer.

Though *Z. elegans* will always be the plant most treasured by true zinnia lovers, another species, *Z. angustifolia* (also known as *Z. linearis*) has recently gained popularity in gardens and is well worth planting where a sheet of burning color is wanted. Unlike *Z. elegans*, which tends to be stocky and upright, it is a wiry little plant that stands up straight as long as it can but that eventually tumbles over under the weight of its growth. Straight or tumbled, it grows about a foot tall eventually, and is composed of a congestion of thin branches and narrow two-inch-long blade-shaped leaves that are hardly visible beneath the mass of bright-orange flowers it produces, in greater and greater profusion from late June until frost. Each is about an inch and a half to two inches wide, made up of a dozen ray petals surrounding a button of disk flowers, and in color and shape they are more reminiscent of the low-growing cosmos called 'Bright Lights' than of a zinnia. The flowers have two peculiarities: The first is that from initial opening to summer's end one will never see a spent or shabby flower on the plants, for the tight-packed disk flowers take a full two months or more to complete the work of pollination, and the ray flowers remain in perfect condition all the while. The second peculiarity is that at the end of the day, just at twilight, the flowers take on fire and seem to smolder like embers, recalling Andrew Marvell's fine phrase about oranges growing in the Bermudas, that they glowed "like golden suns in a green night." Because of its amiably lax habit, its profusion of flowers and its tolerance for drought, *Z. angustifolia* is a wonderful choice for a plant that will tumble from a window box. A dozen or so are also very fine when planted singly in a large clay pot as a decoration for patios or balconies.

Because zinnias are tender tropical annuals, they are best started indoors for a long display of flower. But they crave the sun and warmth, and so little is gained by starting them too early. Late April or early May is usually soon enough. Because they resent root disturbance, it is best also to sow them two or three to a plastic or peat pot, clipping out all but the strongest rather than pricking them out. The young plants should be grown on in full sun and at temperatures around 70 degrees Fahrenheit until the weather outdoors has settled. Even when frost is no longer a possibility, it is well to hold them an extra week indoors, or to move the young plants outdoors on sunny days and indoors on drizzly ones, prolonging the hardening-off process a little until warm weather is assured. When they may be safely transplanted, each young plant should be eased gently out of its pot, or if in peat pots planted pot and all, in rich well-tilled soil in full sun. Once they have caught hold and show signs of resuming growth, a light dressing of granular vegetable garden fertilizer should be sprinkled around each plant, far enough from the stem to avoid burning it. As with many hairy and raspy-leaved annuals, zinnia foliage is sensitive to liquid foliar fertilizers, and so they should be poured on the soil, and not, as is the usual practice, over the leaves and stems.

FAMILY: *Asteraceae: Helianthus Tribe*

COMMON NAMES: *Zinnia; youth in old age*

FULL SUN; MODERATELY EASY; TENDER ANNUAL

II.
TECHNIQUES

Because they are so quick of growth and because mistakes in siting them are so easy to rectify from summer to summer, annuals lend themselves to exuberance and whimsy. One supposes it was a happy gardener who contrived this planting scheme, made up almost entirely of plants grown as annuals, and happier still when it came to floriferous maturity.

INTRODUCTION

It is a wonderful aspect of gardening that the more one knows, the more one has to learn and to give. There is a freemasonry among devoted gardeners, cemented by the passing about of seed and slips and roots of wonderful plants, and most especially by the sharing of information, oftentimes hard won through successes or failures, and very often offered as tips by other gardeners, sometimes long dead. There may be good gardeners who hoard all their best things, who go poker-faced when asked how they have succeeded so well with this plant or that, and who carry all their secrets to the grave. But most gardeners, good gardeners in the moral sense, are like the Clerk in Chaucer's *Canterbury Tales*, whose love of knowledge he summarized simply by saying, "And gladly wolde he lerne, and gladly teche."

Offered here are some of the things I know about the successful raising of annuals. Like other folk, gardeners are prone to confuse fact with opinion. I am no exception and doubtless have let the latter slide into the former; still, I have taken care to separate what I know always to be true from what has merely worked for me, or worse, what I simply have a hunch about. But there never can be any substitute in gardening for one's own direct experience. Luck, too, plays a larger part in one's successes than some gardeners are willing to acknowledge. A stubborn plant may thrive gloriously for a novice because he or she has just the right soil or degree of sun or shade or moisture, while others, said to be easy, will garner a summer's worth of humiliation and nothing more.

Much of the information included in the following sections is so familiar to experienced gardeners that they may safely pass it over. They will know what works for them, and they should certainly continue doing things their way. But it is hoped that in my experience as a gardener I have accumulated a few tricks worth passing on. Certainly it is true that some of the best were passed on to me by garden visitors who paused in front of a bed to say, "Have you ever tried . . . ?" or, "Did you know . . . ?" Often I *hadn't* tried, and *didn't* know, and I cannot express my gratitude for all these generously offered tips better than by sharing them in return.

Procuring Seeds and Plants

To American gardeners it seems that there never has been so exciting a time as right now. There have been other glorious epochs in American horticulture, most notably at the end of the last century and the beginning of this, and again in the late forties and early fifties. But the best seems to be our own, not just because we are alive to enjoy it, but also because seeds and often plants of unusual species are easier to come by than ever before. A host of small mail-order nurseries have sprung up in the last 15 years that specialize in seed (and sometimes

A small home greenhouse, used in the winter to store plants and in early spring to start and grow on seedlings, can be made glorious in high summer by well-grown pots of annuals. After offering a brilliant summer display, most of the annuals shown here can be cut back, fed and regrown for even more precious flowers in the dead of winter.

in started plants) of species that have long been unavailable except through barter with other gardeners. Furthermore, the growth of rapid home-delivery services means that one can get one's seeds or plants quickly and in good condition. Major seed companies that used to find the listing of unusual annuals a sure path to bankruptcy are discovering that American gardeners are more and more willing to experiment with unfamiliar plants. The catalogs are still thick with listings of old stalwarts (marigolds, zinnias, and petunias), but there seems now to be more and more room for craspedia, sanvitalia, onopordum, and the like. Garden centers have followed suit, particularly those small ones run by true gardeners, not for quick profit but for the sheer love of plants. They will spend time selling a customer on species that do not show themselves in cute precocious bloom in the six-pack, that may not flower nonstop with "lots of color" from June to September, that may wait until August to display their first flowers, shy or splendid. Most excitingly, emphasis has subtly shifted away from "improved" hybrids that are double when they should be single, pink when they should be blue, and white when they should be yellow, and from plants dwarfed out of all grace for "easy maintenance." Numerous breeders are turning their attention to delicacy of form and subtlety of color, and there is a greater interest

in pure species than previously. The result of all this is to make gardening, just at this moment, a great deal of fun.

Listed on page 201 are sources for more annuals than the average gardener will have space to grow. All are reputable firms that take care to supply good seeds, and sometimes plants, true to name and reliable in germination. It may still be true, however, that some interesting annuals can only be procured from other gardeners, often with a long history that will be shared as willingly as the seed itself. Gardeners are in the main generous people, and like plants, the rewards of cultivating them are considerable. Most annuals, especially of species, also set far more seed than is needed. So it never hurts to ask, and one's requests are generally granted.

When visiting any garden, therefore, it is wise to have a few small glassine or brown paper envelopes in one's pocket, a ballpoint pen, and perhaps a few plastic bags for really bulky seed (or the chance of a cutting). A self-addressed stamped envelope is also handy, in case one's timing is not just right. And certainly it never hinders free exchange to have a few choice seeds of one's own to offer, sealed up and carefully labeled with the correct botanical name, the date they were gathered, and any cultural information one has learned about them.

Starting Seed Indoors

Putting aside simple thrift, about which passionate gardeners seem to know less than other folk, there are two main reasons for starting one's own seed. The first is that the plants one wants may simply not be available in any other way. The second is that the raising of a plant from seed conveys, in all its tedious and anxious stages, a pleasure the gardener can never

receive merely from purchasing well-grown and thrifty plants, however rare they may be. Starting seed is for many gardeners a necessary part, sometimes the most essential part, of their love for plants.

Still, to cut open a seed packet in early March, to shake out and examine its contents in the palm of one's hand, dust-fine as snuff or as fat with life as a table bean, to see that even in germ there are among plants infinite possibilities in size and shape and color, is for even experienced gardeners tantamount to embarking on a perilous journey. So many things could go wrong. One might sow too thickly, resulting in a thatch of crowded life so dense that no single individual had its own fair chance at existence. Or, despite one's most careful efforts, damping off might set in, felling promising and seemingly healthy seedlings just where they emerged from the soil. In one's zeal to do one's best, one might water too frequently, rotting away sustaining roots; or, in the hurry to get to the office, one might forget to water altogether, only to confront on one's return home a windowsill of parched and yellowed seedlings, desperate for water. Light conditions might be inadequate, resulting in plants that are drawn, spindly, or anemic at transplant time. One might rush the hardening-off process, scalding soft tissue by too rapid an exposure to the full force of the outdoor sun. And one might plant carelessly, forgetting that every tiny root hair ought to be brought in close contact with the surrounding soil in order for a young plant to "catch."

It is a good thing that nature is not so prone to anxieties as are many gardeners, else ours might be a barren planet indeed. The truth is that many seedlings, and most annual seedlings, are amazingly resilient, so bent on life that only the clumsiest handling will do them permanent harm. All of the disasters chronicled above can occur, but with a little thought and care they can just as easily be avoided. By far the most important thing to remember about starting seed, whether sprinkled in the garden on freshly tilled soil or started indoors in February on a sunny windowsill, is that one is asking plants to germinate, grow, and thrive in conditions that are usually far from those in which they have developed naturally. No plant, after all, is native to a sunny windowsill.

Sterile Potting Mixes   The most important precaution in assuring that one's seedlings develop strongly is to maintain sterile conditions from the first. Over and over in the individual plant portraits in this book, when advice is offered about starting seed, the words "sterile potting mix" appear. When my grandmother started her seed, she always simply dug rich earth out of the pile of leaves and garden clippings she accumulated under the grape arbor, rubbed it between her palms, filled whatever containers she had (an old window box or a dishpan with holes rusted out in the bottom) and sowed her seeds across the top, covering them lightly with a thin layer of more earth if they were large. She always produced magnificent seedlings, lusty and eager for life, plenty for herself and to share. If I followed her method I would be doomed to certain failure, for she gardened in Louisiana and I now garden in Vermont. She could start seedlings in her mild climate outdoors, hauling them into the woodshed only on unusually frosty nights. But I must begin to sow seed when nights and even days are full of snowflakes and the only promise of spring is the little germinating seedlings on a sunny windowsill. For this reason, I cannot take a chance with unsterilized earth, however rich, for it is sure to harbor soil-borne fungus diseases that will mean death to seedlings in a closed, indoor environment.

Gardeners who make their own compost swear by it, and with reason, for its rich black crumbly texture, laden with nutrients and trace elements, is mother's milk to any young plant. They usually mix it in the old tested recipe of two measures compost to one each of good garden earth, peat, and sharp sand, perlite or vermiculite. Still, however, they must sterilize it. In old estate greenhouses, this was done by forcing steam from the boiler through and through it until it was quite hot. The gardeners hardly required a thermometer, since they knew everything by feel, but it is useful to know that soil-borne diseases are killed when the soil reaches an internal temperature of between 205 and 212 degrees Fahrenheit. The home gardener may easily sterilize soil by baking it to these temperatures. A large heat-proof container, such as a canning kettle, is filled with prepared soil and baked slowly in the oven until it reaches 205 degrees, or until an apple-sized potato buried in the center is tender through and through. Because sharp sand, perlite, vermiculite, and peat are already sterile, bulk can be reduced by adding them after the soil and compost have cooled off. The mixture is then ready for seeding.

For many years I followed this method, and the faintly nauseating smell of cooking soil was one of the familiar scents of late winter and early spring. For the last few years, however, I have saved myself all this bother by using a commercially prepared soilless mix for starting seed and growing on young plants. (A few seedlings, those that demand unusually free drainage, will benefit by the addition of one-third sharp sand by volume; this requirement is noted in the individual portraits.)

Several cautions will be helpful to the gardener who opts to start seedlings in a soilless mix. First, it should be quite dry when purchased, for when stored wet, toxic fermentations can occur that are harmful to young seedlings, and the fungus diseases one wants most to eliminate may gain entry. It should also be stored dry until just before it is used. Second, it must be thoroughly moistened before it comes in contact with seeds in order for successful germination to occur. Moistening is best done by filling pots or seed flats brimful with the mix and watering them repeatedly or standing them overnight in about two inches of water. (Plastic trays sold for kitty litter are very convenient for this.) Just before seeding, the moistened mix may be pressed down very lightly, never so much as to compact it. Third, though commercial soilless mixes contain enough nutrients for germination and first growth, they are rapidly exhausted by the young seedlings, and so a water-soluble fertilizer must be used in dilute amounts for steady development. (See "Fertilization," page 183.) And finally, once a soilless mix has been used for seeding, it should never be reused for that purpose. Any that remains in the pot after pricking out or that is left behind from pots that did not germinate should be worked into the garden as a soil improvement.

Pots and Containers for Seeding Almost everything that holds a little earth and that can be punctured at the bottom for drainage, from rusted tin cans and worn-out cooking utensils to eggshells, has been used by resourceful gardeners at one time or another to start seed. Old-fashioned greenhouse gardeners depended on clay pans and wooden flats, and those who love the look of a mossy clay pot or a weathered wooden tray will cling to them still. Unless, however, one is prepared to fumigate them with toxic chemicals or scrub them thoroughly in a solution made hand-blisteringly strong with household laundry bleach, they are a sure path to disaster with seedlings. Their porous sides can harbor a host of soil-borne diseases ready to attack young seedlings just as they sprout. If one has a fine old clay seed pan or a sturdy wooden flat, a far better use for it would be to fill it with spent compost and sow it with annual rye, to grow a late-winter salad for the family cat.

The modern plastics industry, whatever one may say about it otherwise, has presented gardeners with a host of serviceable containers in which to start seed. Greenhouse supply companies and large garden centers offer lightweight plastic pots designed to make the most efficient use of space. They are never very expensive, and as they are easy to clean they may be reused from year to year, providing one keeps them from freezing, which makes them brittle. A more satisfying option, in part because they are free, is plastic-foam cups, which may be salvaged out of the trash can wherever hot bever-

Few gardeners have such elegant pots in which to start seedlings. In fact, though the beauty of clay is hard to resist, results are better when plastic, which harbors no soilborne diseases, is used instead.

ages are served to large numbers of people. Putting aside thrift, they have several advantages over plastic pots. The name of the plant may be written directly on the rim of the cup, which saves a label and guarantees that there will be no mixups in the incubator as to each baby's true identity. Each cup, full of soil, is just about the right size for a developing seedling, and a convenient size as well for standing on windowsills. When transplant time'd comes, the cups may be peeled away from those plants known to be difficult to reestablish without harming their delicate roots. The only problem with foam cups is punching holes in the bottoms to ensure the good drainage that all seedlings require, for it is very easy to punch away bottom and all. (Even so, all is not lost, for a bottomless foam cup can be pressed into the soil

around a young transplant to provide shade and humidity while it is catching, and to offer protection against cutworms, which may plague newly planted annuals, particularly members of the family Solanaceae such as nicotianas, salpiglossis, and daturas.)

The easiest way to achieve the requisite holes in a plastic-foam cup is to heat an icepick on the burner of the kitchen stove until it is warm and plunge it through the bottoms of several cups stacked together. As one cannot offer young seedlings too much drainage, it is well to make three or even four holes spaced evenly across the bottoms of the cups.

Though foam cups are perfect for single seedlings, unless one wants only a very few of a species—say five or six—they are too small to serve as "mother pots." These are the pots in which the seeding is initially made and in which the germinating seedlings will live until they are pricked out. With large seeds, it is of course possible to place one seed in each cup, or, because germination can be uncertain, three or four, with the firm intention of heartlessly clipping out all but the strongest when several true leaves appear. With most seeds, however, it is better to make the initial sowing in larger pots, planning to separate the seedlings later when they are large enough to handle.

Mother pots need not be very large, not more than four or five inches across. And they need not be very deep. In fact, shallow pots with a depth of two or three inches are best, as the volume of soil they hold aerates evenly, thereby avoiding the risk of dank, sour conditions developing in the heart of the pot. Many commercial growers prefer to make the initial seeding in plastic trays hardly an inch and a half deep. After filling them with moist soil and firming them gently with a length of board cut to fit the tray, they press a ruler or thin board edgewise into the soil surface to make neat, perfectly spaced little furrows into which the seed is scattered. In this way they ensure that the tiny seedlings have light and air on both sides from the time they germinate until they are pricked out. Unless one is growing a great many plants of a species from seed, however, or wishes for some reason to consolidate space by seeding several species in separate rows in one container, pots that are four or five inches across are usually best. They are easier to keep evenly moist by standing them in a tray of water when they are dry, and they fit more conveniently on a windowsill or the bench of a small home greenhouse.

Seeding Indoors   Before cutting open a single seed packet, it is important to prepare everything one will need. Pots should be well scrubbed in mild dishwashing liquid, rinsed well, and allowed to dry. Plastic-foam cups should also be washed if they are recycled, for small amounts of sugar left in the bottom can sour and ferment the soil. A good supply of homemade sterile potting mix or commercial soilless mix should be conveniently by, rather on the dry side as it is easier to fill the pots evenly when it is in that condition. A small bag of vermiculite is also handy as a top dressing for fine seed or as a cover for larger seeds, as it will go some way in preventing damping off. (See "Damping-Off," page 167.) When all necessities have been assembled, the pots should be filled with the sterile medium to within half an inch of their rims and the soil firmed *very gently* to eliminate air pockets and even out bumps and lumps. One's fingers are not a perfectly effective tool for firming, as they may leave hollows into which fine seed will wash, resulting in unevenly spaced seedlings. The bottom of a glass or jar that exactly fits the diameter of the pot or cup, or a small bit of board trimmed to size, will result in a more even surface. Once the pots have been filled, they should be well soaked, either by drenching them repeatedly with a watering can fitted with a fine rose to prevent the soil surface from becoming pitted, or better, by standing the pots for several hours in a pan of water until they show an evenly moist surface. At this point one is ready to open the packet.

By far the greatest cause of failure with indoor seeding is sowing too thickly. If the seed within the packet is large, there is no problem. The seeds can simply be shaken into the palm of one's hand, picked out singly, and lightly pressed into the soil or laid on its surface and covered with a layer of dry vermiculite about twice their own thickness. Seeds of medium size, such as will tumble freely from a seed packet without lodging in its creases and folds, also pose no problems. Gardeners who are steady of hand and keen of eye simply shake such seeds into the bottom of the envelope, cut across the top with a pair of scissors (taking care not to cut away any of the cultural information that might be useful later), and tap the seeds out evenly across the prepared soil. To some the skill of making even taps against the envelope that will result in perfectly spaced seedlings comes easily. Others might want to practice their hand with a few trial runs using household grains such as barley or mustard seed.

Many annual plants, however, grow from seed that is quite small, even minute. The seed of salpiglossis, for example, is as fine as snuff, and it will cling to the palm of one's hand or even to the sides of the seed envelope. Taken up in pinches or shaken from its packet, it will fall unevenly on the soil and far too thickly. One ill-timed sneeze will disperse the whole crop. A better method with such tiny seed is to mix it with a tablespoon or two of fine dry sand in a shallow, highly glazed bowl, taking up the mixture with a teaspoon and scattering it evenly over the surface of the soil.

Once the seed has been evenly dispersed into mother pots, most should be covered. The rule for covering seed is to bury it to twice its own thickness, more or less. Some gardeners use additional sterile potting mix or soilless mix for this blanket, rubbed between their palms to eliminate lumps, and some use clean, salt-free sharp sand, but many prefer horticultural vermiculite, which is completely sterile and tends to remain that way while the seed germinates and the young seedlings develop. With large seeds, the amount to lay on is easy to determine. Smaller, mustard-sized seeds can be safely covered with a light dusting until they are no longer visible on the surface of the soil. Quite tiny seeds had better not be covered at all, as they can easily be smothered. With such seeds, it is better to coat the surface of the soil with a quarter-inch layer of vermiculite and seed directly onto it. The seeds will lodge in the pores of the medium, which is cover enough.

Even when seed is fresh, in good condition, and handled correctly, germination times will vary widely from species to species, and sometimes, as with cannas and moon vines, from seed to seed. Individual species are also sometimes quite particular in the requirements that will cause them to germinate successfully. Some require light and some total darkness; some demand soil temperatures uncomfortable to most humans, either tropically warm or shiveringly chilly; some are encouraged by drying out slightly between waterings, and others must be kept evenly moist and humid by being enclosed in plastic bags or covered with a sheet of glass. Where the needs of seeds are eccentric, one's best reference on them is the back of the seed envelope, which will always note any particular crankiness. When one receives seed from other gardeners, it is always wise to ask about any particular needs the seed might have. But most seedlings, particularly most annual seedlings, are determinedly bent on life. It is usually enough to be sure that the medium in which they are sown is kept evenly moist (never soggy or waterlogged, else they will rot) and that when their first signs of life appear above the soil, they are given all the light they need. Until then, it is better to water the pots in which they are sown from below rather than from above, as a forceful stream may dislodge the germinating seed.

Pricking Out Pricking out is an old gardener's term for lifting germinated seedlings gently out of a seed pot and transplanting them into single pots or into flats where they will have enough room, light, and air to grow on strongly. Usually the process is done with a plant label, a lead pencil, or a small sharpened hardwood stick, hence the term. It is a gentle and methodical process, best done in good light when one's nerves are steady and one's mind free to enjoy the young life under one's hands.

Most seedlings, even those that do not transplant successfully in adolescence or maturity, will accept the process of pricking out without looking backwards. A few, however, most notably some of the glorious annual vines such as

When growing plants in pots for summer display, and particularly annuals, the rule is almost always "the bigger the pot, the better." And though many species of annuals crammed together for a kaleidoscope of bright color can be cheering, a quieter beauty results often from limiting plants to one or at two species.

morning glories, moon vines, sweet peas, scarlet runner beans, and *Dipogon lablab*, resent disturbance even when they are tiny. They should be sown three seeds to a peat pot, and all but the strongest seedlings eliminated, the survivor to be planted pot and all in the garden. It should be remembered, however, that peat pots should be kept dry until ready to use, and though the earth within them must be evenly moist, no attempt should be made to moisten the pots themselves by standing them in water. They will then become punky and begin to disintegrate long before it is time for the final transplanting. No drainage holes need be punctured in them, as they will absorb and drain excess water, and any attempt to make holes in their base may fracture their fragile skins. Once

filled with soil, they should be stood in trays that can be used to move them about without excess handling, though they must never sit in water, which will sour the soil within them. When the time comes to transplant young seedlings into the garden, however, they should be stood in several inches of water and thoroughly soaked so the outside walls are dark and moist. (Other annuals that resent root disturbance when young have been noted in the individual plant portraits.)

Timing is important in pricking out, for there is a period with most seedlings, just after their first true leaves have appeared, when they are so full of vigor that they will accept disturbance without complaint. And so the advice is usually given to prick out "after the first true leaves have developed." Some seedlings, however, are so tiny and so difficult to handle that one must wait until three or even four leaves have developed. Notable among them are petunias, nicotianas, and *Eustoma grandiflorum*. In such cases, no harm is really done by giving them a little extra time in the seed pot. But all seedlings should be pricked out before they become crowded, drawn, or starved. A few such as marigolds seem able to endure any treatment without complaint, but most annuals require quick, unchecked growth for best results. They are, by definition, plants in a hurry, and a poor start early in life will discourage many to such a degree that they will never develop fully.

Before any seedlings are disturbed, the pots or flats into which they are to be transplanted should be filled with a sterile medium and well watered, as success often depends on exposing the young roots as briefly as possible to drying air. The seed pot should also be moistened, since soil that is moderately damp will cling to roots more effectively than soil that is dry. If the seed has been sown thinly, as should of course be the case, it should be no problem to scoop out the seedling, if lucky with a little ball of earth clinging to its roots. One does not always sow seed as thinly as is proper, however, and sometimes root systems are so vigorous that they will have twined among one another. In such a case it is better to empty out the entire pot, and tease and gently shake the root mass until the little plants may be detached from one another. Sometimes, when roots are very entangled, it is helpful to swish the root mass in cool water, gently washing the soil away so that individual plants come free. Should this be necessary, it is well to have some moistened paper towels to gather around the plants waiting to be reestablished so that they are not exposed to air.

Assembly-line techniques, though they are efficient for other things, will not work in pricking out. Each individual seedling should be detached separately and potted on before handling the next. When a seedling is free, it should be held gently by the leaves in the thumb and forefinger of one hand while the other makes a small crater with the stick or pencil in the moistened soil of its new pot. The little plant should then be lowered in so that its "neck," the point at which the stem has developed from the roots, is just a hair below soil level. Holding it still in place, one then eases the new soil about the roots with the stick or pencil so that the plant sits firm. Soil should not be tightly packed in, as that might damage sensitive root hairs, and a thorough watering later will much more effectively settle soil about the disturbed roots. Nor should one ever use one's fingers to firm the soil, for they may pack it down too tightly, breaking or suffocating the young plant's roots.

As soon as one has pricked out all the plants one wants, or, if one wants a great many, as soon as a flat or plastic tray has been filled, the young plants should be watered in, a process done with a watering can fitted with a rose that will break the flow of water into a gentle shower. This is done to settle the roots and coat them with a film of moisture so that they do not lose vital fluids through transpiration before the root hairs have established. Intensely concentrated as they are on the business of living, transplanted seedlings take a very brief time, a day or so, to make contact with the new soil about their roots and begin growing again. During this adjustment period, however, it is well to keep them in a cool, shaded place, and to mist their foliage lightly if they begin to wilt.

Growing on Indoors The gardener who wishes to tap the incredible wealth of tender plants that may be grown to ornament the summer garden must often seed them as early as late February, and watch anxiously over their development for almost three months until all danger of frost is past and they may safely be set out into the garden.

Of the three conditions necessary to the

growth of plants—water, nutrients, and adequate light—it is the latter that is by far the hardest to provide indoors. For it must be remembered that the late winter and early spring sunshine that comes through the windows of most households, *when* it comes, is much reduced in intensity from that enjoyed by plants outdoors, particularly those that in tropical and subtropical regions. As they mature, most seedlings demand greater and greater intensities of light. They will germinate usually in none, and in stages of infancy, they appear able to endure, even to flourish, on surprisingly little, perhaps because they would be accustomed in nature to crowding beneath the shadows of other vegetation until, by persistent struggle, they overtopped it. But outdoor light falls *through* leaves, and for the purposes of photosynthesis, is light still. Indoors it falls through panes of glass, which diminish its intensity. Indoors, plants will suffer noticeably from being distanced even a foot or two from the source of light, though it may still seem bright to those who are attempting to nurture them. In order to avoid the heartbreak of seedlings that are skinny or thriftless, or that fail altogether, it is always better to grow only as many as one can guarantee an adequate supply of light.

Easily the best conditions in which to grow on seedlings is a small home greenhouse. It is so great a luxury that the avid gardener may forgo others, such as a spiffy car or new carpeting, just to have one. For not only can the thriftiest seedlings be raised under such conditions, seedlings grown in a greenhouse are always easier to establish in the garden, because they are already used to the greater intensities of light that are possible there. One can also store many rare annuals and plants grown as annuals there, either as cuttings taken late in the season or as late-seeded plants or volunteers. Many annuals flower beautifully under glass during the winter, and some, such as schizanthus and salpiglossis, may achieve a perfection that is seldom seen in summer gardens. In a greenhouse, the gardener may also putter happily through the darkest months of the year when frozen conditions or cold drizzly weather make outdoor work impossible.

Lacking a greenhouse, many gardeners have great success in growing on seedlings and young plants with the help of light units. Indeed, some of the healthiest seedlings I ever saw were produced by a good gardener I once knew who grew them in a cool basement under banks and banks of plain white fluorescent lights. The young plants throve in temperatures that hovered around 50 to 55 degrees Fahrenheit, and he took care to shift them often, toward or away from the center of the light as their needs dictated. He always had enough fine young plants for his own small urban garden and to share. Though I envied his success, I have never been inclined to emulate it, for I am not clever with wiring and gadgetry, and I tend to agree with the late Katherine White, who wrote once about growing plants under lights, "Though I'm willing to be a floor nurse I have no intention of becoming an electrician." Gardening is of course not ever a quite natural process, but somehow a dank basement flooded with cruel white light brings home that fact more forcefully than does the equally artificial environment of a sunny heated greenhouse buried to the eves in February snow. Still, there is no denying that plants grown under artificial light can be wonderfully healthy, and sometimes a lack of sunny incubating spaces leaves no other alternative. It is a *very* technical subject, beyond my scope here. But very good manuals exist that should be consulted before one goes to the considerable expense of acquiring the lights and wires and racks and tables and such and tapping into the house current.

Without either greenhouse or light units, gardeners who wish to start annuals indoors and grow them on will have to depend on the sunny windowsill. Most houses haven't many such, and even assuming that the ordinary

Gardeners who grow their own plants for summer display can take pleasure in healthy, thriving stock, even when few flowers are visible. The as yet unrifled wealth of this lath house promises a full season of beauty.

claims of domestic living allow one to press all of them into service, space will still be limited. For a sunny windowsill means one that faces south or southeast, and is without obstructions such as deep overhanging eaves, shadowing trees, shrubs, or curtains. Nevertheless, those who love the process of raising young plants indoors, and are willing to make the extra effort it requires, can manage to produce wonderfully strong seedlings on sunny windowsills, and in

high summer, when the garden is ablaze, each healthy flower acquires added value from one's having been intimately acquainted, sleeping and waking, with the plant that bears it.

There is a final alternative to germinating and growing on one's own seedlings, which is to farm them out. Devoted gardeners may sniff at the process, thinking it as barbarous as the practice indulged in by wealthy women in the 18th century, who sent their infant children at birth out into the country to be reared by wet nurses. They may think what they will. For after years of struggling with seedlings, first on a sunny windowsill, and then in a greenhouse already crowded to the eaves with potted plants, auricula primroses, and winter-blooming bulbs, I finally decided to find another way. I located a young nurseryman nearby who had all the equipment necessary to start and grow on seedlings, and whose green thumb was apparent in the trays and trays of healthy annuals and vegetables he set out for sale each season. He agreed to take my seed and grow it on for me, selling me back at cost of production the plants I wanted. It has been a great luxury, for the plants I select are always in peak condition for planting out. I take only as many as I need; the remainder he plants in his own display gardens or offers for sale.

It is true that I miss an intimate acquaintance with the plants I grow from first sprouting of their tiny seeds. It is true also that I retain the rarest seeds and many cuttings under my own hands, simply to know them better in all their stages of development. But for the rest, the many annuals I know well but still consider indispensable, it is splendid to have them ready grown just when I am ready for them. It is a system that works, and that should be possible anywhere, now that there are so many good nursery owners eager to gain experience with new plants.

Insect Pests of Young Seedlings   Anyone who grows plants indoors will already know that the closed environments comfortable to humans also provide marvelous breeding grounds for a number of insect pests. It is fortunate that the two most pernicious—scale insects and mealybugs—are usually not very interested in seedlings, since they prefer the richer diet to be drawn from mature and woody plants. But whiteflies, aphids, and red spider mites will often attack young plants, and will signal their gratitude for banks of succulent young seed-

lings by increasing in enormous numbers, often, it seems, overnight. Whiteflies live and breed on the undersides of leaves, but make their presence known by flying up in clouds when the plants they inhabit are disturbed by a brush of the hand. Spider mites live there, too, but it takes a keen eye or a magnifying glass to see them. Their presence is usually more apparent in a dusty, mottled, anemic look to leaves, and where large colonies have built up, by filmy gray webs. Aphids, which seem to be stupid uncunning things, take no care to hide, but cluster up and down the stems of plants, usually the freshest and youngest stems, in small translucent globules, sucking them dry. The appearance of any of these pests on seedlings calls for immediate action, for there isn't much, usually, in a seedling to spare. Furthermore, aphids and whiteflies can later be carried into the garden, for a merry life all summer, to them at least, though it is bane to the gardener and the plants.

Of these three most prevalent indoor insect pests, spider mites are the easiest to control, since they flourish in dry, even arid conditions, where one ought not to be growing seedlings in the first place. By frequent misting and syringing of the foliage, most spider mites will be washed away from leaves, and those that remain will be distinctly discouraged. Keeping the air fresh, moist, and buoyant, by standing the pots of young seedlings over trays of damp gravel and by lowering night temperatures so they hover in the mid 50s to low 60s Fahrenheit will take care of the rest, and will produce healthier seedlings in other ways as well. Stubborn infestations of spider mites should be treated with insecticidal soaps or, if the gardener has no qualms, with chemicals sold for the purpose, though fortunately with seedlings such treatment is seldom necessary.

Next easiest to eliminate are aphids, though their extermination is never a once-and-for-all thing, but rather more an ongoing battle, since they increase with amazing rapidity, particularly in early spring, and one or two left behind or on a neighboring houseplant can re-aphid the world. Where young stems are strong and firm, the tender bodies of aphids can often be squished between thumb and forefinger, if one is not squeamish, and if one is, most can be washed away with a forceful jet of water from the kitchen faucet. With very young seedlings, squeezing will damage fragile tissue, and a stream of water strong enough to dislodge the aphids may dislodge the seedlings as well, washing both down the kitchen drain. In such cases, it is better to use an insecticidal soap in a hand sprayer, bearing in mind that once it dries it has no residual effect, as do chemical sprays, and should be reapplied frequently to exterminate the new populations that may develop.

Whiteflies are easily the most stubborn of the three insect pests that commonly beset young seedlings, for they are canny and hard to catch. The smallest disturbance, as, for example, when one takes a flat of seedlings to the sink for a wash, will send them up in clouds and into hiding, from which they will return to feed on the undersides of young leaves. Organic insecticidal sprays work well on them, but they should be applied in a surprise attract, even in the dark of night, and reapplied as frequently as the manufacturer recommends. More than with spider mites or even aphids, it is important to exterminate whiteflies completely before transplanting young seedlings into the garden. They are far better able to multiply there, and will feed on perennials, vegetables, and many shrubs, as well as on any flowering annual they can find.

Damping-off Though seedlings that are attacked by common indoor insects may experience a severe check in growth, and may be weak or stunted at transplant time, they will seldom die outright, and when moved outdoors, may rally surprisingly well. Spider mites will cease to develop in the moister conditions and fresher air of the garden, and serious infestations of aphids will often be reduced by birds and predatory insects. Only whiteflies will burgeon—even explode—in the garden, but even they are susceptible to treatment, and the damage they wreak can usually be reversed. Seedlings affected by damping-off will never even see the garden, however, for once attacked, they are dead, and the "cures" recommended will at best save only a few strong individuals that have not yet contracted the disease. Of all the problems experienced by gardeners who raise their own seed, it is the worst, and certainly the most heartbreaking for a pot of seedlings that looks healthy and full of life one day may be dead the next.

Damping-off is caused by a combination of conditions, but the operative villain is a soil-borne fungus that multiplies rapidly in moist conditions and stagnant air. Completely invisible, it is recognizable only by its pernicious effects. Seedlings attacked by damping-off will show a curious pinch, near ground level, as if the life had been squeezed out of the stem just at that point. Affected seedlings will topple over, and though they may stay fresh for a day or two, they will eventually rot away. Once a few individuals in a pot or flat have been affected, usually those in the middle, the disease will make its sure and rapid way to all the rest. By working quickly, the gardener may save a few seedlings, usually those at the very edges of the container. But far more effective than any remedy is preventing the problem from developing in the first place.

The most crucial requirement for avoiding damping-off is to make certain that seeds are sown in conditions as nearly sterile as possible. Pots and flats should be well scrubbed in soapy water just before use and dried thoroughly. The gardener's first temptation will always be toward clay pots and quaint weathered wooden flats, but they should be avoided, as their porous sides will almost certainly harbor damping-off fungi, whereas plastic and plastic-foam pots can be scrubbed whistle-clean.

Homemade seeding mixes should be sterilized (see "Sterile Potting Mixes," page 157) and commercial potting mixes formulated for seeding should be kept dry until ready to use. It never hurts, either, to scrub one's hands well before handling cleaned pots, sterile seeding mixes, or the seed in the packet.

Even with all these precautions, damping-off may occur, almost always because seed is sown too thickly. A congestion of young seedlings never completely dries, especially in the center of the pot where they are often thickest. Even the most experienced gardeners confess a tendency to sprinkle in too much seed, especially when it is very fine, for one never thinks one has put in quite enough, and surely that little corner, just there, didn't get its share. But it is far better to sow only half the seed one has, or a third, than to sprinkle it all in. Finally, freshly seeded pots should never be watered from the top, before or after the seed has germinated; a misguided stream of water may wash recently sown seed into a thicket at the center of the pot, and after germination, watering from above will moisten the stems, creating a perfect environment for damping-off. Newly seeded pots should be moistened from the bottom up, by standing them in trays with water halfway up their sides, and germinated seedlings should be watered in the same way.

As damping-off is a disease that occurs just at soil level, many gardeners find it helpful to cover seed with a layer of material that will remain sterile no matter how moist it becomes, or when seed is very fine, to sow directly into it. Vermiculite, a commercial product made by expanding particles of mica at high temperatures until they are feather-light, is the first choice. It forms a comfortable-looking security blanket that all seedlings seem to enjoy. Finely milled sphagnum moss is often also used, though without careful handling it can mat into a fibrous layer impervious to questing young shoots. Old gardeners had good results with sharp coarse sand, and the best used nothing else, supplementing its barrenness with carefully concocted doses of weak manure tea or soot water until the young "bottle nourished" seedlings could be transplanted into a solid potting mix. Theirs was always an exacting art, and the home gardener will probably do best with vermiculite, which is easy to handle and to store, and to which no seedling seems to have an aversion. Though it is laid on dry, water will percolate upward to moisten it.

The final prevention for damping-off is good air circulation. Most seedlings, even of fairly tender species, relish quite cool conditions in infancy, provided they stay above freezing. If they are kept in the high 40s at night and in the mid-60s to low 70s during the day, their growth will be the slower but often the stronger. But all abhor dank and steamy conditions when they are first developing, and will sulk equally when they are exposed to a whistling draft. Most commercial greenhouses are now equipped with circulating fans that draw in fresh air away from the plants and circulate it gently over them in pleasant waves. The home gardener may achieve the same effect from a small fan, trained not over the seedlings but into a nearby corner, thus keeping the air buoyant and free-moving.

Should damping-off still occur despite all these precautions, affected pots should be treated promptly. Seedlings that have toppled over should be removed, as well as any that show the telltale pinch, and any scum or mold should be cleaned carefully from the surface of the soil. The remaining seedlings should then be dusted with sulphur, an organic substance, or with Captan, which is synthetically formulated and, truth to tell, far more effective. The pots should then be moved into freely circulating air and kept rather dry. If the seedlings continue healthy, they should be pricked out into freshly washed pots filled with a sterile medium as soon as they have formed their first true leaves. They may then be treated again with sulphur or Captan for good measure.

Sometimes all one's best efforts are to no avail when damping-off has occurred. With this in mind, experienced gardeners know never to seed all of a precious species at once. If all goes well, the remaining seed can be carefully stored and saved for next year, or given away. And if it does not, a fresh seeding can be made, avoiding, as far as possible, the conditions that caused the demise of the first one.

Transplanting and Hardening Off

After setting a young tree in the landscape, or perhaps troweling in bulbs in the weak light of autumn, the transplanting of annuals represents one of the greatest moments of optimism in the life of many gardeners. They can already see, in imagination, the effects of their labor; but unlike trees, which may take many years to achieve their vision, or bulbs, which work invisibly throughout the winter, the gratifications that come from planting annuals are almost immediate. Almost immediate, that is, if the work is done carefully. Most annuals are wonderfully compliant, but clumsiness at transplant time can result in checked growth, stunted plants, and fewer flowers. Some, also, are so exacting in their needs that the most careful handling is necessary to bring them to perfection. The transplanting of small plants is a merry act, almost an initiation into summer. But still it requires thought and care.

The first requirement for success is to grow or buy plants that have reached just the right moment in their lives for transplanting into the garden. If they are too young and fragile, pelting rains, broiling sun, and desiccating winds may all come as shocks from which the seedlings never completely recover. If they are too old, perhaps pot-bound and forced into premature flower by the conviction that there is nothing more to hope for in their confinement, they will often have received what gardeners call a check, and may never develop into lush growth and abundant flower. When buying plants, therefore, it is always wise to pass over the flats or six-packs that already show bloom, in favor of those that are still producing strong growth of leaf and stem. In starting one's own plants, it never works to hurry things, however impatient one may be in early spring. Seedlings that are grown on in cool buoyant conditions will always be in better shape for transplanting than those forced into weak and spindly growth in an overheated environment. And it is always better to delay transplanting, holding the youngest seedlings a week or two longer in captivity, than to produce overmature plants that give unmistakable signs of their eagerness to be given their freedom.

Whatever the age of a transplant, however, it will need careful adjustment to its new environment outdoors. "Hardening off" is the term for this process, and it means a gradual transition from the pampered environment in which a seedling usually begins its life to the facts of the real world. When one buys plants from the outdoor benches of old-fashioned garden centers, one can assume that this process has already occurred. More and more frequently, however, nurseries that specialize in annuals raise them in plastic tunnel houses, where, by a careful control of the environment and frequent misting with water-soluble fertilizers, the quickest growth, and the quickest sales, can be assured. Such plants will need

Though the aim of growing annuals is the beauty of their flowers, gardeners can draw delight also from well-tilled soil and in the process of transplanting plants to their final homes in the garden.

the same hardening-off process as seedlings raised on a sunny windowsill or in the home greenhouse.

It is not so much to sun that young plants need to be accustomed, though the strong sun of spring can affect plants grown in indoor enviroments much as it can the skins of office- or housebound humans on their first day at the beach or in the garden. But for young plants, wind and cold are much greater enemies, desiccating soft sensitive tissue before it has had a chance to build up thickened cell walls and protective layers of wax across the leaves. Therefore one should find for the seedlings a spot that is protected from both sun and wind. Coldframes are especially well suited to the task, but the back wall of the garage, or a well-

protected nook along the north side of the house foundations can handle the job as well.

The process of hardening off should occur in stages, three hours in the high warmth of mid-day for the first day or two, five hours the next, all day the next few after that and thereafter. During the hardening-off process, which may last two weeks or longer, depending on the weather, water-soluble fertilizers should be withheld, since it is not fresh growth at which one is aiming, but rather a toughening and toning of the tissues of the plants. But the seedlings should always be kept well watered, since, in the drier atmosphere that often occurs outdoors in spring, small pots and flats may desiccate much more rapidly than indoors. And any sudden dip in the temperature toward frost should temporarily stop the process, which may be resumed again when the weather warms. Hardening off sounds like, and is, a great deal of trouble, especially these days, when all members of a gardening household may be at work or at school. Coldframes with lids that open and close automatically in response to the weather are a great convenience; but just as convenient, if one has the luxury, is a gardening friend or retired neighbor, whom one can call when one sees the weather darken out one's office window and bits of hail fly suddenly through the air.

Once the hardening-off process has been completed, young plants are ready for their permanent home in the garden. Most gardeners feel the urge to transplant when the morning is warm and bright, with clear skies overhead and even the promise of a bit of heat in the day. Such days are the wrong ones for the work, however tempted one may be, and they are better spent starting one's tan (if one still does that sort of thing) or working at other chores in the garden. For all young plants are best transplanted when skies are gloomy and overcast, and there is a promise of showers. Better still if one can hope for a sequence of such days, for they are the ones that cause plants to "settle in," the old gardener's term for the sometimes difficult adjustment to the cool open earth. If one must transplant on a clear day, because one is a weekend gardener or because one simply can't wait, then the work should still be done as late in the afternoon as possible, and the young plants shielded for two or three days from bright sun by cardboard boxes or old wooden shingles propped up on one side. (But young plants should never be covered with clear plastic bags, glass jars, or discarded plastic milk bottles, for beneath such covers heat will quickly build up, resulting in scalding conditions.) In very bright, dry weather it is also beneficial to dampen the foliage of the plants two or three times a day, to prevent excess transpiration before new roots are in contact with the soil.

And the soil itself should be well dug, enriched with moist peat, compost, or very well-rotted manure, broken up to a fine tilth, and cleaned of all weeds, particularly of perennial grasses, which will be almost impossible to eliminate once the small plants are in place. It should then be raked smooth, and when it is wet and heavy, great care should be taken not to walk on it, which will compact its tilth and deprive new plants of the oxygen they require at their roots. When it is absolutely necessary to move across beds of freshly tilled soil, one should walk on boards that evenly distribute one's weight and prevent compacting.

Most nurseries, and many home gardeners, now use six-packs in which seedlings are pricked out and grown on until they are ready to be transplanted into the garden. They are a great convenience, for each young plant can be eased out separately, with all the roots it has, and transplanted before its neighbors are disturbed. For gardeners who raise their own plants, an even greater convenience results from individual plastic pots, sized so that they fit evenly into plastic carrying trays. At from two to four inches across and as deep, they provide more room for the developing roots of plants, thereby avoiding the overcongestion that can be a problem with six-packs. But even better, they can be set across the soil at transplanting time, arranged and rearranged for the most pleasing spacing before disturbing the plants.

Sometimes, still, the old practice is followed of growing plants in flats or trays in which all the young seedlings share the same earth mass. Advice is often given with such plants to cut them apart like cake. If their roots are hopelessly entangled, there may be no other thing to do. But generally it is better to tease each plant away from its siblings with a kitchen fork, or even with a twisting motion of the hands, half tug, half wrench, rather than needlessly damage roots with a sharp cut of the kitchen knife.

But from whatever sort of container one is

transplanting (even if, as with seedlings grown in nursery rows outdoors, the "container" is the earth itself), the young plants should go into their permanent homes as quickly and with as many roots as possible. A sharp prod of one's thumb against the flexible bottom of a six-pack cell will usually pop out the plant; when individual pots are used, the plant is turned upside down in one's hand, its leafy top dangling through spread fingers, and the bottom of the pot is given a smart rap or two with a trowel held in the other hand. Usually the root mass of the young plant will slide out easily, but sometimes, if it is pot-bound, several firm squeezes of the pot's sides may be necessary to free the plant. With plants grown in any sort of container, however, it is important to resist the temptation to grab them firmly by the neck and yank, for they may come away from the earth without all the root mass they have developed to sustain themselves and you may crush the stem. Plants taken from the open ground should be dug with little balls of earth, or where that is not possible, bare roots should be covered with a clinging wrap of damp paper towels, or with a thick layer of soil mixed into a slurry with water.

Gardeners who routinely plant trees and shrubs grown in pots often lightly score the roots or gently tease them apart. This encourages them to reach immediately into the surrounding soil rather than continue in their determined course, round and round, depriving the young plants of nourishment and often, in years to come, strangling them from girdling roots. The practice is often recommended with annuals also, though it is of questionable utility. When an annual plant has remained for too long in its pot and has produced a thick coil of white roots with little soil remaining, it is often useful to loosen or even tear some of the roots before transplanting. Almost all annuals, however, will suffer a check from such treatment, and it is best always to transplant long before they have reached that stage. Those annuals that

particularly resent root disturbance, such as many climbing annual vines and many members of the mallow family, should never be "riled about the roots," but should be raised in peat pots that are then planted directly in the ground. If grown in plastic containers, these plants should be eased out gently so they hardly perceive they have been relocated.

Skillful transplanting comes almost to be an instinct with practiced gardeners, and they can, without fuss and worry, successfully position young plants in the soil with surprising speed. The novice tends, however, to fret a great deal, and often to make two mistakes. The first comes from positioning plants too high or low in the soil, leaving them in the first instance sitting atop little mounds of earth that dry out quickly, and in the second, burying their necks so deeply in the soil that they suffocate and rot off. A few annuals, such as marigolds, will root happily along a bit of buried stem, and even gain vigor from it. Others, such as *Verbena ×hybrida* and *Lobelia erinus*, can often be fanned out over the surface of the soil and the stems buried, leaving only the tips protruding, to make from one plant a whole thriving colony. Most annuals will prefer, however, to be planted in the open with their necks at just the level they grew in the pot or six-pack. Thus planting holes should be dug carefully, with a little earth placed in the bottom to raise the plant if it is too low in the ground, or a little scooped out if it seems too high.

The second mistake with transplanting occurs from failing to work from the bottom up. Good gardeners will make a cushion of soft soil beneath a transplant, often incorporating into it some good compost or damp peat, or perhaps a bit of the potting mixture in which the young seedling was originally established, to provide a medium that will quickly coax young roots into the surrounding earth. They will then ease the soil around the sides of the root plug, often stirring in a little more peat or compost, and firming gently with their fingertips as they go, so that all roots are in close contact with the soil. The novice often pops the young plant into a hole in the earth, rather like a cork in a bottle neck, leaving sensitive roots dangling in a subterranean pocket, with no hope of coming into contact with the soil below. Many annuals will forgive such clumsiness, and rain or a thorough drenching with the watering can will often settle enough soil around their roots to keep them happy. But making sure that a transplant is firmly seated in the earth, at just the level it wants to be, can often avoid unnecessary checks in growth.

Once transplanting has been completed, the young plants should be watered in, even if the surrounding soil is already moist. A gentle drenching with a watering can fitted with a rose to break the flow into droplets will further settle the earth, eliminate air pockets, and will coat each leaf with a film of water that reduces transpiration while roots make contact with the soil. The addition of water-soluble fertilizer, at half the strength recommended on the package, will further invigorate young plants in their adjustment to their new home. If the weather is hot and sunny or if, as often happens in April across much of North America, desiccating southern winds are blowing, plants should be shaded for a day or two, and not be allowed to dry out until they show evidence of strong growth.

Soil Preparation

There is no substitute for the richest and finest soil one can contrive. Still, one sometimes reads that annuals need no special soil preparation, and may, if overpampered, "run to leaf," with never a blossom in sight. It is true that annuals will often accept soil far below the ideal, and a few are treasured precisely because they will grow and bloom abundantly in very poor, dry, gravelly, or sandy soil, languishing if overnourished. Most annuals, however, will reward careful soil preparation with a greater (if slightly later) exuberance of bloom, richer flower color, finer leaves, and even an increased resistance to diseases and the vagaries of the weather. More than any other plants except perhaps vegetables (most of which are annuals, too), they are grateful for a supplementary diet. They prefer fertilizers strong in phosphorus and potassium and relatively low in nitrogen. Still, there is no substitute for good earth, deeply tilled, rich in moisture-retentive humus, and brought by careful cultivation into what the old gardeners called "good heart." When taken up in a handful and squeezed lightly, such earth should form a compact mass that shows one's finger marks, but it should never sit heavily in the palm, oozing moisture like a mudpie. Lightly rolled between the fingers, it should fall apart into crumbly particles, but never trickle away like sand. This is the ideal, and most places in North America, it cannot be achieved without considerable work.

By trial and error, every gardener must learn his or her own dirt, and the techniques by which its faults may be corrected and its virtues enhanced. If it is heavy or sticky, it may often require barrowloads of sand or gravel, patiently carted in and double-dug into the soil. If it is light and thin, then loam, manure, or the trampled ooze of cattle feed lots (called "muck" by old Vermonters) may need to be worked in. Failing these supplies, peat moss, decomposed hardwood bark, or pulverized fallen leaves may need to be added, preferably in autumn, to rot over the winter and be dug through the soil again in spring. There is never a substitute for good, well-made compost, denied to American gardeners until what may be called the American Compost Movement reminded us of the waste implicit in "waste." Finally, soils should be tested to determine whether they are deficient in nutrients, particularly phosphorus, which many annuals require for good growth, and whether lime should be added to bring the pH level close to neutral, which most annuals prefer.

All these concerns may be matters of mystery to new gardeners. In many states, county agricultural extension agents can offer help. They will answer a call or even chemically analyze a sample of soil for its specific growing components and give advice about its deficiencies. The staff of good garden centers are also often ready with counsel, since they know the problems in the soils of the region, and it is in their interest to see that the plants they sell will thrive. But there may be no better help for the novice than cultivating the acquaintance of good gardeners in the neighborhood. One can recognize them by the thriving appearance of their gardens, and by the fact that they are out in them, early in the morning and late in the evening. Often they may be crusty, and sometimes one may have to endure a dose of humiliation before getting the advice one seeks. ("But child, how could you have supposed you could grow anything in *that?*") Still, there is hardly a good gardener on the earth who will not help out a beginner, sharing the knowledge he or she has, and usually, after the ice has been broken, even a treasured plant or two.

Old-fashioned vegetable gardens always included a "posy patch" of bright, easily grown annuals to cheer the gardener's spirit as he worked at the routine and sometimes back-breaking tasks of cultivating crops. Here a froth of brilliant blue in late spring is created by self-seeded forget-me-nots (Myosotis sylvatica).

Direct Seeding in the Garden

A number of annuals always perform best when they are sown directly into the garden. Often they flower so quickly from seed that the bother of starting them indoors is not justified. Others so resent transplanting that it is better to establish them in their permanent homes from the beginning. Notable in this class are poppies, larkspurs, and several members of the mallow family, such as *Lavatera trimestris* and *Abelmoschus manihot*. Several quite cold-hardy biennial plants, such as forget-me-nots and foxgloves, can be got to flower the first year from an early seeding indoors, but are always more vigorous and free-flowering if sown in late summer and allowed the long winter sleep they seem to crave. And there are lowly, mat-forming annuals such as *Lobularia maritima, Linaria maroccana*, and *Portulaca grandiflora* that are most valuable just in those places one cannot trowel too deeply, in brick paving or over dormant spring-flowering bulbs.

With some experience, gardeners learn which annuals may be safely seeded outdoors, thereby saving valuable space on the windowsill or in the greenhouse for those that need extra time to flower. They learn also, however, that direct seeding is not a blissful partnership with nature, who may safely be left the work while the gardener reaps the pleasure. Direct seeding requires as much vigilance and attention as indoor seeding, and sometimes more. Though the ground outdoors may be rich in nutrients and in trace elements, it may be compacted from the winter, requiring a deep spading to bring it into the fine tilth needed by questing young roots. If it seems poor in humus, it may require the addition of compost, if one can spare it, or well-moistened peat. (For it must always be remembered about peat that when it is dry, a whole April of rains will not moisten it once it is under the ground.) Finally, the bed must be made, by raking the surface soil smooth, and then raking it smoother again, so that tiny seeds will not fall between clods and be washed so deeply under that they will never reach the surface. For smoothing, the back of the rake is best, for the tines leave ridges, and a final gentle patting with sensitive hands is best of all.

Accurate timing is also essential in seeding outdoors. The seed of many annuals is surprisingly cold hardy, even when the plants are native to the tropics and subtropics. Seeds, also, are uncannily weather-wise, seeming to know practically to the hour when it is safe to poke above the ground. Still, as in any population, there are rash and injudicious individuals that may be lured into growth by an uncommonly mild early spring and flattened by the last cold snap. Some, also, have no protection against moisture until they have sprouted, and will sooner rot than germinate in heavy wet soils.

Old-fashioned gardeners have always keyed their seeding more to a keen observation of nature than to the calendar, for though nature is capable of vagaries, it still tends to know best. By the rule of the old gardeners, the hardy biennials—forget-me-nots, poppies, and foxgloves—might safely be sown in late summer when the first goldenrods are apparent in the fields around. For though they might appear earlier on their own, there is a danger that they will grow too fat by autumn's end and become "winter proud." Hardy annuals, such as *Nigella damascena* and the larkspur plants that often self-seed and volunteer from one year to the next are safely sown when the redwing blackbirds reappear, even if that means, as is often the case for us, that one sows them on the last crusts of snow. Hardy annuals on the way to being tender, such as nicotianas, petunias, and various species of *Argemone*, might be sown as

Delivering seeds to an experienced nurseryman for germination and growing on allows one to have healthy seeds in just the varieties and numbers one wants, just at the time when they should be planted out. For many serious gardeners such as this one, however, there is no substitute for the pleasure of growing one's own plants from seeds. Somehow, one is almost certain that the seeds being sown here are falling into the ground at exactly the correct distance and depth for perfect germination.

the last forsythias fade. And tender annuals that relish a cool first growing period, such as daturas and the glorious annual summer vines, *Dipogon lablab, Cobaea scandens*, scarlet runner beans, and morning glories, are best sown just as the apple blossoms fade.

The old lore of gardeners is always to be preserved for the truth in it. But new gardeners will find a reliable guide to outdoor sowing on the backs of seed packets or sometimes in the seed catalogs from which they have ordered. Usually that information is keyed to a phrase that reads "the last frost-free date in your area." It does not take a gardener long to learn when that date is, but if one is in doubt, it can be determined by a phone call to one's county agricultural extension agent. Still, it is important to keep one's own records from year to year, for one's garden might be in a cold pocket that

endures a frost after the surrounding area is free of it; or better, one might inhabit a south-facing hill with good air drainage, which can be exploited to have the first flowers of sweet peas or zinnias a full two weeks earlier than one's neighbors.

Though adequate soil preparation and accurate timing are initially the most crucial aspects of direct seeding outdoors, one must not assume that once the seed has germinated and the young plants have come safely through the last frosts they can then be left on their own. The worst affliction that besets indoor seedlings, damping-off, will not occur in the buoyant atmosphere outdoors. But many insects may move in on a colony of young seedlings, and they must always be watched for and eliminated. Worse, the most carefully prepared ground may be rich with weed seeds, and the aliens must be picked out, one by one, as soon as they can be identified and long before their roots intertwine inextricably with the plants one has sown. It is a rueful fact that one may know the weeds generally because they are bigger and healthier than desirable plants, but when one is in doubt, it is useful to look at an adjacent patch, which will show the same weeds but not the sproutlings one has put in place. Failing that test, one can take leaf samples to an experienced gardener in the neighborhood. He or she may not always recognize the rare annual one has sown, but the weeds will be familiar.

But of all the aftercare required by direct sowing, perhaps at once the most painful and the most necessary is thinning. A crowded colony of plants will never develop into the beauty one envisions, and their weak growth will be prone to disease, may topple over in high summer thunder storms, and will be impossible to stake tactfully. It is hard also to apply dressings of granular fertilizer when they are planted too thickly, and so they will never mature into sturdy, well-grown plants. So one must thin, and again, the back of the seed envelope will be

Annual plants often need protection from sudden dips in temperature in spring and again in autumn, and new transplants benefit from shading for a day or two until their roots have become established in new soil. This antique terra-cotta blanching pot would do all these jobs quite nicely, but most gardeners will have to press into service old sheets, shirts, skirts, towels, and paper boxes and cartons.

the best guide to the spacing the young plants require. (And see "Spacing," page 178.) If the work of thinning is done early and the seedlings have not come up too thickly, it is often possible to lift young plants with a minimum of root disturbance and pot them on (see "Pricking Out," page 161) to establish elsewhere in the garden, to share with friends, or to grow on in containers. With species that do

not accept transplanting readily, however, it is better to eliminate the unwanted seedlings ruthlessly than to run the risk of a poor show. In such cases, one must take care not to disturb the roots of the plants that are to remain in the ground. It is good, in doing such work, to focus entirely on the happy fate of the seedlings that remain, and not on the sad one of those that are thrown away.

Spacing

I was once told the story of a completely inexperienced would-be gardener who had volunteered to help out in the garden of a friend. He was given a six-pack of pansies to plant, on the erroneous assumption that with them he could do no harm. He stared at them for a time in utter perplexity, and then, with a gleam of inspiration, he tapped them gently out of their plastic container and planted them with great care, cheek by jowl, just in the pattern they had occupied in the six-pack. There was, he explained, an ordered symmetry in the plan, and besides, they would have looked so lonely spread farther apart from one another.

Though most gardeners quickly learn to avoid the example of the man in this story, it often happens, even with fairly experienced gardeners, that when faced with unfamiliar plants, they are in doubt about their correct spacing. Fortunately, seed packets always give excellent guidance on this point, assuming, of course, one has not torn off the advice they offer when sowing the seed. But even with this help, most of us tend to space plants too closely together, either because they "look so lonely otherwise," or because the space we have prepared for them is always much smaller than the number of plants we have in hand. There is something pitiful about discarding the extras, full of life and possibly the best of the bunch. So we cram them in, and the results, often, are sickly and stunted plants, weak of growth and sparing of flower, far from the best that they are capable of achieving.

Though not necessarily a comfort, it is at least interesting to note that spacing plants too closely together is not an unnatural act. Nature does it also, for in nature, many annuals, which are abundant self-seeders, occur in thick, crowded communities. The effect, to the human eye, may be quite beautiful, for one perceives only a sea of bloom, and not the stunted growth and yellowed leaves, or the fact that each plant has given all that it had to produce one or two blossoms before starvation doomed it to death. The production of seed, for nature, is always the main goal, and nature is content whether many or few individuals produce enough of it to keep the race going.

The gardener, however, has different expectations. One wishes for healthy plants, well grown, disease-free, and capable of producing as much bloom as they can over as long a period as is possible. With space and air, many plants, and especially many annuals, will reward the gardener with a surprising beauty of leaf and stem, even before they have produced any flowers at all. It is always a reward to know that a plant is growing well, even if one must wait a little longer for its bloom. When flowering comes, it will be the better, and look the better in the garden, for the thriftiness out of which it is produced.

Unfortunately, no hard-and-fast rule can be given for spacing, for some annuals look and actually grow better when they are crowded enough to cover the ground between them. Others profit by close proximity with their own kind, either visually or because their lax stems and heavy blossoms lean on one another for support. And some, notably vines and weavers, will never reach the light and show their flowers unless they are planted fairly close to something that can help them up. Very tall annuals, such as sunflowers, *Impatiens glandulifera*, *Tithonia rotundifolia*, and *Nicotiana sylvestris*, will always look gawky and lonely when grown with too much space between them. They may also be more vulnerable to toppling winds than when they are grown in mutually supporting communities.

Still, it would be a comfort to all gardeners if one could come up with a sure formula for spacing, such as, "Plant all annuals at a distance

Annuals lend themselves to almost any effect in the garden, from the most sophisticated to the most naive. Here a simple row of sunflowers has been planted with seeming artlessness to bend their great heads above a path. Careful staking has kept them from plunging quite over it.

of one-third to one-half of the height each may be expected to achieve at maturity." Actually, that formula works well for many plants grown as annuals, most of which achieve a height of from one to three feet and, accordingly, should be spaced at from six to 18 inches. Only very tall plants, vines, and some self-seeding annuals and biennials such as foxgloves, forget-me-nots, and poppies seem to be exceptions. A better rule, a sort of Golden Rule, is, "When in doubt, space more generously." A bit of bare ground, if it is weed-free and well cultivated, is not the liability in an amply furnished garden that many consider it to be.

Staking

It is a blessing of annuals that many require little in the way of staking. Either they are independent by nature or they have been bred to stand on their own, asking only that they be spaced far enough apart to develop an upright character. For most gardeners, this is a good thing, because staking, what one might actually call the fine art of staking, ranks in the minds of many at the very bottom of all the chores imposed on one by a garden, well below weeding and even double digging. This may be because it is often undertaken when it can no longer be avoided, usually after a summer thunderstorm has wrecked the garden. And the results, when finally one gets around to it, are depressingly unsatisfactory, consisting of prominent sticks and canes to which plants are tied like chastised mariners lashed to the mast. It is very often the gardener's sins for which they suffer, and not their own, for all plants, including those annuals that require staking, can be helped unobtrusively to assume their best posture if the work is undertaken long before it becomes necessary.

Among the annuals that require staking, the easiest to provide for are the benders and weavers, all plants that originate in crowded meadows or woodland verges where other, sturdier plants provide support. This group includes such plants as *Ammi majus, Nigella damascena, Ammobium alatum,* and *Scabiosa atropurpurea*. They are usually thin and wiry of stem and slight of leaf, and should be planted so they can fall on or into other plants for support. The gardener can make use of their dependence on others to save work, and also to contrive very beautiful effects, as, for example, when the fascinating winged stems and papery yellow-centered buttons of *Ammobium alatum* tumble through the foliage of tall bearded irises, or when the lacy ice-white flowers of *Ammi majus* are threaded through marine-blue platycodons. By use of such plants, the interest and beauty of the perennial border can often be extended, and tired or even diseased perennial foliage can be effectively masked. Benders and weavers should be planted as near their hosts as is possible while still assuring that they receive enough sun to develop well. An extra ration of liquid fertilizer is also useful to compensate for the competition they must endure (and may result as well in even finer iris and platycodon flowers the following year). The gardener need otherwise only guide them into the places they should be, for they might otherwise just as likely flop on the ground behind their host plant.

Many annuals that demand open space for themselves and that are often planted in drifts may also require staking. They are often bushy or shrublike in growth, and include such plants as nicotianas, *Moluccella laevis,* and *Lavatera trimestris*. It is useful to know about them all that if they are likely to flop, they will flop just

As they develop, many annual plants will require staking, which should, of course, be as unobtrusive as possible. This planting of Nicotiana suaveolens *is held up almost invisibly by several strands of nylon filament, sold in leather-working shops for sewing leather garments. Without such support, the natural tendency of the plant would be to spread outward, obstructing passage along the path.*

at ground level, and a single thin stake inserted four inches or so into the ground and as much above can be tied to their central stem for as much support as they will need. They may still, as the pure species of *Nicotiana alata* always does, throw their secondary flowering branches loosely about on one another, but that effect is often very graceful, quite different from when the whole plant topples over into the mud. Several genera of the daisy family may also require this unobtrusive ground-level support, such as the taller, large-flowered forms of *Zinnia elegans* and the beautiful tall-growing cosmos. But it is handy to know that they can also be deliberately bent to the ground, the stems lightly crisscrossed over one another, to produce sheets of bloom from every node. The tech-

nique provides a pleasing alternative to gypsophila, which is often recommended for filling the gaps left by early-departing perennials such as Oriental poppies.

An alternative to single ground-level stakes for bushy annuals that are likely to topple is to grow them among thickets of twiggy brush inserted around the young plants while there is still space between them. Anyone visiting the great display gardens of England in late May or early June will notice these thickets around young annuals and perennials. By mid-June they are invisible, having been completely covered over by the developing foliage and flowers. It is an effective staking method, and like many old garden practices, it brings a sort of pleasure of its own when it is well done. The best brush to use is from spruce boughs that have shed their needles, and anyone who gardens in USDA Zone 5 or farther north, and who must therefore cover tender perennials and shrubs with evergreen boughs, should have an ample supply of them. An alternative is to preserve the Christmas tree or even several, gathered about the neighborhood and kept in an out-of-the-way place until late spring. The needleless branches will be thick with twigs, which may be clipped down evenly after the stronger stems have been inserted among small plants. Evergreen twigs have great tensile strength, and will last the season without rotting or breaking under the heavy foliage they must support. Brush stakes should be inserted deeply enough into the ground that they will not topple or become dislodged, and they should be trimmed off tidily at about half the height the plant they support is expected to grow.

There are some annuals that are so tall, however, and usually so brittle of stem, that they will require a strong stake almost as tall as they are. In this class belong *Impatiens glandulifera*, some of the taller castor beans, and the heavy-headed sunflowers. Their combination of great height, sometimes surprising weight, and roots that spread out just below the surface of the ground makes these plants vulnerable to the high winds and pelting rains of summer thunderstorms. Usually they go over just as they reach their peak of flower, and often, once they are down, no salvage operation is satisfactory. It is better usually to clear them away to the compost heap, vowing next year to provide adequate support for them. That support should consist of one and sometimes two stout bamboo stakes, inserted deeply enough into the ground and standing tall enough that little weight is carried by the plant's stem, since heavy, water-drenched foliage and flowers can snap off just at the point that the stake stops. If the stake is attractive in itself, and if it is in-

serted behind the viewing point of the plant, it should not be too obtrusive. The plant should be tied into it with stout twine of a natural wheat color, which is far less distracting than twine that has been dyed a dark unnatural green. Ties should be firm enough to hold the plant in place, but not so firm as to constrict its flow of sap. With very fleshy-stemmed plants, it is well to check the ties periodically and retie the plant if any chafing or swelling along the stem is apparent.

The final group of plants that require staking are those that are scandent or vinelike. Some are true vines, such as morning glories, moon vines, scarlet runner beans, and *Dipogon lablab*, and though they are often grown on trellises or arbors for support, they may also be grown on very strong stakes, such as sturdy weathered fence posts or tall tripods of bamboo, to provide vertical interest in the perennial border or shrubbery. Though they may be self-climbing on strings or the slatted wood of trellises, they may need some help when grown on thicker wood around which their tendrils or twining stems cannot reach. And they always require guidance, else all the stems may favor one side of the pole or one member of the tripod. Even though they are born climbers, a light tying in will help them in the way the gardener wishes them to go. Though poles and tripods may be in themselves very attractive, string sometimes is not. When it must be very strong, one must accept the look of natural fiber twine, which will weather down quickly and which may be made less apparent from the start by rubbing it in the dirt. For light tying, however, the nylon filament sold by leather-supply houses for making leather garments is useful. It is very strong, will not cut tender stems when tied loosely about them, and, in dark brown or black, is invisible, holding up quite heavy plants as if by magic to one or two unobtrusive stakes.

Fertilizers

Any activity one pursues with attention and a desire for success builds up, over the years, some settled convictions. One of mine about gardening is that most failures and near failures with plants occur from the neglect of feeding them adequately with synthetic fertilizers. It is not a fashionable opinion, or in the eyes of many even a moral one. What may be called the Compost Movement in America has caused many to shun expensive petroleum-produced fertilizers that exhaust our shrinking natural resources, damage the environment, and make of millions of once-rich agricultural acres only a medium to hold plants upright. Those who have come to understand the complexities of organic gardening remind us rightly that there is no substitute for the good earth, well tilled, rich in humus and trace elements, capable of giving plants much of what they need to resist disease, insect predation, and even, sometimes, the vagaries of the weather. The enrichment of the soil through naturally decaying vegetable matter cannot be dispensed with by any gardener who wishes plants to thrive and to produce lusty systems of root, stem, and leaf, and an abundance of flower.

Still, even the most fabulously rich soil may be deficient in some of the elements plants need to thrive, especially in quickly available nitrogen, which promotes rapid and healthy leaf growth, in phosphorus, which develops strong root systems and aids in ripening and maturing, and in potassium, which increases resistance to disease and helps plants endure unfavorable weather conditions. All three of these essential elements can be had in organic form, through properly prepared compost and animal manures. And when a plant is permanent in the landscape, as are trees, shrubs, and groundcovers, the best results are achieved through their use. They offer plants a slow and steady diet, and they increase the fertility of the soil incre-

mentally over many years, building up a thriving world of beneficial microorganisms and earthworms.

But annuals are a different case. They are plants of quick growth, expected to produce, from seed sown directly in the ground or from tiny transplants started indoors, lusty stems and leaves and abundant flower in one short season, often no longer than two months. Their needs are immediate, and those needs are often best answered by synthetically produced granular fertilizers or by water-soluble ones that can be absorbed almost immediately through growing tissue.

The argument is often voiced that fertilizing annuals will result in lush growth at the expense of flower. It is true with annuals, as with all plants, that when they are starved they will attempt to flower and produce seed as rapidly as they can. But many annuals are very beautiful in leaf and stem, and there is no annual, really, that will not reward a timely and sparing dose of fertilizer with increased and more handsome growth and with a greater abundance of flower. Moreover, with annuals, a really well-grown plant is always wonderful, even when one must wait a little longer for it to produce a blossom.

In many of the plant portraits in this book, the application of a good, granular vegetable-garden fertilizer is recommended. It differs from other plant foods in being relatively low in nitrogen and high in phosphorus and potassium. It is compounded in such a way as to release its nutrients quickly into the soil. For most annuals, one application is sufficient, and it should be applied when a seedling sown in place has achieved two or three true leaves, or when a transplant has adjusted to its new home and has begun to make fresh growth. It is sprinkled in a circle around the plant in about the quantity one would use when generously salting a chicken for roasting. Great care must be taken to keep the fertilizer away from the stem of the plant or its leaves, for they are easily burned, and even a very little granular fertilizer dropped into the growing center of a young plant will kill it. After the fertilizer has been applied, it should be lightly scratched into the surface of the soil, never dug in deeply, as the growing roots of the plant may lie just below the soil and can be injured. A thorough watering is then administered, which dissolves the fertilizer and makes it available to the plant. Within a week, results should be apparent in the darkening of leaves and a burgeoning of growth. Should plants continue to look thriftless, a second application of fertilizer may be tried two or three weeks after the first. But once the plants appear to be growing strongly, no further applications should be made so that the plants will ripen into flower.

Water-soluble and liquid fertilizers differ from granular ones in that they are formulated to be absorbed almost immediately through all the growing tissues of the plant—leaf, stem, root, and even flower. They are useful whenever a boost seems needed, especially when seedlings are being grown on in a sterile medium or are newly transplanted, when mature plants are under stress from being grown in crowded conditions, as in pots and window boxes, or when plants that have exhausted themselves from flower production are sheared back to force a repeat bloom. Old-fashioned gardeners apply liquid fertilizer in the form of manure tea, an infusion brewed from fresh cow manure and enough water to cause a putrid slurry. After two or three weeks in a covered container, the excessively smelly liquid that results is run through a strainer, diluted to the color of weak tea, and applied with a watering can around the roots of plants but never on their leaves. The results can be dramatic, and there may be no other way to raise prize-winning sweet peas if one plans to enter some sort of competition.

But putting aside the obvious difficulties of odor and the general unavailability of a co-operative cow, manure tea is dangerous stuff, since its chemical content is uncertain and it requires careful judgment in its brewing and application. Even those who are not particularly squeamish will find a safer substitute in one of several water-soluble fertilizers that are sold for houseplants but that work miracles in the outdoor annual garden. They are more concentrated by far than granular food, and the directions on the package must be scrupulously followed. With liquid plant food the rule of "little and often" produces the best results. One should mix the fertilizer at half the strength recommended but apply it twice as often as is suggested. Synthetic soluble fertilizers are applied with a watering can fitted with a rose that breaks the flow into a gentle shower and drenches every part of the plant. Applications are best made in early morning, just after the dew has dried but before the sun is at its height. There are those who are convinced that the solution is most quickly absorbed if it is tepid to slightly warm, and no harm, and possibly a great deal of good, will come from making it up in this way.

Water-soluble fertilizers are almost essential in growing healthy seedlings indoors on a sunny windowsill or in a greenhouse, since their roots quickly exhaust the small amount of nutrients in the potting mix in which they are grown. Many will never recover from early starvation, and all will be the better for a nourishing diet in infancy. When they are transplanted, a drench of dilute liquid fertilizer will stimulate their roots and leaves, encouraging them to accept their new homes quickly. Annuals that are ailing or thriftless from no apparent cause can sometimes be brought into flourishing growth by a timely application of liquid food, and those grown close together, in the border or in pots or window boxes, may be absolutely dependent on extra nutrients.

Prolonging the Show

The primary reason for growing many common annuals in the garden—often the only reason, as the gardeners who grow them may admit when pressed—is that they are capable of producing a display of color throughout the whole summer. Indeed, the most popular annuals in garden centers—snapdragons, marigolds, cosmos, *Salvia splendens*—will produce their first perky blossoms in infancy, while still in the six-pack; and certainly there is something cheering about this precocious dot of color. It will be followed, one hopes, by waves of flower until frosts are so severe that there is no way, no matter how many blankets or old sheets one spreads, of prolonging the show.

Gardeners who make a specialty of growing some of the rarer and less usual annuals know that sometimes a summer full of them will require a few tricks. The lengths one is prepared to go to depend always on one's facilities and the amount of time one has to spend in the garden, and perhaps on just how greedy one may be.

The first technique for prolonging the season of bloom requires more courage than time, effort, or skill; it is to pinch out that premature cheerful little bloom when transplanting, and often, if a plant is lank or spindly, to reduce it by half with a determined clip of the shears. With annual plants, more than with any others, early flowers are often produced at the expense of strong growth of root, stem, and leaf. The canny nursery owner may also, through the application of foliar feeds or by turning up the greenhouse heat, have forced just that winsome display of first flowers, knowing how effectively they will sell his wares. But in the garden, the longest and most abundant show of bloom will always be produced from strong-growing plants that have been given time to build up good root systems and lush foliage before they are asked to produce flowers. Pinching out is one

more among many cases known to gardeners, of gratifications being better when they are slightly delayed.

Deadheading, the removal of spent flowers before they have had a chance to set seed, is a second important technique in securing the longest possible display from annuals. There are many plants, such as *Impatiens wallerana* or *Lavatera trimestris*, that are capable of producing such abundant flower over such a long period of time that the removal of faded blossoms is hardly worth the trouble. But for most annuals, the production of flowers is really incidental to the production of seed. When frustrated in their attempt, they will try again, with more flowers and more, until either sheer exhaustion or the coming of autumn frosts puts an end to their efforts. Happy indeed is that effect for the gardener, however it must frustrate the plant's sense of mission.

Shearing back is a variant of deadheading, in which not only spent blossoms are removed, but also whole tops are scalped away by the use of garden shears, scissors, or even hedge clippers. The hope is that new flower-bearing growth will appear from stems and leaf nodes across the plant. This technique works best with mat-forming annuals, such as *Hymemostemma paludosum, Lobularia maritima*, or *Linaria maroccana*; with annuals (often actually tender perennials) that grow from a persistent crown, such as snapdragons or species of *Diascia*; or with bushy plants like cosmos or *Hibiscus trionum*. But with any plant grown as an annual such drastic treatment is worth a try if the plant begins to look shabby and unproductive by midsummer. Shearing back is most effective when only the top third or so of the plant is removed, just above the point where its scaffold of woody growth modifies into flower-bearing stems. But it is important to remember when shearing back that one is asking a lot of the plant; a dose of water-soluble quick-acting fertil-izer, applied over the stems and around the roots, will encourage one's amputees.

Estate gardeners in the last century were ex-pected to keep benches and benches of healthy plants in reserve, to smarten up the borders the minute they became shabby; this practice of "dropping in" was considered essential to a good garden. The results were often startling, for tender tropicals like crotons and even cym-bidium orchids were pressed into service. Dis-plays of really bad taste, and some really bad gardening, were often the inevitable results. But from this practice modern gardeners can learn an important technique for keeping their bor-ders fine and full of flowers. Many, though cer-tainly not all, flowering plants grown as annuals transplant with ease, if the work is done in overcast weather, if they are lifted with gener-ous root balls, well watered in, shaded for a day or two from a break in the clouds, and encouraged with a drench of quick-acting water-soluble fertilizer. Members of the com-posite family particularly, such as annual chry-santhemums, marigolds, and calendulas, can be grown in an out-of-the-way place in the garden, or in a reserve row of the vegetable patch, for just this use. But annuals grown in pots are easi-est to drop in, since they can be eased gently out of their containers with almost no root dis-

Though classic park bedding can lift the spirits of strollers on hot summer days, it is primarily the practice of planting some of this, some of that, and some of something else, all for vivid color, that has turned many gardeners away from annual plants. Certainly most of the flowers in this bedding scheme could be more sensitively used, particularly the ageratum, a good garden plant once freed from its compulsory march.

turbance. They offer the added advantage in that one can try them out, moving the pot about the garden until one can determine where the plant will look best. Gardeners bent on achieving the most exuberant display of flowers cannot do better than to master this minor art, for the floppy growth of perennials past their prime can always be eased aside to make room for a splash of fresh color.

Repeat Sowing Good vegetable gardeners know the art of repeat sowing, to ensure a continuous crop of radishes or salad greens or snap beans. The same technique can be used to keep the garden full of flowers, for many annual plants make surprisingly rapid growth when seeded directly into the garden. They will not always produce the earliest flowers or the first fine wave of color, but that is precisely the point. They will pick up and carry on the garden's display when transplants started indoors have begun to flag. Though seed packets used to be more generous than they seem to be these days, one still often has more seed than one needs, and it is always worthwhile to hold some in reserve, to sprinkle lightly among the transplants one has started indoors. It is important to leave generous areas among transplants for a second seeding, and to thin rigorously. A thicket of new seedlings will never mature into well-grown flowering plants; they may even choke out the transplants on which one depended for early color. It is also important to remember that in most parts of North America plants do not develop evenly throughout the summer. Around the Fourth of July there is a lull in all plant growth, occasioned by warm nights, hot days, and a decrease in atmospheric moisture. After the dog days of August, matters reverse, and plants seem to burgeon. So repeat sowings in the garden must take account of this pattern. Any packet will note the length of time from germination to first flowering; with repeat sowings, one must add a week or two, or, if one seeds near the Fourth of July, even three.

And finally, to prolong the show in most gardens, one must cover. In North America the weather is always a game of cat-and-mouse. In many regions, sometimes as early as late August and sometimes as late as mid-September, there is a sudden drop of the temperature into near frost. Then, many of the gardens of North America display a draping of old sheets and other worn-out bedclothes, rugs, shirts, skirts, paper bags and boxes, whatever one can find to trap the residual warmth of the soil around plants as the night temperatures move in sinister fashion toward the red dot on the thermometer. The general effect must look, to foreign visitors, as if someone had forgotten to take in the laundry, or worse, to stow the trash. Still, from this curious effort imposed on American gardeners come benefits well worth reaping. For after this first brief hint of what winter will be, there often follows a glorious period of warmth—two weeks or more—in which many annual plants take on new vigor, and the wealth of their flowers becomes more vivid in the warm haze of early autumn, with perhaps a spangling of the first turning leaves to set them off to perfection.

Cuttings

Theoretically, there is no annual that cannot be rooted from a cutting, and those who have skill in this art might try anything. In fact, cuttings are sometimes the only way to carry on a plant, such as a particularly fine form that may not come true from seed, or a double one that cannot set seed. Many annuals and plants grown as annuals, however, will tax even an experienced gardener, for propagation by cuttings is always a race between a plant's natural inclination to perish when severed from its roots and its willingness to form new ones. Some annuals, however, such as marigolds and *Lobelia erinus*, literally root in the air, showing tiny fingers questing toward the earth beneath any stem that is kept moist and shaded beneath the parent plant. Others, such as species of *Tropaeolum* (the nasturtiums of gardens) will form fat white roots in the water of a vase before they fade and must be thrown out. And most gardeners know how easy it is to propagate a bit of *Impatiens wallerana* or a fibrous begonia, by sticking it in a pot of damp sand or even earth, and keeping it moist and cool in a shady place. But always, to root a plant is a thrill, a step upward from growing it from seed.

Cuttings are best taken from vigorous side growths that have not yet formed flower buds, for once a plant is bent on flowering, it has another way in mind to perpetuate itself and may not be willing to alter its agenda. Cuttings should be "ripe," which is to say neither so soft and watery that they will wilt immediately and be prey to fungus and rot, nor so woody that they will have lost their youthful will to live. (One old test of ripeness was to see if a shoot could be snapped between thumb and forefinger, leaving a skin of outer tissue clinging to the parent stem.) Cuttings of annuals are always best taken from young plants, in full growth and vigor, and they are taken in the morning, when everything is well rested and full of life. The sooner they are inserted into a rooting medium the better, and in the meantime they should be kept turgid by being enclosed in plastic bags, with perhaps a sprinkling of water to keep them fresh.

Rooting hormones are a help with firm woody stems and with shrubs, but are seldom necessary with succulent cuttings, and may actually inhibit rooting. Those who routinely propagate plants from cuttings always have their favorite medium; some favor pure perlite or vermiculite, and some prefer sharp sand, with perhaps a handful of peat in it. All agree, however, that the medium should be sterile, and should admit as much oxygen as possible while still being in close contact with the stem, and that cuttings should be kept in an environment saturated with moisture but buoyant with oxygen until they strike root. Such conditions are most easily achieved by enclosing the cuttings, pot and all, in a plastic bag, with perhaps a structure of bamboo stakes or bent coat hangers to keep the damp film from clinging to the leaves. These incubators are kept in bright but never direct light, which might cook the cuttings, until rooting occurs.

It is always a temptation to pull up a cutting to see if it has formed roots. Usually, however, it is better to wait to be told, by a freshening of old leaves and the appearance of new ones. Even among plants easy to root, however, the success rate will seldom be 100 percent, and any cuttings that blacken or turn yellow should be removed promptly. It is a help also, at the first appearance of furry gray mold or when several cuttings in a batch go limp and slimy, to apply a dusting of sulphur or a drench of fungicide, which will often save those that are still vital.

When one knows that rooting has occurred, either by the appearance of new growth or by a subtle resistance when a cutting is gently tugged, the new plants must be gradually accustomed to the real atmosphere. The plastic bag should be loosened to admit air, but left draped about its supports. After two or three days, it may be removed altogether, and after two or three more the rooted cuttings can be gently lifted out with a sharpened pencil or small stick, and potted in a sterile potting medium. They should still be kept in bright light but never strong sunlight until their roots have made contact with the potting medium. They may then be brought into full sun and grown on as one would any plant started from seed.

Root Cuttings It is a surprise to gardeners that many plants grown as annuals can be carried over and repropagated as sections of root, even when they are only single sections as thick, or less, than a pencil, with no crown or stem or bunch of leaves attached. Preeminent in this class are members of the family Solanaceae—petunias, nicotianas, and daturas—all of which produce thick fleshy roots and sometimes, as with nicotianas, small swellings or tubercles that remind us of their relationship to potatoes. But any annual that is thick of root, or that will sometimes show small plantlets about its base when disturbed by a trowel, is worth repropagating by root cuttings. Sometimes the technique is a great convenience, as with *Datura meteloides*, which may not set viable seed in cool gardens, and if it does produce seed, will flower a month after plants propagated by root cuttings. Sometimes also, as with the very rare variegated and double-flowered nicotianas, or the fine large-flowered form of *Nicotiana langsdorfii* bred at Sissinghurst, root cuttings may be the only way to preserve the strain in a pure form. The attempt is also fascinating in itself, adding one more to the good gardener's many skills, and it is not actually very difficult to do.

After frost has blackened the foliage of most annuals, those from which one wishes to take root cuttings should be carefully dug, and the fattest and starchiest roots put aside. (If they are warty, swollen, or lumpy, so much the better, for those may be sure signs of plantlets to come.) The roots should be kept moist, in a plastic bag or with a shovelful of earth, until they can be cut with a sharp knife or razor blade into sections approximately three inches long. It is from the top of the section that the new plants will usually come, and so it is important to know which end is which. Old gardeners made a straight cut across the top end, and a slanted one across the bottom, to avoid this confusion. The root cuttings are then placed in damp sand, or even in a plastic bag of barely moistened peat, and kept quite cool, just above freezing, until the days turn toward spring. They are then inserted into a sterile potting mix, with the top end just below the level of the soil. The mix should be kept evenly moist and warm until little plants begin to appear. The sections of root can then be lifted carefully, potted singly, and grown on as one would any new seedling.

Self-Seeders

Even in quite cold gardens, many annuals and biennials need only be planted for one season in order to reappear year after year as self-seeded plants. The old gardeners referred to this amiable practice as "volunteering," and it is an apt word for the tiny seedlings that appear on their own, sometimes for generations. Often they will occur quite shyly here and there, never two together and sometime skipping a year or two, as will *Cirsium japonicum* and *Bellis perennis*. Sometimes they will appear in a perfectly spaced colony of many individuals,

as will species of *Argemone* and some salvias, as if the gardener's hand had ruled their existence from the beginning. And sometimes they will sprout in ground-covering sheets, as do *Impatiens glandulifera* and *Perilla frutescens*, "as thick," to quote my grandmother, "as hairs on the dog's back."

Nervous gardeners always fear annuals that self-seed, dreading that they may introduce into the garden yet one more noxious weed to plague their existence. But self-seeded annuals, when they are too numerous or simply no

Much of the pleasure to be had from growing annuals results from combining them imaginatively with perennials and with shrubs. Here Perilla frutescens *makes a rich dark mass among roses, daylilies, and lilies. The stately irislike plant to the right is* Sisyrinchium striatum, *and the foam of acid green is the flowers of* Alchemilla mollis, *both true perennials.*

longer wanted at all, are much easier to exterminate than other "weeds." None are stoloniferous, shooting up in the hearts of more precious plants at a great distance from their parent. Few have deep, carrotlike taproots that can regenerate, as do dandelions, when the crown is pulled. And fewer still will sprout anew from the tiniest root hairs left behind, as will several kinds of polygonum, the "sour grass" dreaded by vegetable gardeners. Those that may be designated as "dog-haired," after my grandmother's saying, are in fact the easiest of all to exterminate, for they may be skimmed off in sheets or plucked from the centers of other plants without extreme effort.

Many gardeners count absolutely on the annual reappearance of some of their favorite plants from self-seeding. It has been 15 years since I seeded foxgloves, yet I always have a reliable show in June. I remember planting various fancy strains of the little *Viola tricolor* called Johnny jump-up, but for years now, in out-of-the-way places in the garden, there has been a pleasing display of tiny faces, not just the familiar purple with a yellow stain, but also some that are almost black and some that are so pale a primrose yellow as to be practically white. And in Vermont, the opium poppy, *Papaver somniferum,* will appear of itself wherever people garden, perhaps from air-borne seeds or perhaps from seeds lying buried for years and brought to the light by new cultivation.

But not all annuals may be so depended on as these reliable self-seeders. Some had best always be considered as unexpected surprises. And when they are plants that are almost indispensable in the summer garden, such as species of *Nicotiana* or *Papaver rhoeas*, it is safer always to make fresh seedings. Sow them either indoors for the earliest bloom or outdoors, when the plants are known to bloom quickly or are difficult to transplant. Then one can take joy from plants that occur on their own without risking the disappointment that they will for some reason not appear at all.

Though part of the excitement of gardening is an endless altering of one's plans and a shifting about of plants for ever more refined effects, it often happens that one finds just the right place for an annual plant and feels that its absence for a season would be a loss to the garden. So one comes to plant some annuals, year after year, exactly in the same spot. In such situations, self-seeded individuals are invaluable; they will often make lustier plants than those started indoors, and they will flower somewhat later, thereby prolonging the display sometimes well into autumn. The great trick in such doubling or tripling of splendor is simply to thin carefully, making sure that self-seeded plants do not come up so abundantly among transplants that they will all crowd one another out and ruin the display one seeks. The point is not to be too greedy.

When pure species of annuals are grown in the garden, it is almost certain that volunteers will look just as one wishes them to. But when hybrids or carefully selected colors are wanted, self-sown seedlings will probably revert, sometimes over several generations, to the original flower color of the species or to forms intermediate between the parents. Sometimes the results of reversion can be quite lovely, producing plants more beautiful or more delicate of color than those one originally planted.

And sometimes, of course, they can be dreadful, at least if one is aiming at a subtle orchestration of color. *Phlox drummondii*, for example, when planted in beautiful soft forms of shell-pink or salmon or pale lavender, will sooner or later, in its seedlings, get back to magenta. Magenta is not a *bad* color, of course; when placed among the silvery leaves of many herbs it can be very beautiful. But it may not be what one wants in just the place in the garden it occurs. Experience teaches gardeners those plants that had better not be allowed to self-seed, by removing mature individuals before their progeny falls to ground or by exterminating young volunteers when they occur. But good gardeners often allow plants in the best color forms to self-seed, eliminating the rest, thereby developing their own fine and sometimes unique color strains.

Though it is a happy gardener who finds young plants coming up just where they are wanted, it is a happier one still who finds them in unexpected spots where they look splendid nevertheless. Plants have often an uncanny ability to select their own best places to grow, and many beautiful effects come quite on their own. A sense of spontaneity in the garden is a part of its soul, and though there are gardeners who are wonderfully clever at contriving this precious effect, most of us need a bit of help. A colony of young forget-me-nots may settle in under the bare shanks of a shrub where we have neglected to weed, presenting us in June with a beautiful sheet of limpid blue. Foxgloves we never planted may splendidly tower in a bay of the shrubbery, and a gentle cloud of alyssum may hover next to the large stones of a path. Over our shoulder on a fine late summer morning in June we may catch the first flash of scarlet from a self-seeded corn poppy and know that it is perfect, just where it is. The trick with such effects is never to be too aggressive a weeder, for in gardens, one is in a partnership with nature, and with self-seeded plants, one is very often the junior partner.

Seed Saving

Once one has procured and grown an annual plant one likes, however, it is still important to save seed, for many uncommon plants are released on an experimental basis or in limited numbers, and one may not be able to buy seed of them in following years. Other plants come to one through the generosity of fellow gardeners, and it is good to carry on and extend the chain, and sometimes even to repay that generosity when, through accident or poor seed set, a treasured plant has been lost to those from whom one originally had it.

If properly stored, most annual seed will remain viable for two or three years or even longer. Germination rates decrease with each year of storage, but one may still raise enough young plants from old seed to continue a race in one's garden if the annual harvest fails. Seed of hybrids and of plants selected for special characteristics such as size of bloom, unusual vigor, or particular coloration of leaf or flower may not preserve those characteristics into succeeding generations. But more than one gardener has found that by undoing the work of breeding carried on by seed companies he ended up with a plant of much more beauty and grace than the one they produced. Any pure species (such as are many of the plants in this book) should come true from seed, even when grown in close proximity with other related species in its genus. Spontaneous crosses in the garden are very rare, though should they occur, the results might be wonderful.

The most useful tool I have found for saving seed is a stack of heavy flat soup bowls of vitreous white china, such as may be inexpensively bought in restaurant supply stores and sometimes from mail-order catalogs. (Williams-Sonoma is my source.) They are almost indestructible, can be held beneath a rod of ripening seed to catch every one while they are plucked, and the name of the plant can be writ-

Seed catalogs are better stocked with unusual plants and seeds than ever before, but sooner or later the gardener will find himself saving his own seeds, either because they are hard to come by, from an unusually fine form of a plant, or simply because it is fun to do. Many plants grown as annuals are species that will come true from seeds, while others may revert to the simpler and more graceful forms of their parents. Crucial in drying seeds is preventing excess moisture from forming around unripe seed heads. Paper bags do an excellent job of this, as do open bowls.

ten on the edge of the bowl with a grease pencil or felt marker while the seed is curing. Once the seed has dried, one can clean it directly in the bowl, shaking it from pods or capsules and discarding them, with any stems or leaves or other trash. The white surface of the bowl makes even tiny seeds visible, and they do not stick to its highly glazed surface.

Seed should be cured for two or three weeks, even longer if it is fleshy or large, in an airy dry place until it is free of all moisture. It can then be cleaned and put into envelopes to store. Old-fashioned gardeners had the art of folding seed packets out of sheets of white paper in such a way that they would remain sealed and never spill a seed. It required a handiness equal to making origami birds, and most gardeners will do better to use the small brown or glassine envelopes sold in stationers' shops to coin collectors and jewelers. Each is about two inches wide and four inches long, and is well glued enough at the end to prevent even the finest seed from slipping out. Before the seed is spooned into the envelope, one should write on it the correct botanical name of the plant, the year it was gathered, and any special cultural information one has noted. It is always wise to make up several packs, especially of unusual or hard-to-get seed, to share with other gardeners or to trade for seed one does not have.

The greatest loss of viability with saved seed occurs if it is kept too moist or too dry. If it should get wet or even absorb moisture from the atmosphere, it may begin premature germination. If it desiccates from dry air, such as causes the piano to fall out of tune and the furniture to come unglued, it will lose the sometimes infinitesimal amount of sealed-in moisture that keeps the tiny germ alive during its long sleep. So it should be stored in very cool but not freezing conditions that feel buoyant and fresh to human skin. Such places are never very hard to find in the winter in Vermont, and so I store our seed at about 50 degrees Fahrenheit in the back of an old cupboard. Those who live in houses where the air is very warm and desertlike, from central or electric heating, will do better to place the seed packets in a mason jar, seal them tightly, and store them in the back of the refrigerator.

Carrying On

For most gardeners, the whole point of annuals is that they will fill their brief season with flower and can then be forgotten. For many, indeed, the coming of the first frosts is a sort of relief; after the tidying up is done, one can retreat to the books that piled up through the summer, to correspondence neglected, or to the seed catalogs, and the dreams they hold of gardens yet to be.

Many other gardeners, however, feel an urge to save a bit of summer's splendor. Often, a stem of *Impatiens wallerana*, broken off accidentally and rooted in a glass of water, will satisfy them. Or a pot of fibrous begonias or pelargoniums, too pretty to sacrifice to the first frost, is hauled in and finds a place on the kitchen windowsill to flower shyly, with long rests in between, throughout the winter. Such small events hook the gardener, who then begins to look at all the last flowers of summer with a new eye to what might be worth saving.

Many plants commonly grown as annuals can in fact be carried over the winter, providing one understands their needs. Often "carrying over," the old gardener's terms for such attempts, may be the only way to preserve a particularly desirable plant. Sometimes, also, gardeners become impatient of seeing each growing season as a separate bead without a string, and crave the continuity that comes from linking each to each by the act of preservation. And finally, though winter-flowering houseplants—clivias, tender azaleas, orchids, and forced bulbs—are all precious in their way, a miracle occurs when one has larkspurs for Christmas or when a single petunia or morning glory unfurls in the weak light of January.

Carrying on plants commonly grown as annuals depends first on understanding their botanical

Thousands of woody shrubs sold as annual plants are thrown away each year in America after a brief summer of bloom. Many can be carried through the winter easily on a sunny windowsill, a sun porch, or even as dormant plants in a cold but frost-free basement. This venerable fuchsia, of the cultivar named 'Hidcote Beauty', has been lovingly maintained for 10 years. At the end of each summer it is cut back hard, repotted in fresh earth, and kept dormant until late February. Then it is brought into good light, fertilized regularly, and regrown for standing outdoors.

classifications, for one treats plants differently according to whether they are true annuals, biennials, tender perennials, shrubs or subshrubs, or plants that grow from corns, rhizomes, or tubers. The last classification is by far the easiest to manage, though even it requires some care and attention. Plants that sprout from underground reserves retreat into them for the winter, storing there the energy required to begin new growth in spring. Familiar in this group are gladiolus, dahlias, acidantheras (now officially *Gladiolus callianthus*) and crocosmias, though a few other plants commonly grown as annuals, such as *Mirabilis jalapa*, the old-fashioned four o'clock, and all canna species and hybrids, also grow from subterranean mechanisms. In very mild gardens they can all be left underground, but where the ground freezes, shallow or deep, they must be lifted, cleaned, stored in a frost-free place, and started into new growth each spring.

Lifting of corms, tubers, and rhizomes is done after the top growth has withered or been blackened with frost, but not before. All the starches and sugars in the leaves must have time to retreat underground. Corms are then carefully separated and graded (for only the largest will produce immature corms, or flowers, and the cormels, must be grown to size elsewhere), spread on trays in a dark, frost-free airy place for a week or two to cure, and then stored in almost-dry peat or barely moistened perlite or vermiculite at temperatures that hover just above freezing. Tuberous and rhizomatous plants, such as begonias, four o'clocks, and cannas, need no such period of curing, but should be lifted with earth around them, placed in pots, and kept barely moist in a frost-free place. Such places are easy to find in an older house but may be difficult to locate in more modern structures. In such places, the back of the refrigerator may have to serve. If dirt, inedible roots, and possibly small earthworms seem disquieting there, an old refrigerator can often be acquired almost for the hauling. Shoved into the back of the basement it will serve to store perennial roots and also to force a few pots of bulbs. But care must be taken always to be sure that the roots never freeze, for they will then be reduced to a black or slimy yellow mush.

In spring, about six weeks before the last anticipated frost, tubers and rhizomes should be taken from storage, cleaned, and started into growth. Tuberous begonias are left entire, but cannas are cut into sections, each with an ivory shoot or two of new life. Dahlias and four o'clocks are divided so that each tuber ends in a stem and several eyes. They should then be potted up in a sterile potting mix and kept warm and only moderately damp until new growth appears above the soil level. Then they must be placed in good light, watered well, fertilized with half-strength liquid food once a week, and grown on as strong as possible until all danger of frost is past, when they may be transplanted into the garden.

Many plants grown as annuals are in fact tender perennials, and they are always worth carrying on if one has the space, time, and the inclination to do it. In this class belong many tender herbaceous salvias, a number of diascias and verbenas, and some of the beautiful South African composites such as venidiums and gazanias. They may be lifted in late summer or early autumn and potted up. If they have made rods of growth, as does *Salvia farinacea*, they must be cut back hard to three-inch stubs. If they form basal rosettes, as do gazanias, one only removes spent flowers, seedpods, and buds. Those that have no leaf or fresh growth at soil level will require a short sleep in quite cool conditions, just above freezing. They should be brought into relative warmth (50 degrees Fahrenheit or so) when the days lengthen in mid-February. They will then come quickly into growth, and may be divided, repotted, and grown on as one would any half-hardy annual started from seed. Half-hardy perennials that retain thick clumps of basal leaves, or that continue to produce fresh shoots from their crowns at summer's end, should never be put quite to sleep. They are best grown in cool sunny positions, such as are comfortable to people only at midday or with a sweater on, and kept always above freezing at night. They will make strong growth, but will produce few flowers until spring. It is important with such plants always to keep them rather dry during the winter, but never to the point of shriveling, and to withhold fertilizer until spring, for too much moisture or too rich a diet will cause them quickly to rot away at soil level.

Shrubs and subshrubs sold as annuals always represent a challenge to gardeners, for they can see, from the stout woody stems they produce, and sometimes from their determination to produce flowers and fresh growth in late summer, that they could be salvaged, carried over the winter, and reestablished in the garden for another season of beauty. In the class of tender shrubs and subshrubs belong many plants sold by thousands each spring as annuals, including fuchsias, coleus, lantanas, and culinary herbs such as rosemary and woody French thymes. There are rarer plants, too, like *Anisodontea capensis* and abutilons. All are worth saving, if the gardener has the facilities and the determination.

Some shrubs and subshrubs, such as pelargoniums, fuchsias, and lantanas, can be cut back hard to a scaffold of bare woody stems in late summer, potted in fresh well-draining soil rich in humus, and then stood directly on a sunny windowsill, where they will almost immediately make fresh new growth and may even produce a few flowers by Thanksgiving. Others, such as rosemary and woody thymes, may be potted entire, if they are not too large, shaved lightly, and grown on indoors in as much sun as one has for a harvest of leaves or young twigs to flavor winter soups and stews. But when winter flowers or leaves are the gardener's principal aim (rather than simple preservation), it is usually better to start with young plants taken as cuttings in high summer, potted on when they are well rooted, pinched frequently to encourage bushy compact growth, and frustrated, until late August, in their desire to produce flowers by removing all buds as they appear. Often, young plants so treated will burgeon with flowers throughout the winter, as is always the case with pelargoniums. Some plants, however, may wait until the days lengthen in February to reward the gardener for his patience, and others, such as the shrubby salvias, may produce no flowers until they can be reasonably sure of escaping their indoor captivity. Nevertheless, all shrubs and subshrubs should be grown on strongly throughout the winter, in the best light, and encouraged to produce lush growth by weekly applications of half-strength liquid fertilizer. They should be pinched or clipped frequently, also, to develop a compact, bushy shape.

The last chore of the season for the gardener who grows annuals is a thorough cleanup, since withered foliage can harbor diseases over the winter that will infect new plants in spring. Autumn is also an excellent time to apply compost, leaf mold, or peat moss to restore humus to the depleted soil of the border.

Unlike tender perennials and shrubs, whose term of life is usually ended in the garden by spells of cold too intense to endure, true annuals are actually bent on perishing. They essentially bloom themselves to death to produce the seed that will perpetuate their race. Often, their mission is complete long before the first frosts. But the attentive gardener, when clearing away their spent remains, may notice a still vigorous side branch that has rooted where it touched the ground and was prevented from flowering by the shade of its parent, or a sprinkling of young seedlings from early flowers he neglected to deadhead, luxuriating in the cool nights and abundant rainfall of early autumn. Such events are always an invitation to carry on a true annual, in the hope that it will reward one's efforts by a surprising bit of summer bloom in the depths of winter.

One reads the advice sometimes that annuals may be dug from the garden, cut back, and potted on for winter bloom. When they are in fact tender perennials, as are petunias, or woody shrubs, as are ornamental peppers, and especially when they are willing to resprout vigorously when cut back hard, as is *Lobelia erinus*, the results are sometimes worth the effort. Little is usually gained, however, by rushing out into the garden before the first frost, digging a mature plant in full flower, and cramming it into a pot. So many roots are sacrificed that even if the top of the plant is reduced to bring it into balance with what remains, it will wilt from the shock and be hopelessly set back in its growth. Better plants for early to mid-autumn flower indoors are usually had by growing them in pots from the beginning. In midsummer, immature specimens are potted up, from late-developing transplants not needed in the garden, or from cuttings or a late sowing of a few seeds left in the pack. Clay pots are usually preferable, not only because they will look best later when brought indoors, but also because they can be sunk to their rims in an out-of-the-way spot in the garden, thus saving a deal of watering and also ensuring cool, even conditions for developing roots. Most annuals look best for indoor display when established singly in pots, and ones that are five to eight inches in diameter will do for all but the largest-growing species. The young plants should be fed every two weeks with water-soluble fertilizer, and any flower buds that develop should be removed. In early autumn, before frosts have touched their leaves, they should be lifted from the garden, the pots cleaned, and brought indoors. They should flower on a sun porch or sunny windowsill throughout the autumn, and sometimes into December.

Annuals wanted for late winter and very early spring flowers should be started from seed or cutting sometime around the first two weeks of August or, if they are quick-maturing plants, in early September. Seedlings should be pricked out and grown on as one would for spring-sown plants, eventually to be established in five- to eight-inch pots that should be moved indoors before the first frost. Few, even among the shade lovers, will develop well unless given good sunlight, and the best plants will result from conditions that are quite cool, hovering around 50 degrees at night and 70 degrees in the daytime. A light hand with watering and with feeding is crucial to success throughout the darkest days of the year, when growth will be slow and plants will be unable to utilize abundant moisture or a rich diet of fertilizer. Pots should be kept evenly moist, never so dry that the plants shrivel or so wet that the pots seem heavy and clammy. With the coming of the bright days of February, however, growth will visibly quicken, and watering can be increased, with doses of half-strength liquid fertilizer applied every two weeks. Any annual plants that have made it that far will shortly begin to show flower buds, and flowers, which should last through March and April, providing an exciting alternative to forced bulbs and florists' azaleas.

Standards

Given the space and effort often required to carry on shrubs and subshrubs, many gardeners will find it worthwhile to train them as standards, mop-headed plants with all the growth clustered atop straight woody stems. Almost any summer-flowering shrub and some tender culinary herbs can be developed into standards. The best results are usually achieved not from natually grown plants in the garden, but from small, unbranched, vigorous plants rooted as cuttings. Young plants are potted in late summer, and trained to one central stem, which is tied to a stake as tall as the eventual standard is to be. All developing side growth is pinched at the stem, though leaves are left to nourish the plant. When growth has reached the top of the stake, it is pinched out. Two or more branches will then develop, which should be pinched again after they have formed two or four sets of leaves. The resulting additional branches should also be pinched, and branches from them pinched again, until the plant has developed a full head of growth. When enough leaves have formed at the top of the plant to support it—usually after the second or third pinching—those along the central supporting stem can be clipped away to expose the trunk.

Flowering plants trained as standards are best left to grow naturally once a thick scaffold of branches has been built up at the top, for too much pinching thereafter will eliminate flower-bearing stems. Plants valued for aromatic leaves or for culinary use, such as shrubby artemisias,

lemon-scented pelargoniums, rosemarys, and thymes, can be sheared as round as a basketball, to look like the little imaginary trees in medieval paintings. Though most standards are kept in pots all their lives, they may also be planted in the garden, at an entrance or the turning of a path, where their strong architectural form adds magic to looser, less disciplined plantings at their feet. They can then be lifted each autumn, potted up in fresh soil and clipped back to regrow through the winter. Some plants, such as lantanas and fuchsias, can be carried on in this way for many years, eventually building up trunks as thick as broomsticks and becoming family heirlooms. (A standard lantana died recently at White Flower Farm in Litchfield, Connecticut, that had been started as a cutting before the Civil War. Still vigorous of growth and abundant of flower, it was blown over in a storm and the head broken off.) Other flowering plants, such as pelargoniums, will eventually become too old and woody to produce fresh growth, and must be started anew, every five years or so, from cuttings.

Many plants sold as annuals are discarded at seasons's end. This dwarf fuchsia has been trained as a standard and carried over five winters. Wherever it is placed in the garden, it creates an air of refinement.

Learning to plant in generous masses, often of single colors, is crucial in drawing from annual plants all the beauty they possess. It is a hard discipline, since often it means the gardener must give up some of the species he may crave. But, with annual plants, there is always the possibility of fresh experiments next year.

SOURCES

The nurseries and seed companies listed below all ship via mail order. Most, though not all, charge a small amount for their catalog, usually a dollar or two. Unfortunately, the cost of each catalog cannot be listed, as it may be subject to change from year to year. But a good collection of catalogs is always a joy to the gardener and a wonderful reference, sometimes the *only* reference to the name of a plant whose label has washed quite clean or been lost; and sometimes a catalog from a small nursery, or even a home-printed list, may be the only source for seed of coveted species or even started plants. So the minimal amount charged may well be worth the money.

Happily, the list offered here cannot be complete, because there are so many more good small nurseries and seed houses than there were 10 or so years ago, and each year adds to their number. To keep abreast, gardeners cannot do better than to purchase Barbara J. Barton's wonderful book, *Gardening by Mail*, now in its third edition (Houghton Mifflin; $16.95 paperback). It lists and cross-references hundreds upon hundreds of sources for plants, seeds, and garden equipment that may be ordered by mail. Meanwhile, the companies listed below will provide more than one winter of dreaming, and more than one summer of beauty in the garden.

Abundant Life Seed Foundation
P.O. Box 772
Port Townsend, Wash. 98368

Alberta Nurseries & Seed Company
P.O. Box 20
Bowden, Alberta, TOM OKO
Canada

Allen, Sterling & Lothrop
191 US Route 1
Falmouth, Maine 04105

Alpen Gardens
173 Lawrence Lane
Kalispell, Mont. 59901

Angel Seed Company
P.O. Box 100
Garden City, Mich. 48135-0100

W. Atlee Burpee Co.
Warminster, Pa. 18974

Bachman's Nursery
6010 Lyndale Avenue So.
Minneapolis, Minn. 55419

Bluebird Nursery, Inc.
515 Linden Street
Clarkson, Nebr. 68629

Canyon Creek Nursery
3527 Dry Creek Road
Oroville, Calif. 95965

Carroll Gardens
P.O. Box 310
Westminster, Md. 21157

Chiltern Seeds
Bortree Stile
Ulverston
Cumbria LA12 7PB
England

Companion Plants
7247 North Coolville Ridge Road
Athens, Ohio 45701

The Country Garden
Route 2, Box 455 A
Crintz, Wis. 54114

Eisler Nurseries
Route 422
Prospect, Pa. 16052

Environmental Seed Products, Inc.
P.O. Box 5904
El Monte, Calif. 91734

The Fragrant Path
P.O. Box 328
Fort Calhoun, Nebr. 68023

Grianán Garden
P.O. Box 14492
San Francisco, Calif. 94114

Harris Seeds
P.O. Box 22960
Rochester, N.Y. 14692-2960

Heirloom Gardens
P.O. Box 138
Guerneville, Calif. 95446

Holbrook Farm & Nursery
Route 2, Box 223 B
Fletcher, N.C. 28732

J. L. Hudson
P.O. Box 1058
Redwood City, Calif. 94064

J. W. Jung Seed Co.
335 S. High Street
Randolph, Wis. 53957-0001

Logee's Greenhouses
141 North Street
Danielson, CT 06790

Merry Gardens
P.O. Box 595
Camden, Maine 04843

Montrose Nursery
P.O. Box 957
Hillsborough, N.C. 27278

Native Plants, Inc.
417 Wakara Way
Salt Lake City, Utah 84108

Native Seeds/SEARCH
2509 N. Campbell Avenue, #325
Tucson, Ariz. 85719

George W. Park Seed Co.
Cokebury Road
Greenwood, S.C. 29647-0001

Plants of the Southwest
930 Baca Street
Santa Fe, N.M. 87501

Otto Richter and Sons, Ltd.
Goodwood
Ontario, LOC 1AO
Canada

Clyde Robin Seed Co., Inc.
P.O. Box 2366
Castro Valley, Calif. 94545

The Rocky Mountain Seed Company
P.O. Box 5204
Denver, Colo. 80217

Sandy Mush Herb Nursery
Route 2, Surret Cove Road
Leicester, N.C. 28748

Seeds Blüm
Idaho City Stage
Boise, Idaho 83706

Select Seeds
81 Stickney Hill Road
Union, Conn. 06076

Shady Hill Gardens
821 Walnut Street
Batavia, Ill. 60510

Shepherd's Garden Seeds
30 Irene Street
Torrington, Conn. 06790

Southern Exposure Seed Exchange
P.O. Box 158
North Garden, Va. 22959

Stokes Seeds
Box 548
Buffalo, N.Y. 14240

The Thomas Jefferson Center for Historic Plants
Monticello
P.O. Box 316
Charlottesville, Va. 22902

Thompson & Morgan
P.O. Box 1308
Jackson, N.J. 08527

Well-Sweep Herb Farm
317 Mt. Bethel Road
Port Murray, N.J. 07865

White Flower Farm
Litchfield, CT 06759-0050

Index

Italicized page numbers refer to captions.